Other Kaplan Books for the Regents Exam
New York State Regents Exam: Biology
New York State Regents Exam: Chemistry
New York State Regents Exam: Global Studies
New York State Regents Exam: Mathematics: Course I
New York State Regents Exam: Mathematics: Course II
New York State Regents Exam: Mathematics: Course III

Other Kaplan Books for High School Students
High School Handbook

Kaplan Books for College Admissions Tests
SAT & PSAT (with CD-ROM)
SAT II: Mathematics
SAT II: Writing
SAT II: Biology
SAT II: Chemistry
SAT Math Workbook
SAT Verbal Workbook
SAT In-a-Week
Roadtrip for the SAT (with CD-ROM)
SAT or ACT? Test Your Best
ACT (with CD-ROM)
ACT In-a-Week

Other Kaplan Books About College and College Admissions
Scholarships
The Road to College (with CD-ROM)
The College Catalog
You Can Afford College (with CD-ROM)
The *Yale Daily News* Guide to Succeeding in College
Parents' Guide to College Admissions
Getting Into College Toolkit (with CD-ROM)

New York State Regents Exam: U.S. History and Government

Geoffrey Cabat, Ph.D.
Assistant Principal/Social Studies
Seward Park High School
New York, NY

Merrill D. Smith, Ph.D.
Widener University
Chester, PA

Steven T. Peterson, M.A.
Hawkeye Community College
Waterloo, IA

Simon & Schuster

Kaplan Books
Published by Kaplan Educational Centers and Simon & Schuster
1230 Avenue of the Americas
New York, NY 10020

Project Editor: Fred N. Grayson, American BookWorks Corporation
Interior Page Design, Production, and Layout: American BookWorks Corporation
Cover Design: Cheung Tai
Production Editors: Richard Christiano and Maude Spekes
Managing Editor: Brent Gallenberger
Executive Editor: Del Franz

Special thanks are extended to Kiernan McGuire and Sara Pearl.

Manufactured in the United States of America
Published simultaneously in Canada

The New York State Regents exams in this book were administered in January, 1989, June, 1996, and
August, 1996, and January, 1997. These exams are reprinted by permission of the University of the State
of New York/State Education Department.

December 1997
10 9 8 7 6 5 4 3 2 1

ISBN: 0-684-84542-3
ISSN:1095-1822

CONTENTS

Part I

An Overview of the Exam

Chapter 1

The U.S. History and Government Regents Exam

SCOPE OF THE EXAM

In eleventh-year Social Studies, you have investigated problems and issues in U.S. History and Government. You have studied the principles of government that are the core of our republican system of government. Most of you will be taking a Regents at the end of your junior year that will test your understanding of the material you learned in American History. Some of you will take a Participation in Government course before the Regents and will not take the exam until January of your senior year. In any case, this book is designed to help you prepare for that examination.

As you may be aware, the U.S. History Regents exam does not cover all of American history and government equally. As you will see, it begins with the development of political institutions of the new republic in the period of our war for independence. In fact, the curriculum does not include any topics other than political history and theory until the period of the American Civil War, 1861–1865. The reason that has been given for this abridgement is that topics from the early period, including Native American history and culture, had been covered thoroughly in the seventh and eighth grades in New York State schools. Be aware that even if your school mandates a more extensive course than the Regents prescribes, and some do, the questions that you will get on your state exam will reflect only the Regents curriculum. So, apportion your studying accordingly.

The course of study and the U.S. History and Government Regents on which it is based are divided into six units. Let us review them so you will be better able to topically organize your studying.

Unit 1: Constitutional Foundations of the American Republic

This unit traces the origins of the U.S. republican system of government to its European roots. It looks at the political and ideological issues that caused the separation of the U.S. from Great Britain and then examines the three important documents of our early political history: the Declaration of Independence, the Articles of Confederation, and the Constitution. It then delineates the important foundation concepts that are found in the Constitution. In fact, the unit sketches out 13 important principles that are at the core of the republican government that has evolved since the ratification of the Constitution. These Enduring Issues, as the curriculum calls them, are important for you to know since they are at the core of the political concepts on which you will be tested in the Regents Examination. These issues are:

1. National power—limits and potentials

2. Federalism—the division of power between state and national governments

3. The judiciary—interpreting the Constitution

4. Civil liberties—the balance between governmental power and individual rights

5. Criminal liberties—the rights of the accused and the protection of the community

6. Equality—as defined by the Constitution

7. The rights of women

8. The rights of ethnic and racial groups

9. Presidential power—in wartime and in foreign affairs

10. The separation of powers—its effect on the capacity to govern

11. Avenues of representation

12. Property rights and economic policy

13. Constitutional change and flexibility

In this unit, you will also study the basic functioning of the three branches of government. You will be asked to compare and contrast the structure and functioning of the National Government with the structure and operation of the Government of New York State. There will also be comparisons made with governments that have different ideologies and structures, such as that of the People's Republic of China.

The last segment of Unit 1 traces to what degree the enduring principles were established by the first governments of the republic (Washington, John Adams, and Jefferson). The emphasis in this unit is almost strictly political, emphasizing the enduring principles and the government policies that implemented them. This segment of the course of study concludes with a description of sectionalism and traces the forces that led to the failure of sectional compromise and the subsequent outbreak of the Civil War.

Unit 2: The Industrialization of the United States

This unit traces the changing nature of American Society from 1865–1920. It examines the importance of the Civil War as a momentous event in American History in terms of both political rights as well as economic expansion. You will study the reasons why the United States began a rapid industrialization after the war and learn how that industrialization affected different groups in American Society: workers, newly arrived immigrants, women, and other minorities.

In this unit, the approach to the subject becomes broader and more diverse, covering not only the political history of the United States, but also the economic, social, and cultural happenings and trends that occurred in the time period under consideration.

Unit 3: The Progressive Movement: Responses to the Challenges Brought About by Industrialization and Urbanization (1900–1940)

If Unit 2 deals with the cause and effect of industrialization, Unit 3 deals with the responses of the various groups in American society to the brave new world created by the machine. Based on the enduring themes discussed earlier, the unit looks at the reform movements: their goals, their accomplishments and their failures. The unit examines the administrations of two presidents of this time period whose programs historians have considered to be progressive: Theodore Roosevelt (Square Deal) and Woodrow Wilson (The New Freedom). The unit, consistent with the enduring principles, adopts a multicultural approach in describing and analyzing how many different kinds of Americans were involved in progressive reform activities.

In Unit 3 you will also learn how, as a result of industrial expansion, the United States, in order to secure resources, markets, and labor became an imperialist and world power. You will then examine the consequences of global responsibility for Americans, as well as for those who came under the control of the United States.

Unit 4: At Home and Abroad: Prosperity and Depression (1917–1940)

In Unit 4, you will trace American foreign policy between the World Wars as the United States rejected world leadership and instead concentrated on the affairs of its own hemisphere.

You will learn about the decade of the Roaring Twenties on the homefront. We begin to see the development of the age of rapid communication and transportation, mass consumption, and individuality that we take for granted today. For this period, you will also study how minorities and women struggled against discrimination.

Then you will see how this age of optimism was quickly ended by a world-wide depression that affected virtually all Americans. To conclude this unit, you will examine how President Franklin Delano Roosevelt's New Deal responded to the Great Depression and, in doing so, completely changed the relationship between the American people and their government.

Unit 5: The United States in an Age of Global Crisis: Responsibility and Cooperation

In Unit 5, you will begin to study modern history. In this segment of the course of studies, you will be reading about events that might be remembered by some of the senior members of your family. Unit 5, for example, relates how the United States was forced out of its policy of isolationism by events in other parts of the world and reemerged as a world leader in World War II, and as a founder of the United Nations in the postwar world.

It will then trace the origins of the Cold War, a four-decades-long conflict between Russia and the United States, which, in its most critical phases, such as the Berlin Crisis of 1948, threatened to plunge the world into nuclear war.

Unit 6: The World in Uncertain Times: 1950–Present

Since 1950 our planet has grown much smaller. What happens half a world away can easily affect the lives of Americans. Since 1950, for example, we have sent U.S. troops to Korea and Vietnam to fight a war, each of which cost the lives of more than 50,000 American soldiers. Why we fought those wars and how those conflicts were both similar and different should be major themes for which you study for your Regents Exam. Global responsibility is a key theme in this unit, which covers the last half century of our history. More recently the Cold War appears to have come to an end; the reasons and consequences for the conclusion of that conflict should also be a major theme on which you focus. However, the dissolution of the Soviet Union has not meant, as some had hoped, the end of world conflict. The Gulf war and our interventions in Haiti, Somalia, and Bosnia have continued to keep the United States on a war-readiness footing. Questions about these conflicts are also likely to appear in some form as Regents questions.

On the home front, the civil rights movement and the criminal and civil liberties revolution brought about by the ground-breaking decisions of the Warren Court should occupy your attention. In this vein, issues dealing with affirmative action, which have been in the news for the last several years, might very well be subjects for upcoming Regents questions.

The unit is subdivided by historically convenient time periods, and contains more information than previous units. Therefore, to learn it well, you may have to study more facts and details than you did for previous units. It is important, for example, to review the progressive policies and legislation of the Kennedy and Johnson administrations. You should turn your attention as well to the more recent Republican attempt to roll back the reforms of the New Deal and Great Society, as reflected in the programs of the Bush-Reagan administrations. You therefore should also be familiar with the Contract for America, the conservative agenda proposed by House Republicans at the beginning of the Clinton Administration.

Finally, be aware that there is a contemporary-problem essay on many United States and History Regents. When you study, devote some time to studying some of these contemporary issues, which are of concern to Americans today—such as crime, homelessness, immigration, technological change, health-care reform, and changing family patterns.

There seems to be a feeling among the people who compose Regents exams that not enough is being studied about the most recent U.S. history, and that in future exams more topics in this last unit will appear in both essays and short-answer questions. This trend appears in the last several exams, and it will probably continue. You should therefore apportion your study time accordingly.

Clearly, these topics are overlapping and interrelated. To reiterate, they serve as a framework for the curriculum and the Regents exam. As you study, keep them in mind, because if you have the right mind-set as you enter the exam room, your responses, especially on the essays, will reflect an orientation close to the model answers developed by the Regents. This will enable you to obtain the maximum credit possible.

FORMAT OF THE EXAM

Before we go on to discuss study tips and test-taking strategies, let us review the format of the exam. The United States History and Government Regents consists of 48 short-answer. multiple-choice questions worth 55 points.

There are also seven essays on the exam, from which you must answer three. You must choose one of two government essays (Part II), and two out of five history questions (Part III). Thus, you have some leeway to write about the topics that you know best and for which you have prepared the most. The essays, Parts II and III, are worth 45 points.

The first step is to become familiar with the exam. Take a practice exam in this review book to get a feel for the test. Mark the exam to see how well you did and to give you an idea of how much preparation you will need to achieve a good grade on the Regents Exam. As you study, do more practice exams, and follow some of the techniques discussed in this chapter, you should see improvement in your scores and, as a result, walk into the exam room with confidence.

Chapter 2

Preparing for the U.S. History and Government Regents Exam

Build Your Vocabulary

The most important key to success on the short-answer part of the exam is vocabulary building. After you have finished marking your practice examination, review and write down all the social studies vocabulary that you do not know—not only the responses that you missed, but all the words you didn't understand. Remember that all these vocabulary words are potentially correct answers for the U.S. History and Government Regents exam that you will take.

Buy some packages of 3 × 5 index cards. Write each new vocabulary word on one side of the card, and its definition in two or three short sentences on the other. Then alphabetize the cards and repeat this process as you go through subsequent exams. As you build up your flashcard glossary, think about dividing the cards either by topic, e.g., the Progressive Era or constitutional principles, to help you study particular areas in which you consider yourself weak.

To give you some guidance in the creation of your flashcards, look at some sample questions from a recent exam and review what possible words you might include in your glossary, assuming that you had not previously known them.

1. Federalism is best described as the . . .

> ### *Federalism*
>
> A political system that divides power between the national and state governments. Many nations, including the United States, have adopted a federal system of government.

2. "Senate Fails to Ratify Treaty of Versailles"

   "President Truman Vetoes Taft-Hartley Act"

   "Senate Rejects Nomination of Robert Bork to Supreme Court"

   These headlines illustrate the constitutional principle of

1. republicanism.

2. executive privilege.

3. due process of law.

4. separation of powers.

Treaty of Versailles

The treaty that ended World War I (1919). It included a provision for an international organization to maintain world peace. President Wilson tried to obtain Senate ratification of the treaty, but he was not successful.

Due Process of Law

The rights Americans enjoy if they become involved in a criminal proceeding. Due process begins with freedom from illegal searches, and includes, among others, the right to an attorney, a fair and public trial, and the right to appeal. Due process is guaranteed by the U.S. and New York State constitutions, as well as by state and national laws.

Separation of Powers

The division of the national government into three distinct branches of government—executive, legislative, and judicial. This division allows for a system of checks and balances that should prevent any one branch from becoming dictatorial.

---

3. The presence of Mr. Jim Crow "in all public places" was legally ended by the

1. ratification of the Thirteenth Amendment (1865).

2. Supreme Court's ruling in *Plessy v. Ferguson* (1896).

3. establishment of the National Association for the Advancement of Colored People (NAACP) (1909).

4. passage of the Civil Rights Act of 1964.

Plessy v. Ferguson

A U.S. Supreme Court decision of 1896 that ruled that state laws segregating public facilities did not violate the Equal Protection Clause of the Fourteenth Amendment. This "separate but equal" doctrine led to more than a half century of segregation (Jim Crow Laws) in the South.

Civil Rights Act of 1964

Despite great opposition, this law passed, through the efforts of President Lyndon Johnson. It banned discrimination in public places, guaranteed voting rights for all Americans, and prohibited job discrimination on the basis of race and gender by all employers and unions engaged in interstate commerce.

DIFFERENT KINDS OF MULTIPLE-CHOICE QUESTIONS

As you prepare for the short-answer segment of the exam, keep in mind that you will encounter several different types of multiple-choice questions. You will be better able to answer these questions if you can recognize each of these types.

Definition question. One that asks for significant terms, concepts, people, or events. Using the June 1996 Regents Exam as a source, question 14 on that exam asks: "According to the theory of laissez-faire, the economy functions best when the government . . . ."

Cause and effect. This type of question tests your knowledge of an event, which might be a causative factor for other events. As you might expect, the causative factors may have taken place in a different period of time than the resulting occurrence. Question 17 of the June 1996 exam, for instance, is illustrative of this type of question: "The major reason that the United States placed few restrictions on immigration during the 1800s was that:"

Time periods. This type of question often looks for common threads that join people of different epochs. Keep in mind that one of the primary goals of this curriculum and Regents Exam is to have you understand these comparisons and contrasts. From the June 1996 exam, question 45 is an example of this type of question:

"Which characteristics of the American frontier continue to be an important part of life in the United States today?"

This question is trying to show a link between the values of frontier America and those of our contemporary society.

Generalization. This is one of the most common multiple-choice questions on the exam. It is a broad principle that applies to important concepts and ideas in U.S. History and Government.

Question 24 on the June 1996 exam is an example of this type of question.

24. A major goal of the reformers during the Progressive Era was to

   1   end segregation in the South.

   2   correct the abuses of big business.

   3   limit immigration from Latin America.

   4   enact high tariffs to help domestic industry grow.

The correct answer to this question is 2, "correct the abuses of big business." You should note that correcting business abuses has been a goal of almost all reformers in the industrial age, before and after the so-called Progressive Era. Thus, even if you don't know about much about the specific period mentioned in the question, you should be able to make a good guess at the answer.

Data- or Document-Based Questions

This type of question presents a graph, a statistical table, a cartoon, a dialogue, or a short excerpt from a document and ask you to combine information from that data, and your knowledge of social studies to answer one or more questions. It seems to be the intention of the Regents to increase the use of this type of question on future exams, so look out for them, because they may be appearing with greater frequency. Since many students don't do well on this type of question, here is an opportunity to spend some time reviewing several types or varieties of data- or document-based questions.

Graphs. As a model, we will use questions 35 and 36 on the January 1995 exam.

35. From 1940 to 1945, the trend in the federal debt of the United States was caused primarily by the cost of

   1   fighting World War II.

   2   programs of economic recovery under the New Deal.

   3   efforts to launch manned space flights.

   4   social programs of the Great Society.

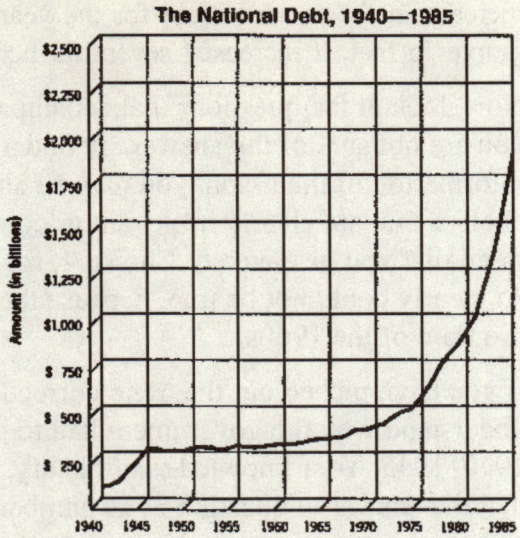

36. The trend shown between 1970 and 1985 would most
likely have been reversed by

   1   increasing Social Security payments.

   2   increasing defense spending.

   3   reducing agricultural exports.

   4   reducing government expenditures.

Look at the graph's title: "The National Debt, 1940–1985."
From this title, you should now be able to infer what question
is being addressed by the graph and by the two questions that
follow. You should, therefore, be suspicious of any of the
answers that are *not* related to the topic of the graph.

Look at the keys, or indicators, on the graph that explain the
numbers and symbols underneath; you can see that the
numbers expressed represent the years covered by the graph.
Then observe the vertical axis, which represents the nation's
debt in billions of dollars. Quickly make sure you know how
to read the graph by running one finger along the vertical
axis and one along the horizontal until they cross. For
example, in 1970, what was the national debt, according to
this graph? This whole process seems to take a long time, but
once you get the hang of it, you can figure out a graph in less
than a minute!

Graphs are a way of organizing figures to show direction or
trends. Before you answer the question, figure out the trend the
graph is trying to show. In this case, the trend was for sharp

increase in the national debt for the years covered in the graph. In fact, it increased sevenfold between 1945 and 1985.

Now, look at the questions that accompany the graph. Even if you are not sure of the answer, by understanding the basic information of the graph, you may be able to eliminate choices that are clearly irrelevant or contradictory to the trend that you discovered. Choice 4, for example, in question 35 clearly could not be true, because the Great Society was a program of the 1960s.

If you have picked out the trend correctly, you now have to understand why the government had to go into debt between 1940–1945. Your knowledge of history, then, should tell you that the answer to question 35 is number 1. Remember that to answer this question, you have to discern the trend and then apply your knowledge of history to the information you get from the graph.

Question 36 will ask you again to use your knowledge of social studies to make inferences from the graph—in this case, to explain the reason for the data contained in the graph. It asks what government would have to do between 1970–1985 to reverse the trend shown in the chart, i.e., to decrease debt. Using common sense, you know that if your family were in debt, to erase it you could either bring in more money and/or spend less. Apply that idea to the question, and the only answer that makes good sense is number 4.

The January 1995 questions 35 and 36 were based on a line graph. You might also be asked to analyze a pie graph, or pie chart. An example is the pie chart that accompanies questions 35 and 36 on the June 1994 Regents Exam.

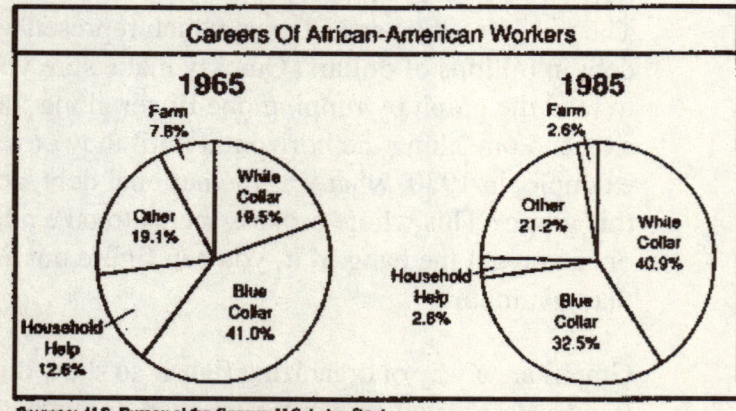

Repeat the process outlined above: Look for the title, look for the units used—in this case, percentages of people employed in various occupations. Then review the terms like *blue collar* and *white collar* in your mind. Finally, and most important, find the trend or the direction to which the graph is pointing.

Cartoons. Another kind of data-based question asked on the U.S. History and Government Regents Exam are cartoons. As you might know from reading the newspapers, a cartoon is a drawing that often depicts the author's point of view on a current topic. A cartoon can be serious or humorous in nature. Keep in mind that cartoons often make use of symbols or caricatures (exaggerated drawings) to express a point of view.

For example, in a cartoon, the figure of Uncle Sam usually stands for the United States; the donkey represents the Democratic party, and the elephant stands for the Republican Party. If you review past Regents exams, you will also see stylized drawings of present and past presidents such as Franklin D. Roosevelt or his cousin Theodore Roosevelt.

When you see a cartoon question on the Regents:

- Pick out the highlighted people or symbols you recognize.

- Ask yourself what activity or actions are happening in the cartoon.

- Use the information found out to try to ascertain the main idea of the cartoon.

- Examine the choices offered by the question and see which most corresponds to the information which you found.

As an example, look at the following question from a previous exam.

> The cartoon on the following page was encouraging the American public to
>
> 1   exercise caution regarding involvement in European conflicts.
>
> 2   demand repayment of World war II debts owed by European nations.

3   support countries resisting Communist aggression.

4   provide food to Eastern Europe.

Source: Library of Congress

- In the cartoon, there is a drawing of Uncle Sam, the symbol of the United States.

- He is holding a paper. Analyze what it is saying.

- Far away there is a war in Europe.

- Based on your knowledge of world history, what point of view is the cartoon expressing?

- The best answer is reflected in choice 1.

Questions Based on Short Reading Passages

The last category of short-answer question that we need to review for the exam is the one that calls upon you to analyze a short reading passage. It is the intention of the Regents to improve reading comprehension and document analysis skills. Consequently there may be more questions containing those skills on Regents exams in the near future. In answering a reading comprehension question, follow these guidelines:

- In reading comprehension passages, it is often a good idea to read the questions to find out what information will be required to answer them. You might then be able to pick out some of the correct answers as you read the passage. Keep in mind the following:

- Don't hesitate to underline key words or phrases in the test booklet that will help you respond to the question or questions.

- After you read the passage, try to summarize the main idea in a sentence or two.

- Depending on the question, try to determine the tone of the passage: angry, official inquisitive etc., and the reason the author had for writing what you have read.

To give an example of how to answer a reading compression passage, let's use question 7 on the January 1997 exam:

7. "To the Honorable Senate and House of Representatives in Congress Assembled: We the undersigned, citizens of the United States, but deprived of some of the privileges and immunities of citizens, among which is the right to vote, beg leave to submit the following Resolution: . . ."
   —Susan B. Anthony
   Elizabeth Cady Standon (1873)

This statement is an example of a citizen's constitutional right to

1. petition for a redress of grievances.
2. seek election to public office.
3. receive a speedy, public trial.
4. assemble peacefully.

After reading the question, you know that the testers want you to tell them what constitutional right is being illustrated by the passage.

Underlining key words, you should be able to answer, since words such as *deprived*, *privileges*, and *submit* clearly should lead you to the answer (1).

Sometimes the reading comprehension question will take the form of a dialogue between several speakers disagreeing about the same issue or controversy. For this type of question, follow the same guidelines as outlined above.

In dialogue questions:

- Be sure to identify the controversy or issue in dispute.

- Identify as best you can how the speakers views are different.

- Identify any similarities in the arguments made by each speaker.

For the dialogue example, we can use questions 47–48 from the June 1996 examination.

Speaker A: We must take action, even if we are not sure it will work. To do nothing to stop them would be a repeat of the Munich mistake.

Speaker B: We must recognize the increasing interdependence of nations and join the United Nations.

Speaker C: Stopping the spread of communism can and must take several forms. We must be willing to do whatever is necessary.

Speaker D: Involvement in European affairs would be a mistake. We should not jeopardize our peace and prosperity over issues that Europe's ambitions and rivalries control.

47. Which speaker best describes the basic foreign policy of the United States until the late 1800s?

   1   A
   2   B
   3   C
   4   D

48. The "Munich mistake" mentioned by speaker A refers to a policy of

   1   interdependence.
   2   appeasement.
   3   balance of power.
   4   collective security.

Having read the questions first, you should be looking for the one speaker who reflects the views of the late 1800s. Context clues that make reference to much later events should eliminate some of the foils and lead you to the correct answer for question 47, which is 4.

Your knowledge of history should help you with question 48. Realizing that the Allies *appeased*, or gave in to, Hitler at Munich in order to prevent war, you should choose answer 2. In situations like this your vocabulary flashcards should come in handy, because *appeasement* should be one of the words in your glossary.

PREPARING FOR THE ESSAY PART OF THE EXAM

Now that we have reviewed short-answer preparation techniques, let us look at the essay segment of the test. To reiterate, this segment is worth 45 points. You must choose three out of seven essays, each equally weighted at 15 points. On the U.S. History and Government Exam, you will be asked to choose one of two government essays (Part II) and two of five history essays (Part III). It is critical that you answer all three questions, even if you believe that you can't give a complete answer for all. Once you begin to write, you'll be surprised at how much you know.

As you study for this segment, bear in mind that these kinds of questions are often repeated year after year in modified form. Therefore, one key to success is to identify these recurring questions and prepare for them by replicating test conditions, i.e., make an outline, write and check the essay, time yourself to make sure that you are working fast enough to complete the test in the three hours allotted.

Before we discuss some of the types of questions for which you should prepare, let us review the general format of the essay question. Each begins with a general statement, and then asks you to define, explain, and/or discuss a cause-and-effect relationship.

In preparation for the exam, answer old exam questions in each of these frequently asked categories. Examples of these questions are cited in parentheses:

For Part I—the government essay (choose 1 of 2)—the following are among the most commonly asked questions:

- The application of significant principles of the Constitution (Essay 1, June 1992)

- The issues dealing with system of checks and balances (Essay 1, June 1994)

- The exercise of presidential power (Essay 2, January 1994)

- Amendments to the Constitution that have affected the development of democracy in the United States (Essay 2, June 1995)

- Supreme Court decisions that have had an important effect on historical events and/or the functions of government (Essay 2, June 1994)

- The effect of lobby groups, the media, and other groups on the legislative process (Essay 1, June 1993)

The following are some common history essays (Part III). Remember that on Part III you are to answer 2 of 5 questions.

- Current social and/or economic problems facing the people of the United States, e.g., welfare, immigration, family structure, etcetera. (Essay 7, January 1997)

- Significant foreign policy issues and initiatives often linked to various presidents (Essay 3, June 1996)

- The influential domestic programs initiated by American presidents (Essay 7, January 1996)

- Individuals who have fought for and/or initiated social and political change (Essay 6, June 1995)

- Influential works of literature and how they reflect the crucial times in which they were written (Essay 5, January 1996)

- The struggle of various segments of American society for their civil rights (Essay 4, January 1995)

- U.S. policy toward immigration (Essay 3, June 1993)

- Reform movements and/or legislation; their purposes and effects (Essay 4, January 1997)

- Document-based questions (songs, documents, and poems) (Essay 6, June 1996)

The Regents has expressed the view that the social studies teachers should better develop the skills of document interpretation. Therefore, it is likely that more of this type of question will appear on future Regents exams.

The best way to prepare for the essay part is to be aware of these categories and practice writing essays in each under simulated test conditions. Work in a quiet place without interruption and time your writing to make sure that you can complete the actual exam in the three hours allotted. It is imperative that you write an outline for every essay on the actual test, as in practice. Setting up the outline will "break the ice," making the writing of the actual essay much easier.

Begin your essay study session by carefully reading all the questions and choosing the three that you know best. Many students feel that the contemporary-problems question is a good choice, since much of the information needed to answer that type of question is current and fresher in your mind than some of the historical topics. You can prepare yourself for this often repeated question by reading a good newspaper like *The New York Times* every day.

Many students have found that using a diagram or a box form is the most efficient way to write an outline. Let us use Essay 3, January 1997, as a model question upon which to write an outline.

> In U.S. history, foreign policies pursued by various presidents have resulted in controversy. Some of these controversial policies and the presidents associated with them are listed below.
>
>> Addition of the Corollary to the Monroe Doctrine— Theodore Roosevelt
>>
>> Support for the Versailles Treaty—Woodrow Wilson
>>
>> Aid to Great Britain before United States entry into World War II—Franklin D. Roosevelt
>>
>> Use of the atomic bomb—Harry S Truman
>>
>> Aid to South Vietnam—Lyndon B. Johnson
>>
>> Involvement in the Pesian Gulf War—George Bush
>>
>> Aid to Bosnia—Bill Clinton
>
> Select three of the foreign policies and the president with which the policy is paired. For each pair selected:
>
> • Discuss one specific reason why the president pursued the policy.
>
> • Discuss one argument raised by the opponents of the policy.

One of the policies listed in the question is about the Monroe Doctrine and Theodore Roosevelt. An outline for that one response might appear as follows:

> Reason for Policy: The United States had to act as a policeman in the Western hemisphere to protect this hemisphere from European intervention which might threaten U.S. security.

> Opposition to Policy: Many of the nations of Latin America opposed the Roosevelt Corollary because they believed it to be a threat to their sovereignty.

In short, write down the major ideas that will serve as the basis for your essay. Sketch them in outline form for each example, and you will be well on your way to writing a successful Regents essay.

Finally, when you write both your practice and regular essays, remember use the language of the question to begin your answer. This technique also gives you a jump start to essay writing and will therefore most likely increase your chances for success on the exam.

For example, using the model question, you might start the question:

> In U.S. history, foreign policies pursued by various presidents have resulted in controversy. One example is the Roosevelt Corollary of President Theodore Roosevelt. The reason he gave for the policy was (go to your outline). One group that opposed the policy was (go to your outline) because (go to your outline).

Thus, by using a good outline and the structure provided by the question itself, you will find that the essay writing is not so difficult.

Chapter 3

Strategies for Mastering the Test

Although the suggested tips are for taking the exam, the readiness of your mind and the wellness of your body before the test are more important than the tips. Therefore, it is essential to make an appropriate plan and follow it before the exam to keep your mind and body in optimal condition. Here are the specifics:

- Eat meals with balanced nutrients regularly.

- Get enough rest daily.

- Do some appropriate physical exercise.

- Prepare and bring everything needed for the exam to your test site. These include a black ball-point pen, a pencil, a rubber eraser, a reliable watch, and your photo ID or test admission ticket. Do not rely on borrowing from others.

During the exam, the following tactics should be used wherever applicable.

Following Directions

You need to pay very careful attention to directions. Read over the directions more than once, and don't proceed to the questions until you have a grasp of what the questions require. Ask the proctor for help if you don't understand.

Reading the Questions

After reading the questions thoroughly, predict an answer and then look for the answer choice that best matches your prediction. If you know an answer, you can use your common sense or make an educated guess by eliminating the least likely answers.

Skipping Questions

Skip those questions that you are not sure of and move on to the next question. This way you can get the most points with the highest certainty within the least amount of time. When you have finished answering the easy questions, go back to those you skipped and try them.

When you skip a question or are unsure of your answer, circle it or mark it so that you can return to it later. When skipping questions, remember to check to make sure you are answering each question in the right spot on the answer sheet.

Attacking the Difficult Questions

Tackle your difficult questions after you finish all the easy questions. Some of the difficult questions may now be readily answered by the cross-reference information you obtained from the easy-questions.

Answer all questions, even by educated guesses, because you are not penalized for wrong answers. Remember: Uncertain answers are better than no answers because they may be correct.

Reviewing

When you have extra time, review your work or the questions that you are not so sure about. Rethinking with more time and in a relaxed mood often results in finding errors and making better decisions.

Going With Your First Impression

As a general rule, your first impression about the answer to the question is usually the correct one. Therefore, do not change your first impression answer unless you determine that it is absolutely incorrect.

Summary of Test-taking Tips

- Follow the directions carefully for all exam questions.

- Read questions thoroughly, then predict an answer, and look for the answer that best matches your prediction.

- Skip difficult questions and do easy questions first.

- Avoid correct answers that don't actually answer the question.

- Answer all questions to get possible credit, even if you have to guess (eliminate answer choices you're sure are wrong).

- Mark questions where you're not sure your answer is correct so you can reconsider your answer if you have time.

- Review your work when you have time.

- Keep your first impression answers unchanged unless you are absolutely sure that they are incorrect

Good Luck on the Regents Exam!

Part II

U.S. History and
Government Review

Chapter 4

Constitutional Foundations of the United States

Part 1: The Constitution: The Bulwark of American Society

I. Foundations

    A. Political and Legal Ideas of Colonial America—influenced by many concepts and practices

       1. English common law developed in the twelfth century to replace the hodgepodge of conflicting laws—Anglo-Saxon, Norman, and church. Royal judges traveled throughout the country and heard cases in the king's court. Their decisions were noted to be used as guidelines in future proceedings. The rule of law accepted as first principle of English government.

          a. Dating from the Magna Carta (1215), all of England, kings and subjects, must obey the law; this extends to the American colonies

          b. Rights of due process and trial by jury

       2. Representational democracy is also part of British traditions carried to the colonies. Parliament represents the people of Great Britain.

       3. Ancient Greek and Roman ideas were Anglicized after several centuries of English thought and practice.

          a. Aristotle's political thought stressed importance of rule of law and centered on the city-state. Laws enabled people to live rationally and morally.

          b. Ancient republics seen as ideal society—they died when citizens became corrupt; virtue was important in a republic.

       4. Enlightenment thought influenced colonial leaders.

          a. Thomas Hobbes (1588–1679)—Sees contract between monarch and subjects as basis for government, rather than divine right. However, this contract was unbreakable. *Leviathan* (1651) published during English civil war.

    b. John Locke—Counterpoint to Hobbes. Government to protect natural rights of life, liberty, and property. Government that does not respect rights of citizens is a tyranny—breaking contract with people; citizens have natural right to rebel. *Two Treatises on Government* (1689).

    c. Montesquieu (1689–1755)—Studied monarchies, republics, and despotisms. Political power should be divided among legislative, executive, and judicial branches of government—checks and balances.

  5. Haudenosaunee political thought.

    a. Iroquois League formed prior to European contact

    b. League had written constitution; confederation system with council formed by fifty male sachems. Central authority limited; each tribe could pursue own concerns.

    c. System of checks and balances and supreme law.

    d. Influenced European political theorists and Americans such as Benjamin Franklin. Also influenced Articles of Confederation and U.S. Constitution.

B. Revolutionary War and Declaration of Independence

  1. Virtual representation

    a. English belief—Parliament represents everyone in empire. Colonists—only men for whom they have voted represent them. Good government is limited—theory of Real Whigs.

    b. Americans used to more self government in their Assemblies

  2. Taxation—Issue of contention between colonies and England—no taxation without representation

Examples:

Stamp Act (1765)—lead to riots

Tea Tax—lead to Boston Tea Party; Coercive Acts imposed by British—seen as tyranny

  3. Revolution and political change in England affected the evolution of independence movement in North American colonies.

    a. Glorious Revolution—power of Parliament increased

    b. French and Indian War—England needs money to pay for war's expenditures. Prime Ministers increased taxes for Americans.

    c. Thomas Paine's *Common Sense* (1776)—published after battles at Lexington and Concord, but before Declaration of Independence. Influenced many to join the cause for liberty. Bestseller (150,000 copies sold in one year = one copy for every 17 Americans of the time); Paine called George III a tyrant.

4. Declaration of Independence

    a. Ideals and goals still have to be reached:

       "We hold these truths to be self-evident: That all men are created equal; that they are endowed by their Creator with certain unalienable rights; that among these are life, liberty, and the pursuit of happiness." Declaration written by Thomas Jefferson, although the ideas did not originate with him. He was influenced by Locke and borrowed phrases from other writers and documents.

    b. Government derives power from consent of the people to protect these rights. When government becomes despotic, people have right to change it.

    c. King has become a tyrant; Declaration lists grievances, such as that king has imposed taxes without colonists' consent, that he has deprived colonists of trial by jury, and that he has suspended their legislatures.

5. Outbreak of War

    a. After passage of Intolerable Acts and Quebec Act, delegates meet in Philadelphia for first Continental Congress (1774). First shots of war fired at Lexington and Concord (1775).

    b. French alliance with U.S. allows France to openly supply aid to United States—soldiers, ships, arms—and gives British another enemy to fight.

    c. Approximately one-fifth of white population remained loyal to Great Britain. Known as loyalists or Tories.

    d. General Cornwallis surrendered at Yorktown (1781).

    e. Treaty of Paris signed in 1783. Officially gives independence to United States.

C. Articles of Confederation

    1. Federalism—compromise between centralized unitary system and decentralized confederate framework = power shared

    2. Weaknesses of Articles: Major problems—could not regulate commerce or tax; no national currency; no federal judiciary to decide constitutional questions; passage of legislation required approval by nine of the 13 states; amendments required unanimous approval.

        a. Under the Articles, states united in a "Firm League of Friendship." Each state "sovereign." United States was a confederation of sovereign states.

II. The Constitutional Convention

A. Call for Constitutional Convention

    1. Meeting in Annapolis (1786) to discuss what could be done about Confederation government. Many feel it is not effective in handling disputes between the states (e.g., Maryland's and Virginia's feud over fishing rights in Chesapeake Bay) nor between states and the Confederation government. Some feel that Congress does not have enough power. Only five states send delegates. Call for meeting in Philadelphia.

    2. Shays' Rebellion (Massachusetts, 1786). Seen by some, such as Washington, as need for stronger central government.

    3. Fifty-five delegates gather in Philadelphia—prosperous, educated men, some with experience in writing state constitutions. Among delegates were George Washington, James Madison, Alexander Hamilton, Benjamin Franklin. Meet in secret. Decision is made to create new government rather than rewrite Articles. New government to be based on the citizens of the United States rather than on the states, as in Confederation.

B. Democracy—balances rights and freedoms with responsibilities of citizens. Some fear "tyrannical power"—Patrick Henry refused to attend convention. Rhode Island did not send delegates.

C. The Convention

   1. Representation and process: Virginia Plan and New Jersey
      Plan. Issues: large states versus small states; federal power
      versus state power.

   2. Conflict and compromise: "Great Compromise"—Each state
      sends two senators to upper house, Senate. Representation in
      lower house based on population of each state. This appeased
      small states such as New Jersey and Connecticut. Slaves to
      be counted as three-fifths of person. This was a compromise
      with the South—slave trade continues until 1808.

   3. The document: structure of government. Constitution
      distributes political authority between executive branch
      (President), legislative branch (Congress), and judicial
      branch (Supreme Court and federal court system). Separation
      of powers. Also divisions between federal government and
      states. Constitution to be "the supreme law of the land." The
      Constitution is written law. It is the rule book of our
      governmental system.

   4. Ratification—each state to have convention; delegates
      elected by voters in each state. Federalists favor Constitution.
      The Federalist, published in New York—essays by James
      Madison, John Jay, and Alexander Hamilton, promote
      Constitution. Helps to ratify Constitution in New York (by
      vote of 39 to 27). Antifederalists oppose
      Constitution—fearful of powerful central government; lack
      of Bill of Rights.

   5. Bill of Rights—First ten amendments to the Constitution.
      Guarantees such rights as freedom of speech and religion and
      trial by jury, among others. Ratified in 1791.

   6. How amended—most common approach is two-thirds vote of
      both houses of Congress; three-fourths of state legislatures.

III. Basic Constitutional Principles

A. Thirteen Enduring Principles—these continue throughout U.S.
history:

   - National Power—limits and potentials

   - Federalism—balance between nation and state

   - The Judiciary—interpreter of Constitution or shaper of public
     policy

- Civil Liberties—balance of power between government and individual
- Criminal Liberties—rights of accused and protection of the community
- Equality—its definition as a Constitutional value
- Rights of Women—rights given under the Constitution
- Rights of Racial and Ethnic Groups—rights given under the Constitution
- Presidential Power—during war; in foreign affairs
- Separation of Powers—capacity to govern
- Avenues of Representation
- Property Rights and Economic Policy
- Constitutional Change and Flexibility

B. Early Constitution provided a limited democracy; added statutes, amendments, and judicial findings have made U.S. government more democratic. Constitution changeable and flexible due to these factors.

IV. Basic Structure and Function

A. Three branches and their operation—all are separate, but interdependent in balance of power; checks and balances.

1. Executive—the president. He has primary responsibility for foreign affairs; he is commander-in-chief of armed forces. He also has power to appoint judges and other federal officers. He can veto Congressional legislation, but his treaties and major appointments need Senate approval.

2. Legislative—Senate and House of Representatives. Under Constitution, Congress has power to regulate commerce between states and with foreign nations, levy and collect taxes, devise rules for naturalization, and administer national patents and copyrights. Congress was also granted authority to make all "necessary and proper" laws to carry out its duties.

3. Judicial—Supreme Court has the final word on interpreting the Constitution. Congress also given power to create other federal courts to ensure that federal laws are carried out. Judiciary Act of 1789 provided that the Supreme Court would have a chief justice and five associate justices. The act

also defined the jurisdiction of the federal judiciary; set up 13 district courts and three circuit courts of appeal.

B. The Federal Bureaucracy—very small at first; has grown, especially in twentieth century. Three administrative departments established under Articles of Confederation were continued: War, Foreign Affairs (State), and Treasury. The first Congress added: attorney general and postmaster general. After debate, power given to president to control these department heads.

C. Comparison to New York State Government—state governments also have system of checks and balances; division of executive (governor); legislature, and judicial branches of government. But under the Constitution, federal government is supreme over that of the states. *McCulloch v. Maryland* (1819).

D. Comparisons to other governments—How does our system of government with its written Constitution and system of checks and balances compare to other governments and systems?

V. Implementing the New Constitutional Principles

A. Hamilton's Financial Plans—intended to create domestic stability. Hamilton was Secretary of the Treasury. Plans included Congress's assuming state debts and issuing new bonds to current bond holders. Also wanted to charter a national bank. Debates over whether this is constitutional.

  1. Broad constructionist view of Constitution—Hamilton—if not prohibited by Constitution, then it is permissible under Congress's power to make all laws that are "necessary and proper."

  2. Strict constructionist view—Jefferson—Congress could do what was necessary, but not merely "desirable," only what was indispensable.

B. Development of unwritten Constitutional Government Under Washington, Adams, and Jefferson.

  1. Cabinet—Washington used the heads of his executive departments as his advisors, this created the cabinet.

  2. Political Parties—parties not considered desirable and not mentioned in Constitution. During Washington's presidency, two parties develop—Federalists and Republicans. When Jefferson becomes president, there is first peaceful transfer of political power from one party to another. This is a significant feature of democracy.

3. Suppressing rebellion—Whiskey Rebellion (1794)—Washington will not allow threats to national unity; Alien and Sedition Acts (1798)—attempts by Federalists to suppress Republican opposition

4. Judicial review—John Marshall, Chief Justice of Supreme Court, instrumental in fashioning theory of judicial review—Supreme court has power to decide if laws are constitutional. Constitution is supreme law; any federal or state laws contrary to it are unconstitutional. Judicial review helps to make the court nonpartisan and independent.

   a. *Marbury v. Madison* (1803)—first time a federal law declared unconstitutional.

   b. Court opinions have changed over time. For example, in *Dred Scott v. Sanford* (1857), the court ruled that Dred Scott was not a citizen of the United States, that he was not made free by living in a free territory, and that Congress did not have the power to bar slavery from a territory as it had in the Missouri Compromise.

C. Neutrality, National Security, and Foreign Affairs—Washington through Monroe

   1. Neutrality—a key element of U.S. foreign policy. After Revolution, United States is a small country surrounded by European powers (England in Canada, Spain in Florida, Spain/France along Mississippi); economy still tied to England; English and French fighting on the seas. United States tries to remain neutral, although Jay's Treaty in 1795 seems to put United States on England's side.

   2. Economic pressure is another tool of diplomacy. Embargo Act (1808), however, only hurts New England, as shipping there collapses.

   3. Is war with England unavoidable, or is this an excuse? War of 1812—United States tired of English interference with shipping, impressment of sailors, and entanglements with Native American tribes, but desire for war is also fueled by visions of expanding into Canada.

   4. Territorial expansion creates safer boundaries for U.S. Acquisition of Louisiana Purchase (1803) forces Jefferson to sacrifice principle of strict construction for national advantage. United States paid $15 million to France for 828,000 square miles, doubling size of U.S. Jefferson decides

the purchase is within president's implied powers to protect the nation. This area, owned by Napoleon, would be a threat to United States. Flexibility of Constitution—different interpretations are possible.

5. Grand doctrines articulate principles and extend power—another tool of diplomacy. Monroe Doctrine (1823) announces that the Western Hemisphere is closed to colonization and interference by European nations.

6. Foreign policy of most democratic nations—mixture of national self-interest and international idealism.

Part 2: The Constitution Tested

I. Constitutional Stress and Crisis

National Power Limits and Potential. Nationalistic and sectional feelings and movements are constant "pulls" throughout U.S. history.

A. Development of Sectional Differences

1. Growth of country leads to sectional differences with differing philosophies of government. Frontier, new cotton areas, northern industrial and agricultural areas.

B. Equal Rights and Justice

1. Growth of franchise—more white men are able to vote; most property requirements dropped. Two-party politics in effect by 1830s, especially by election of 1840. Women, African Americans, Native Americans cannot vote.

2. Growth of frontier leads to expansion of slavery, denial of Native American rights and land ownership. Cotton gin (invented in 1793 by Eli Whitney) makes cotton production profitable. Mills in England and New England use the cotton—part of new commercial economy. New slave states such as Mississippi and Alabama, created as Indians pushed off their lands. Trail of Tears (1831–1838) forces some Indian tribes to resettle in West. Seminoles however, successfully resist in Second Seminole War (1835–1842).

C. Great Constitutional Debates—compromises postpone clash between sections of country with different economic and social systems.

1. States rights versus federal supremacy. Doctrine of nullification—state has right to nullify federal legislation that conflicts with its own. Articulated by South Carolina (most notably by John C. Calhoun, who resigned as vice-president and became a senator from South Carolina) during Jackson's presidency. Federalism: balance between nation and state.

2. Arguments for and against slavery. In South, it is argued that slavery is a positive good for society and for the slaves. Morally good, and part of legal system. Economically, slavery became necessary in South. Those depriving them of slaves are stealing their property. Northerners not all antislavery. Some see it as morally wrong (many abolitionists); some just want to be able to compete economically. "Free soil, free labor, free men."

3. Attempt to preserve the Union through compromise. Much of this over western lands. Questions: Will new states enter Union as slave or free states? How will this change political balance in Congress? Missouri Compromise (1820), Compromise of 1850, idea of popular sovereignty. Many great orators debate constitutional points: Henry Clay, "The Great Compromiser"; Daniel Webster.

4. Also debates over equality and citizenship. Equality: its definition as a constitutional virtue. Who can vote? Who is a citizen?

   a. Women's-rights movement begins—Seneca Falls Convention, 1848; principle organizers—Elizabeth Cady Stanton and Lucretia Mott. Both had been involved in abolitionist movement—were refused seating as delegates at 1840 antislavery convention in London because they were women. Many women involved in abolitionist movement and other movements such as temperance and peace—these women were usually educated, Protestant women from the North.

   b. Dred Scott case (1857) ruled Scott was not a citizen, could not sue in court. Chief Justice Taney also ruled Missouri Compromise unconstitutional—Congress could not prohibit slavery in territories. Also invalidates idea of popular sovereignty. Northerners upset—see "slave power" conspiracy growing and involving Supreme Court.

   c. Native Americans deprived of rights as well as lands.

     5. Other "triggers" toward Civil War

       a. "Bleeding Kansas"—Kansas-Nebraska Act (1854)—people there to decide if they would have slavery or not. Kansas becomes a battleground for proslavery versus antislavery forces. "Border ruffians" set pro-slavery town of Lawrence on fire. Abolitionist John Brown kills five pro-slavery Kansans in retaliation.

       b. John Brown's raid on Harpers Ferry Arsenal (1859). Brown captured, tried for treason, and executed. Some abolitionists applaud Brown's actions; see him as martyr. Southerners fear Republicans winning 1860 election and being sympathetic to those like Brown.

     6. First shots of Civil war fired by South at Fort Sumter (1861)

II. The Constitution in Jeopardy: The American Civil War

A. U.S. Society Divided over Issues of Slavery—unable to abolish slavery peacefully, as England did. Even Emancipation Proclamation—Lincoln stated that on January 1, 1863, he would emancipate slaves in states that were "in rebellion against the United States." Does not free slaves anywhere else—wartime measure.

B. Wartime measures: Unity, Stability, Security—patriotism in North in trying to keep Union together. War production helps promote industrialization in the North. Much idealism, but not everyone willing to fight—draftees can pay for substitutes. Need to gear government and business for war effort.

C. Congressional and executive rivalry—the war required Lincoln to take active leadership; sometimes he moved ahead without Congressional approval. Leadership versus incursions on personal liberty. Suspended writ of habeas corpus for everyone living between Philadelphia and Washington. National Banking Acts (1863, 1964, 1865)—established a national banking system with national banknotes. Lincoln begins plans for restoring Union. Lincoln saw preservation of the Union as test of freedom with international implications.

D. One Result of Civil War—greater federal supremacy over the states—Fourteenth Amendment.

Questions

1. The political frame of reference of the colonists in the late seventeenth century can best be described as follows:

   1. They were accustomed to exercising a great degree of local self-government.

   2. They had not yet experienced anything resembling representative government.

   3. They had some limited self-government, but were more comfortable waiting for instructions from the king.

   4. Any small amount of control they had was relinquished when they moved to the New World.

2. Which statement best identifies Abraham Lincoln's policies?

   1. The legislative branch of government works best without executive leadership.

   2. War requires active presidential leadership.

   3. A president is bound by the same constitutional restrictions in war as he is in peace.

   4. Decentralized power is the best way to handle a nation's domestic affairs.

3. The theory of judicial review

   1. permits the Supreme Court to nullify an act of Congress by declaring it unconstitutional.

   2. allows the Supreme Court to try federal judges for high crimes and misdemeanors.

   3. gives the Supreme Court permission to appoint special investigators within the executive department.

   4. makes the Supreme Court the final authority in disputed federal or state elections.

4. Under the Constitution, the president is to be elected by

   1. direct vote of all qualified American citizens.

   2. the vote of delegates to special conventions.

   3. the votes of state legislatures.

   4. the vote of electors who were originally appointed by state legislatures.

5. During Jackson's presidency, "nullification" referred to

   1. a federal court had the right to reject any state law it found unconstitutional.

   2. no tariffs were to apply to the South.

   3. a state had the right to reject any federal law it believed was unconstitutional.

   4. a new election would be held if no presidential candidate received a majority vote in the election.

6. In 1808, Congress banned

   1. the slave trade in Washington, D.C.

   2. the importation of slaves.

   3. the sale of slaves within the United States.

   4. slavery in all territories of the United States.

7. The Seneca Falls Declaration argued that women
   1. had a special sphere in the home.
   2. were entitled to special treatment because they were "purer" than men.
   3. needed to have more power than men.
   4. were entitled to the same rights as men.

8. The Emancipation Proclamation
   1. freed all the slaves in the North and South.
   2. was issued by Lincoln on the basis of his powers as commander-in-chief of the armed services.
   3. passed Congress with overwhelming support from Republicans and Democrats.
   4. freed slaves only in the border states and the western territories.

9. During and after the Revolution, most states revised their constitutions to
   1. concentrate all power in a single government office.
   2. extend suffrage to all citizens, black and white.
   3. give greater powers and longer terms to governors.
   4. explicitly list the rights of the people against the government.

10. The Missouri Compromise
    1. permanently ended the slavery controversy.
    2. after admitting Missouri, prohibited slavery in the Louisiana Territory north of 36°30'.
    3. outlawed slavery.
    4. indicated that slavery was not an important issue for most Americans.

11. A federal system of government meant, in theory, that
    1. the national government was the only real government.
    2. states maintained their sovereignty.
    3. there was a sharing of powers between national and state governments.
    4. the executive branch held all power.

12. The Supreme Court's decision concerning Dred Scott
    1. supported a moderate interpretation of the Constitution.
    2. sanctioned the most radical arguments of Southerners.
    3. favored the opinions of radical abolitionists.
    4. took slavery out of the political arena.

13. The idea of "popular sovereignty" was that
    1. the territories should decide if they wanted slavery or not.
    2. the nation as a whole should decide if there should be slavery in the territories.
    3. the Constitution permitted slavery anywhere in the country.
    4. a war would have to be fought to determine where slavery would be permitted.

14. The Constitution, as it was ratified

    1. protected only the right to bear arms.

    2. protected freedom of speech.

    3. said almost nothing about individual rights.

    4. spelled out all the individual rights for which the Americans had fought.

15. During the Constitutional Convention, the Great Compromise was

    1. an attempt to include slavery in the list of debated topics.

    2. the decision to create a House of Representatives apportioned by population, and a Senate with each state represented equally by two senators.

    3. the decision to accept the Constitution.

    4. the decision to have voters elect a president directly.

Answers

1. The correct answer is 1. By the late seventeenth century, most colonies had a two-house legislature with elected representatives. There was a substantial degree of local political autonomy, especially in New England. Throughout the colonies, free adult men with some property expected to have a say in how they were governed and taxed.

2. The correct answer is 2. Lincoln took an active role as president. He went ahead before he had congressional approval several times. For example, he suspended the writ of habeas corpus for people living between Philadelphia and Washington in order to ensure loyalty, and he started a major shipbuilding program.

3. The correct answer is 1. This theory was defined by John Marshall. The Constitution is the supreme law of the land, and it is the court's duty to uphold the law. Thus, it can decide if a law is unconstitutional. *Marbury v. Madison* (1803).

4. The correct answer is 4. The authors of the Constitution hoped to keep the president independent of Congress, parties, and the people by avoiding direct popular election.

5. The correct answer is 3. Sectional tensions came through over the issue of the tariff. The slave states did not favor high tariffs on imports. South Carolina actually nullified the tariff of 1828 and warned of secession. President Jackson declared that the state could not act against the Union in this fashion, but a compromise averted civil war at this stage.

6. The correct answer is 2. Section 9 of the Constitution prevented this from occurring earlier. However, this ban on importation did not eliminate slavery or the slave trade.

7. The correct answer is 4. The Seneca Falls Convention was organized by Elizabeth Cady Stanton and Lucretia Mott in 1848. They drafted their declaration using the format and language of the Declaration of Independence with its list of grievances. In this case, the grievances were made against men for not allowing a number of rights to women.

8. The correct answer is 2. In issuing the Emancipation Proclamation, Lincoln invoked his powers as commander-in-chief. The proclamation applied only to states in open rebellion—those which did not have representatives in Congress. It did not apply to areas that had fallen under Union control or to the border states.

9. The correct answer is 4. Eleven of the 13 states wrote new constitutions; Connecticut and Rhode Island amended their colonial charters. Most of the constitutions restricted the power of the governor. Governmental power was divided between executive, legislative, and judicial branches. Limits were placed on government, and the rights of citizens were delineated, sometimes in separate bills of rights.

10. The correct answer is 2. In addition, Maine was admitted as a free state, since Missouri entered as a slave state. This meant an equal number of slave and free states remained, while the rest of the compromise attempted to resolve future problems. The compromise kept slavery from being discussed directly for a time, but did not keep sectional tensions away completely.

11. The correct answer is 3. The Constitution created a federal system of government.

Laws of the United States were the laws of the land; states could not make foreign policy, engage in wars, or coin their own money, for example, but limits were also placed on the national government. States remained in control over electing senators, congressmen, and the president. Amendments to the Constitution required the consent of three-fourths of the states.

12. The correct answer is 2. Chief Justice Taney, a Maryland slaveholder, not only declared that Scott was not a citizen and therefore could not bring suit, but he also proclaimed that the Missouri Compromise was unconstitutional. He determined this by arguing that slaves were property and stating the Fifth Amendment prohibited Congress from taking property without due process. By this reasoning, slaveholders could not be deprived of their "property" anywhere.

13. The correct answer is 1. This was Stephen Douglas's plan to organize the Nebraska Territory. The Kansas-Nebraska Bill repealed the Missouri Compromise by asking residents to decide if they would have slavery or not. Douglas expected that the southern part of the territory, Kansas, would vote for slavery; the northern part, Nebraska would be free. Fighting erupted in Kansas as pro- and antislavery settlers collided.

14. The correct answer is 3. This was one of the objections made by the Anti-Federalists. The Bill of Rights, the first ten amendments, delineated the rights of citizens. Congress added a Bill of Rights to the Constitution in 1791.

15. The correct answer is 2. This was a compromise between what large states and small states wanted. However, delegates at the convention had a long tradition of a two house legislature—this concept was not new to them. In addition, slaves would be included in the population count by considering each slave to be three-fifths of a person.

Chapter 5

Industrialization of the United States

Part I: The Reconstructed Nation

A. Reconstruction Plans: Disputes between Congress and President; States and Federal Government, Status of Former Slaves

1. Lincoln's plan

   a. Begun during the war—restore political relations quickly. Used constitutional authority to grant pardons for federal offenses; would restore property, except slaves, to rebels, who would swear loyalty oath. (Excluded officials of Confederacy.) A state government could be established after ten percent of number who voted in 1860 election had taken oath. Only Congress could recognize seating members from reconstructed states. New state governments required to make new constitutions abolishing slavery. No provision for black suffrage included. To many in South, Reconstruction meant "carpetbaggers" (people from the North who took advantage of Southern defeat) and "scalawags" (white Southerners who cooperated with Northerners and ex-slaves).

   b. Wade-Davis Bill—submitted to Lincoln; he pocket vetoed it (did not sign it). Bill included appointment of provisional governors; left questions of political rights of blacks to the states; required action by fifty percent, instead of ten percent. Loyalty oath was designed to keep Confederate officials out of political participation by making them pledge past and future loyalty.

2. Reconstruction under Johnson

   a. Johnson carrying out Lincoln's policies, using executive powers, as Lincoln had. Modifies—to reenter Union, states had to nullify their secession ordinances, accept the thirteenth amendment, repudiate Confederate debts.

States quickly reenter, but ex-slaveholders returned to power. New Congress refused to seat senators and representatives from former Confederate states. Lincoln and Johnson—secession illegal, so states were never considered out of Union.

b. Congressional Reconstruction: Johnson and Congress opposed each other. Congress tried to get Freedmen's Bureau Bill and Civil Rights Bill passed; Johnson states that Congress does not have right to pass any Reconstruction legislation because Congress would not include the former Confederate states in their votes. Radical Republicans; former abolitionists, want to crush former planter class of South and help former slaves.

c. Impeachment: Congress trying to nullify Johnson's executive authority, especially his power as commander-in-chief—powers Lincoln had used to bypass Congress. Radical Republicans gain power in Congress: Thaddeus Stevens, Charles Sumner and others. Tenure of Office Act—designed to prevent Johnson from firing those opposed to his policies—trying to protect job of Secretary of War Stanton. Radical Republicans trying to make legislative branch supreme over executive and judiciary. Johnson impeached, but not convicted, by one vote,1868.

d. Radical Reconstruction: Confederate states had forfeited statehood. Military occupation—divided into five districts, adult black males to be registered along with qualified white males, elect delegates to state constitutional conventions—new constitutions to include voting rights for black men and ratification of Fourteenth Amendment. Black Codes—Southern states pass laws restricting freedom of blacks—could only work or live in certain places; could not vote or bear arms—did not have rights of full citizens.

e. Post–Civil War Amendments: Thirteenth amendment (prohibited slavery), Fourteenth amendment (anyone born or naturalized in United States is a citizen—gives civil rights to slaves), Fifteenth Amendment (gives ex-slaves the right to vote).

B. The North

   1. Civil War stimulated economy and technology in North

      a. War production boosted heavy industries: coal, iron, steel

      b. New technology in industries helped production; also in agriculture, mechanization, such as McCormick reapers, increased production.

      c. Northern railroads benefit—build northern route for transcontinental railroad—Congress gave charter to Union Pacific and Central Pacific railroads

   2. World Markets—industrialization and technology increase production, exported to world markets; mass-produced goods less expensive than handcrafted

   3. Labor—northern farm families had new agricultural tools, didn't suffer from loss of labor; industrial and urban workers faced inflation during war, form national unions, strike activity squashed by employers, sometimes with help of federal troops.

      a. Panic of 1873—caused by banks lending too much money toward building western railroads. When important bank, Jay Cooke and Company, goes bankrupt, panic begins; three million people out of work; clashes between labor and business, as many workers are laid off as result of the Panic—series of railroad strikes in 1877 (especially violent one in Pittsburgh).

C. The New South

   1. Agriculture: Land and labor. Industrialization of South part of Reconstruction policies, but still heavily agricultural. Rely on cotton production, but lost markets during war—the cotton sold to Europe; prices do not recover; many landholders in debt.

   2. Status of former slaves

      a. Rise of sharecropping system—Sharecropping begins as compromise between landowners who do not have cash to pay wages and former slaves who do not want to work in gangs under white supervision as they did when they were slaves. Landowners divide their land into small plots—provide seed, mule, plow and other supplies; sharecroppers do the work and give the owners part of the crop in return. Owners have first share, so sharecroppers suffer when agricultural prices decline.

b. Importance of education; schools started by Freedmen's Bureau. Beginnings of public school system in South—segregated. Colleges: Howard University, Fisk University, and others

c. Segregation common by 1870s in theaters, trains, other public areas

d. Looking for better opportunities, some former slaves begin to migrate North. Exodusters, former slaves who move to Kansas; more than 20,000 arrive between 1878 and 1879.

3. Struggle for political control

a. Key controversy during Reconstruction—citizenship rights for southern whites and for former slaves

b. Former planters oppose rights for former slaves, try to regain control in new state governments

c. Ku Klux Klan—not just attacks on blacks; also attack and kill white Republicans, anyone helping to get black votes.

4. Supreme Court and Fourteenth Amendment—in 1870s, narrowed meaning and effectiveness of the Fourteenth Amendment. *Bradwell v. Illinois* (1873), a female attorney had not been permitted to practice law. Argued that this was against her rights as a citizen. Supreme court disagreed. In other decisions, the Court declared that state citizenship and national citizenship are separate, only very few specific rights of national citizenship protected by Fourteenth Amendment.

a. Fourteenth Amendment: Relationships to federal and state governments, relationship of government and business, relations to individual rights, court cases: *Munn v. Illinois* (1877), *Lochner v. New York* (1905), *Muller v. Oregon* (1908).

5. Debates over "proper" role of blacks

a. Booker T. Washington—favored black accommodation to whites, Atlanta Compromise. Self-help. Founded Tuskegee Institute (1881).

B. W.E.B. Du Bois—"anti-Bookerite." "Talented Tenth," educated, intellectual blacks should be leaders and

examples to other African Americans. Helped found
National Association for the Advancement of Colored
People (NAACP) in 1909.

D. The Grant Era

 1. As president, Grant politically naïve; supports friends he's
     hired even when they are corrupt. Administration filled with
     scandals and corruption—Black Friday gold scandal, Crédit
     Mobilier, kickbacks and bribery within his cabinet. Grant
     reelected in 1872, helped by black voters in the South. Panic
     of 1873

 2. Whites still made up majority of voters in South. White
     Democratic Party in South—"white supremacy" was slogan.

     a. "Solid South"—most southern whites were Democrats.
         No former slave state voted Republican in presidential
         election in late nineteenth century.

E. End of Reconstruction

 1. Election of 1876—dispute over electoral votes between
     Samuel J. Tilden (Democrat) and Rutherford B. Hayes
     (Republican). Special commission, voting on Republican
     lines, names Hayes president.

 2. Part of compromise over election—Hayes would withdraw
     last federal troops from South, allowing white Democrats to
     take power there.

 3   Southern blacks lose rights, despite constitutional
     amendments.

     a. *Plessy v. Ferguson* (1896)—Court endorses "separate but
         equal." Will not be overturned until *Brown v. Board of
         Education* decision (1954).

Part II: The Rise of American Business, Industry, and Labor, 1865–1920

A. Technology and World Industrialization

 1. Technological developments, 1750–1860

     a. Development of new and effective steam engine by James
         Watt in England—produced more coal, iron; used in
         textile mills; used in flour, malt, flint and sugar mills.

    b. Railroads—"iron horse"; aids industrialization by making transportation faster and easier after 1840; distances can be measured in time, rather than distance.

    c. Factory system—putting-out system; mass production instead of handcrafted; factory workers instead of skilled craftsmen; new emphasis on time schedules—dehumanization, alienation

2. Impact on People: England

    a. First country to industrialize—due to colonies, stable government, effective central bank, developed credit markets, demand for goods

    b. Social critics condemn conditions of mills for workers: Blake, "satanic mills," Marx and Engels—proletariat consciousness

    c. Factory workers had to change lifestyle

    d. Factories employed children and whole families—child labor laws inevitable

    e. Trade unions and increased political activity

B. Pre–Civil War Industrial Growth

1. Samuel Slater and others smuggle plans for mills and other technology out of England.

2. Cotton gin makes growing profitable, increases need for mills

3. United States has natural resources: water power, coal for steam power

4. United States has money, laborers, many inventors, too

C. Business Organization

1. Proprietorships and partnerships—creditors can seize assets of individually owned businesses or partnerships, if business goes bankrupt.

2. Corporations—sell "shares" in a company. Helps entrepreneurs raise money, limits risks. Examples: Standard Oil, U.S. Steel Corporation, Amalgamated Copper Company, American Sugar Refining Company, American Tobacco Company, U.S. Rubber Company

D. Organizational Changes

1. Venture capital—necessary in formation of new enterprises—investment with expectation of return. These were key ideas of businessmen of the time.

2. Expanding national and international markets—United States expands geographically and in population. Overseas markets become more accessible.

3. Merchandising changes

   a. Department stores—Wanamaker's, Marshall Field, help fuel new consumerism. Available goods, charge accounts.

   b. Mail order—Montgomery Ward; Sears Roebuck—make consumer products available in rural areas.

E. Major Areas of Growth in Business and Industry

1. Transportation

   a. Railroads—help connect people and products across United States Urban centers develop along key transportation routes.

   b. Automobiles—mass production (use of assembly lines, interchangeable parts) makes Henry Ford's Model T affordable to many workers by 1920s

   c. Urban transportation—needed due to rapid growth of cities; horse-car lines, steam-powered elevated train (el), electric trolleys

2. Steel—made from iron, but much stronger. Used in buildings, bridges, rails for trains. Too expensive for general use before Civil War. New method to make it discovered by both Henry Bessemer (England) and William Kelly (U.S.) Andrew Carnegie realizes significance, begins production of new Bessemer steel mill outside Pittsburgh.

3. Energy sources

   a. Coal—United States had large amounts of coal, necessary for steam production.

   b. Oil—1855, discovery that crude oil can be broken down into kerosene. Cheap fuel for cooking and heating. Pennsylvania oil rush develops.

   c. Electricity—Edison invents incandescent light bulb; by 1900, more than 3,000 towns and cities were electrically illuminated. Once alternating current was developed, electricity could be transmitted over large distances.

d. Communications

1) telegraph—invented by Samuel F. B. Morse, 1861; connects East and West coasts, revolutionizes communication across country, provides information to railroads. Underwater cable links United States and Europe in 1866.

2) telephone—invented by Alexander Graham Bell in 1876. By 1900, 1.5 million Americans connected.

F. Entrepreneurs

1. Examples

a. Rockefeller—oil refining, Standard Oil

b. Carnegie—steel

c. Ford—automobile

2. Work ethic: Cotton Mather (Puritan ethics), Benjamin Franklin, Gospel of Success (Rockefeller, Russell B. Conwell, "Acres of Diamonds"—opportunities everywhere to get rich), Horatio Alger (writes popular boys' novels). Values of virtue, hard work, honesty would be rewarded by wealth and success.

3. Conflict between public good and private gain: Carnegie believed that pursuit of riches made United States strong, but that wealthy had duty to distribute wealth so that poor could join in competition. Other rich men also turn to philanthropy, perhaps to counteract criticism of their lifestyles and business practices by such people as Ida Tarbell and the "muckrakers."

G. New Business and Government Practices

1. Interpretation of Fourteenth Amendment: *Santa Clara County v. the Southern Pacific Railroad* (1886). Supreme Court ruled corporation a "person" under Fourteenth Amendment—states could not deprive them of property or rights without due process.

2. Pools, trusts, holding companies, and mergers

a. Pools: Competing companies made agreements about how much each should produce, prices to be charged. Used mainly by railroads to divide up the traffic. Interstate Commerce Act of 1887 outlawed pools.

b. Trusts: One company gains control over stock of other companies in same industry. Sherman Anti-Trust Act (1890)—language left vague; few cases were actually tried under this act.

c. Holding Companies: own partial or complete interest in other companies. (Trusts hold in trusteeship, don't own.)

d. Mergers: holding companies can merge their constituent companies' assets and management. Vertical integration—to control all aspects of the business, including raw material, production, distribution. Example: J. P. Morgan and U.S. Steel Corporation consisted of iron-ore properties, railroads, wire mills, and other firms.

3. Business mergers—tended to produce monopolies, threaten competition. Government can help or hinder business through trade agreements, taxes and tariffs, banking laws, laws concerning labor, and laws concerning business or corporations.

4. Railroad rate inequities: railroads would boost rates on noncompetitive lines to make up for low rates on competitive lines. Played favorites: gave special rates to some businesses and favored customers. *Munn v. Illinois* (1877)—Supreme Court upheld railroad rate regulation. Interstate Commerce Commission (1877) created.

H. Labor Unionization

1. Knights of Labor (1869)—included unskilled workers, as well as skilled; also included women and African Americans. Knights grew under leadership of Terence Powderly. Believed in cooperative society rather than in striking.

2. American Federation of Labor (AFL) (1886)—federation of craft unions; skilled workers only; hostile to women.

a. Goal was "bread and butter": concrete goals—higher wages, shorter hours, better working conditions, and the right to collective bargaining. Not interested in idealistic or vague goals of Knights.

b. Would strike if necessary, but believed in bargaining with employers. AFL supported capitalist system.

c. Samuel Gompers, head of Cigar Makers Union, was president of AFL: 1886–1894; 1896–1924.

    d. Opposed immigration was especially anti-Japanese and anti-Chinese; opposed organization of women and blacks.

3. Women's Trade Union League (1903)—worked for protective legislation for working women, sponsored educational activities, campaigned for women's suffrage. Began with middle-class leadership, but shift in leadership to workers in 1910s.

4. Industrial Workers of the World (IWW or "Wobblies")— believed in socialism, used violence and sabotage. Workers should seize nation's industries—anticapitalism.

5. Struggle and conflict

    a. Haymarket Riot (1886)—anarchists arrested and convicted. Followed by mass arrests of anarchists. Many believe need for stronger law and order, suspect anarchists, socialists, and immigrants.

    b. Homestead Strike (1892)—strike in Homestead, PA. Carnegie Steel closes plant. Pinkerton guards brought in and attacked. State militia brought in. Strikers give up after five months.

    c. Pullman Strike (1894)—workers' strike supported by American Railway Union led by Eugene V. Debs. Federal injunction to prevent union from "holding up the mails." Federal troops called in—strike crushed. Debs arrested. Supreme Court rules that federal court has power to remove obstacles to interstate commerce.

    d. Lawrence, MA, strike (1912)—women textile workers' strike, participation in IWW strike.

6. Negotiation and mediation generally more effective than confrontational methods. Government has played crucial role in balance of power between labor and management. Late nineteenth-century government generally supported business. Big business had political allies in Congress, used bribery and other means to keep government on its side. *Example*: Sherman Anti-Trust Act busted few trusts, but was used against strikers.

Part III: Adjusting Society to Industrialism: American People and Places

A. Impact of Industrialization on People

1. Urbanization; quality of urban life

   a. Industrialization part of world phenomenon—in nineteenth century only parts of Europe, North America, and Japan were industrialized, but effects seen everywhere—U.S. grain cheaper than local products; mass-produced goods cheaper than handmade ones.

   b. Attractions of cities: jobs (industrial and commercial centers), education, culture.

   c. Skyscrapers—used new steel-frame construction to support; had electric elevators and steam heating systems. More effective use of expensive urban lots.

   d. Problems—housing shortages, especially for poor; crowded, dirty conditions, little ventilation in slum apartments

      1) inadequate water and sanitation—no bathrooms in tenement apartments, too many using privies, horse manure also on streets, unsafe drinking water

      2) crime, larger urban areas with crowded conditions breed violence; some if it might have been just more conspicuous; blamed on immigrants and African Americans who migrated to cities

   e. Cities begin to pass more regulations—housing, sanitation, expanded power of police, but many felt this restricted individual freedoms

   f. Social Darwinism—Darwin's "survival of the fittest" mixed with laissez faire: power and wealth naturally acquired by most capable. Idea developed by Herbert Spencer in England. Yale professor, William Graham Sumner, help spread in United States. Carnegie, "Gospel of Wealth," and other wealthy individuals were trustees, had duty to raise the "moral culture," of society—endow museums, hospitals, libraries.

   g. Conspicuous consumption—Thorstein Veblen's term; very rich display their wealth just to show how wealthy they are. Buy yachts, private train cars, expensive jewels, give parties costing thousands of dollars, etcetera.

h. Industrialization improved the living standard for many, but also increased gap between rich and poor. Henry George, *Progress and Poverty* (1879), promotes idea of "single tax" based on property values but not improvements by owners. Believed landowners becoming rich because of demand for land, especially in cities. Changed the nature of work from individual producers to mass production by employees. Impact on families and communities.

2. Work and Workers

a. Factories and people: cause changes and problems; Buffalo, Detroit, Pittsburgh, Patterson, Utica, and others. Human-made environment replaced or changed natural environment of many areas. Upton Sinclair published exposé of meat-packing plants, *The Jungle* (1906).

b. Industries and cities built near transportation; raw materials and power source available. Working-class people and immigrants tended to congregate in inner-city neighborhoods.

c. Working conditions—steam power and improved machinery take over many jobs of craftsmen. Unskilled workers in factories are more interchangeable, so they can be poorly paid. Factory workers—12-hour working days, 6 days a week. Poor working conditions; courts usually ruled that employers not liable for injuries suffered by workers.

d. Workers: skilled, usually native born, English/Irish ancestry. Usually unskilled; women, children, recent immigrants. "Sweat shops," child labor, few blacks in factory jobs.

3. Women, families, and work

a. Traditional role—is ideal for upper- and middle-class women: they take care of home and family, religious, spiritually "pure," wear restrictive clothing, can't be physically active—reality: some women have always worked outside the home, poor women could never be the "ideal," women denied equal rights

b. Patriarchal societies tend to restrict women's roles to home and family.

c. Taking care of households was hard work; laundry, for example, had to be washed by hand with water heated on stove, hung up to dry, ironed without electric irons. While taking in boarders brought in extra money, it also meant cooking and cleaning for more people.

d. Women frequently held low-income factory, service, and domestic jobs: maids, laundresses, textile workers. Industrialization and changes in technology opened up clerical jobs to women, previously held by men (who moved to managerial positions). Women use typewriters, cash registers, and other new inventions. Also took jobs as telephone operators.

e. Emerging family patterns: two wage earners, broken homes. Some women have always worked outside home, but larger numbers of women entered workforce with industrialization. Women paid less than men, but two incomes needed to support families in many cases. Children also have to work to help support families. Kinship ties important—immigrants or migrants to cities can live with kin, find jobs for kin.

f. Women often empathized with social reform movements. Early twentieth century, many wealthy women turn from frivolity and spending to becoming involved in causes such as Prohibition and helping the poor. Settlement houses, such as Jane Addams's Hull House in Chicago (1889) and Lillian Wald's Henry Street Settlement in New York (1893). Frances Willard, head of Women's Christian Temperance Union (W.C.T.U.).

4. Growing middle class

a. Emerging standards of cultural values—fashion, houses, furniture, magazines, amusements. Changes emerge. Wealthy—conspicuous consumption, but middle class fashions and lifestyle changes, too. "Gibson Girl," named after Charles Dana Gibson, a magazine illustrator—becomes popular image for women, not a feminist, but self-assured, participate in sports and other activities.

b. Conveniences—flush toilet, around 1900. Middle-class urban homes concerned with cleanliness—bathrooms are private. Canned goods, refrigerated railroad cars, and home iceboxes make food more available. Women participating more in work and leisure activities; fashions change, less restrictive, shorter hemlines.

c. Leisure activities—white-collar workers have more leisure time than previously. Organized sports become popular, especially baseball. Other sports: croquet and bicycling, men and women participate. Circuses, shows, vaudeville. By 1910, movies were distinct art form.

5. Art and literature

a. Dime novels and penny press make reading and news available to working class. New magazines appeal to those less intellectual, sell for a dime, make profit from advertising: *Ladies' Home Journal, McClure's , Munsey's, Saturday Evening Post*.

b. Yellow Journalism: Pulitzer's *New York World*, Hearst's *New York Journal*, sensationalism, also more on sports and women's issues. Other papers emulate. Hearst and Pulitzer played up Spanish brutality in Cuba; invented incidents in order to get readers. Promote war fever after U.S.S. *Maine* explodes in Havana harbor.

c. Realism, Naturalism, Regionalism in literature; Mark Twain, Henry James, Stephen Crane, Frank Norris, Jack London, Theodore Dreiser.

d. Importance of philanthropy in aiding fine arts; importance of more leisure time. Changes in arts reveal changes in society.

B. The Immigrant and Changing Patterns

1. Colonization and "old" immigration (1609–1860)

a. British colonies—white population came mostly from northern and western Europe. Reasons: religious persecution, economic benefits, political freedom. Many came as indentured servants.

b. Mid-nineteenth century—Irish Catholics fleeing famine, Germans fleeing revolution, Chinese arrive in California after gold discovered, 1849. Small groups of Sephardic and German Jews assimilated into American society.

b. Africans—came involuntarily as slaves.

c. Others become part of United States by conquest and annexation—French Acadians, Mexicans/Hispanics.

d. Nativist reactions—mostly against Irish Catholics and African Americans.

e. Immigration has been the source of rich cultural pluralism in the United States, but nonwhites, especially, have found assimilation difficult to attain.

2. "New" Immigration (1870–1924)

a. Between 1865 and 1915, 25 million immigrants came to United States. New sources of immigration: eastern/southern Europe; Asia.

b. Often very poor. Not all planning permanent settlement in United States, just sending money home. Others facing religious persecution or conscription in armies.

c. Migration of African Americans to northern cities.

d. Attractions in United States: fill labor shortage, liberty and freedom here.

e. Urbanization: ghettoes—members of each ethnic group lived in own neighborhoods—some comfortable with distinct customs, religion, language, foods. Those separated from families often lived with kin.

f. "Americanization" process. Crisis of identity—immigrants have to choose which cultural traditions to retain; which American behaviors to adopt. English taught in schools, need to speak it to get jobs; cooked ethnic meals with American ingredients. Hard work—looking for American success.

g. Impact on family, education, politics—kinship ties to get jobs. Family members all need to work. Often live in crowded conditions with boarders. Children learn English and American customs in schools. Ethnic "bosses," such as Boss Tweed of Tammany Hall (New York), advance by bringing in votes for urban political "machines."

h. Religion—United States changes from mostly Protestant to a nation composed of Protestants, Catholics, and Jews. Religious tolerance develops slowly, assisted by diversity of beliefs. Puritanical beliefs and values persist in our historical development. Some Catholics and Jews try to accommodate their religious practices to American culture, support liberalizing trends, but often face resistance from new immigrants.

    i. Immigrants—provide United States with great diversity; help build modern cultural diversity—folk music, African American jazz; Italian, Mexican, Chinese cuisines.

  3. Reactions to "new" immigration

    a. Cultural pluralism—Americans have ambivalent attitudes toward new immigration; empathy and welcoming attitudes mixed with prejudice and disapproval. How much do immigrants have to assimilate? "Melting pot" or cultural pluralism, or both?

    b. Nativist reactions: new immigrants seem much more alien to many Americans—different foods, language, customs, and religions. Stereotypes develop about various ethnic groups. Nonwhites face most discrimination in housing, education, employment.

    c. Constitutional rights of ethnic and racial groups have changed and developed over time. Exclusion Act (1882)—kept Chinese from legally entering United States. Japanese and other groups excluded in 1924. African Americans kept from voting through poll taxes and literacy requirements. "Red Scare" after Bolshevik Revolution. American radicals: Wobblies, anarchists, socialists, union leaders, and others labeled as "red." House of Representatives refused to seat Congressman Victor Berger—charged with being pro-German and pro-Bolshevik.

    d. Quota Act of 1921 and Immigration Act of 1924 set quotas on number of immigrants who could enter United States. Favored northern and western Europeans over southern and eastern Europeans, and Asians.

C. The Last Frontier (1850–1890)

  1. Frontier: Myth and Reality, 1607 to present

    a. Colonial idea—frontier frightening; wilderness needs to be tamed and ordered. Few go beyond mountains and other natural barriers. Nineteenth century: frontier represents root of American individualism. Frederick Jackson Turner, "The Significance of the Frontier in American History" (1893)—as Americans moved west, constantly breaking through frontier, American character formed—powerful, self-confident, belief that anyone can succeed. Frontier seen as "virgin land"; Native Americans seen as not having conquered or properly occupied the land. Justification to spread white American culture—"manifest destiny." Ignore consequences to nonwhite minorities and to environment.

2. Land west of Mississippi

   a. Rolling plains—mechanization in agriculture, railroads, make this area profitable for grain and meat production—world's breadbasket. Great American Desert—populated by Native Americans; subsistence farming through irrigation; Mormons practice extensive irrigation in Utah Territory.

   b. Traditional native people—empathy with environment; interdependence with land, sky, water.

   c. Homestead Act (1862)—distributed free land to citizens who resided on and cultivated land for five years—encouraged western settlement. Morrill Land Grant Act (1862)—endowed states with land to finance agricultural and industrial colleges, favored East because acreage tied to size of congressional delegation; colleges founded do help agricultural development.

3. Impact of Industrialization

   a. Plains supply grain and meat to urban East.

   b. Railroad construction booms between 1865 and 1890. Towns grow along the lines, country goes by railroad established time zones, refrigerated cars transport foodstuffs. Other cars bring freight and people.

   c. Great migration of people to the West between 1870 and 1890; average of 1.6 million acres of new farmland cultivated each year. Some migrants from eastern states; others from Europe. Railroad agents recruit settlers from Denmark, Sweden, Germany. California imports laborers from Mexico and Japan.

   d. Many invest in West—railroads, cattle, commercial farming.

   e. Key urban centers develop—often along railroads and in mining towns.

4. Native Americans

   a. Pushed westward by white settlement from colonial times. Cherokee and others forced to resettle in Indian Territory (Oklahoma) in 1830s. Different views of land ownership; white belief that they can settle wherever they wish. Subsistence and ecological balance was way of life for Native Americans. Deliberate slaughter of buffalo by whites, helps destroy this balance on plains.

b. Indian tribes treated as separate nations by U.S. government—made treaties, then ignored treaties. New policies in 1870s—"civilize" Indians instead of treating them as separate nations. New policies—place Indians on reservations.

c. Indian wars, 1850–1900—U.S. Army preferred pitched battles, but Indians favored hit-and-run skirmishes. Two hundred "incidents" recorded by army, 1869–1876. Sioux led by Chiefs Sitting Bull, Crazy Horse, and Rain-in-the-Face defeat Custer at Little Bighorn River in Montana in 1876. Final suppression of Plains Indians, Battle of Wounded Knee (1890).

d. Helen Hunt Jackson, *A Century of Dishonor* (1881), focused American attention on how Indians had been treated—cheated of lands and forced onto reservations with worthless land. Americans demand reforms.

e. Dawes Severalty Act (1887)—dissolves tribal lands; land distributed; 160 acres to each head of family; additional 80 acres to each adult member; extra land sold to whites. Problems: Most Indians were not farmers, and most of the land was worthless, and western tribes did not think in terms of private ownership in a family; tribe was basic social unit. Also expected that Indians would leave their "uncivilized" ways if children were sent away and educated at boarding schools in the East. Officials also fund white church groups and schools in order to suppress Indian religious ceremonies.

f. Ghost Dance. As result of these policies, a prophet named Wovoka tries to revitalize and restore culture; brings about "Ghost Dance." Promises that buffalo and ancestors would return, and whites would disappear. White government fearful of Ghost Dance—fear it will lead to uprisings. Leads to Battle of Wounded Knee.

5. The Cattle Frontier

a. Romantic image of cowboys—created during the time of frontier and embraced by cowboys, as well as Easterners. Cowboy clothing, boots, bandana, western saddle—all derived from Mexican *vaqueros*. Twenty-five percent of cowboys may have been former slaves.

b. Open range—cattle owners would buy few acres near stream allow cattle to graze on large area of public domain land. Ranchers sometimes banded together—cattle grazed over wide territory; each rancher had own brand: cattle roundups twice a year.

c. Big profits; cattle start to overrun range. Land can't support so many. Fights between cattle ranchers and sheepherders who move into area. Ranchers start to set up barbed wire fences illegally on public land. Winters of 1886 and 1887 destroy many cattle; many ranchers ruined. By 1890, big business taking over cattle industry.

6. The farming frontier

a. Plains very dry—much drier than eastern farmland; had to plow deeper. Few trees, so houses made of sod.

b. Technology: barbed wire kept out farmer's livestock and open-range cattle; new chilled steel plow could slice through sod; other new farm machinery made American farmers most productive of the world, and able to cultivate more land. Railroad brought migrants to plains, brought goods, carried crops to markets. Arid Great Plains were environmental challenge met by technological ingenuity.

c. Life on Great Plains: water, fuel, and lumber scarce. Climate unpredictable—some years enough rain, other years droughts. Very hot during summer; blizzards during winter. Grasshopper swarms destroyed farms in 1870s and 1880s. Settlers isolated—might be miles from neighbors. Women especially isolated.

d. Problems: market and rail dependence: farmers dependant on railroads to move their crops and to bring them goods. Railroads have special rates for favored customers, politicians, and shippers. *Munn v. Illinois* (1877)—stated that railroads must submit to regulation for public good. Interstate Commerce Act (1887)—outlawed pools, rebates, discrimination in rates, and created Interstate Commerce Commission. Farmers in debt to buy machinery, seeds, provisions; agricultural prices fell lower, collapsed in 1890. Overproduction, so prices low, but transportation, storage and sales fees high. Farmers had to produce more, but the more produced, the lower prices dropped. Many farmers lost their farms, couldn't pay mortgages.

7. Agrarian Protest

    a. Grange movement—farmers form networks of local organizations in 1860s and 1870s. Strong in Midwest and South. Mostly social; involved women and families. Moved into political and economic action—formed cooperatives for buying and selling. Not successful, most farmers did not have available cash, and big business undercut them. Elected legislators who passed Grange laws to regulate railroad rates and storage rates, but courts ruled against them.

    b. Political response. Farmer's alliances developed in Midwest and South by 1890. Included Colored Farmers' National Alliance—one million black members. Farmers blamed their plight on monetary scarcity—working against crop liens, railroads, "money power." Northern and southern branches don't unite.

    c. Court cases: *Munn v. Illinois* (1877)—Supreme Court ruled public had right to regulate business for common good. *Wabash, St. Louis, and Pacific Railway Co. v. Illinois* (1886)—only Congress can regulate commerce between and among states; Illinois legislature could not regulate freight rates between cities within Illinois. Very unpopular ruling; Court reinterpreted interstate commerce clause of Constitution, favored large railroad companies.

    d. Interstate Commerce Commission created (1887); calmed anti-railroad feelings. I.C.C. develops rules and regulations regarding interstate commerce. Sherman Antitrust Act (1890)—attempt to stop consolidation movement—very vague language. *U.S. v. E. C. Knight Company* (1895)—Court favored the Sugar Trust; ruled manufacturing was not commerce.

    e. Populism—Alliance become more political. Form political party, Populist Party wants to reform corrupt government. Omaha platform included: government ownership of railroad, telegraph lines; silver coinage, graduated income tax, direct election of senators, shorter hours for workers.

       f. Election of 1896—William Jennings Bryan becomes both Democratic and Populist candidate for president. "Cross of gold" speech helped bring about his candidacy. Free silver is big issue. McKinley, republican candidate, wins election. Silver issue kept Populists from building urban-rural coalition. Neither labor leaders nor socialists would unite with Populists.

D. American Society at Turn of Century

    1. George Eastman—modernizes camera; Kodak camera, 1888. Ordinary people can make own photographs. Photography released painting from realism—leads to impressionism and abstract art.

    2. Utopian writers: Henry George, *Progress and Poverty* (1879); Edward Bellamy, *Looking Backward* (1888); Henry Demarest Lloyd, *Wealth Against Commonwealth* (1894). Oppose monopolies; George argued for "single tax," Bellamy and Lloyd favored government ownership of production.

    3. United States sees many changes: agrarian to urban base; European to American culture, frontier to city. Pluralistic society. Entering Modern Age.

Questions

1. Industrialization in America is characterized by which of the following?
   1. little interest in technological inventions and innovations
   2. concentration on local and regional markets
   3. growth of cities in size and predominance
   4. large business concerns divide into smaller and more manageable units

2. During Reconstruction, radical Republicans believed it was necessary to
   1. ensure the rights of the former slaves.
   2. treat the South compassionately and sympathetically.
   3. follow the president's guidelines on Reconstruction policy.
   4. conclude Reconstruction as quickly as possible.

3. In the 1880s, "new" immigrants into the United States arrived mostly from
   1. South America.
   2. southern and eastern Europe.
   3. northern and western Europe.
   4. Asia.

4. "We will answer their demand for a gold standard by saying to them: 'You shall not press down upon the brow of labor this crown of thorns, you shall not crucify mankind upon a cross of gold.'"

   These words are part of a speech that

   1. was McKinley's acceptance speech for the Republican candidacy.
   2. united Republicans and Populists.
   3. was made by William Jennings Bryan on behalf of the silver coinage platform at the Democratic convention.
   4. helped the Populists win the election of 1896.

5. The Dawes Severalty Act of 1887 granted Indians
   1. tribal sovereignty.
   2. land allotted to each family.
   3. community-owned tribal lands.
   4. greater representation in Congress.

6. Four standard time zones were established in the United States in 1883 by
   1. the army.
   2. Congress.
   3. the railroads.
   4. the president.

7. After which of the below did Jim Crow laws spread quickly throughout the South?
   1. The Supreme Court upheld the separate-but-equal doctrine.
   2. African Americans migrated into southern cities.
   3. Northern states passed quotas on immigration.
   4. Southern farmers joined the alliance.

8. The American Federation of Labor
   1. was composed of craft unions that called for practical goals, such as higher wages and shorter hours.
   2. called for a socialistic state.

3. permitted skilled and unskilled workers to join.

4. instigated the Haymarket riot.

9. The Industrial Workers of the World believed

1. U.S. industries should be taken over by workers who would then run the industries.

2. workers should be organized in craft unions.

3. workers should align themselves with the Republican party.

4. they should be affiliated with the AFL.

10. In the case of *U.S. v. E.C. Knight Co.* (1895), the Supreme Court

1. used the Sherman Antitrust Act to break up a monopoly for the first time.

2. declared the Sherman Antitrust Act unconstitutional.

3. strengthened the Sherman Antitrust Act.

4. left the Sherman Antitrust Act with only token power to limit monopolies.

11. In *Munn v. Illinois*, the Supreme Court

1. upheld the ownership and management of the railroads by the federal government.

2. upheld the principle of railroad regulation.

3. outlawed the practice of railroad regulation.

4. declared railroad regulation unconstitutional.

12. A critical feature in fostering settlement of the Great Plains was

1. construction of railroads reaching that area of the country.

2. an end to Indian resistance.

3. a decline in farm indebtedness.

4. inflation throughout the country.

13. Congress impeached President Andrew Johnson for

1. permitting former slaves to vote.

2. granting women the right to vote.

3. violating the Tenure of Office Act.

4. confiscating the property of Southerners.

14. In the late nineteenth century, the federal government's Indian policy was characterized by

1. strategies to protect the buffalo.

2. encouraging Native Americans to learn the ways of white society through education and the abandonment of their own culture.

3. trying to preserve and revitalize tribal culture.

4. attempts to compensate Native Americans for past mistreatment.

15. In the period after the Civil War, the working-class neighborhoods of American cities

1. revealed no intermingling of ethnic groups.

2. were characterized by ethnic groups living in a particular area.

3. did not permit families to create any kind of community life.

4. were healthy and sanitary places in which to live.

Answers

1. The correct answer is 3. Cities were growing along with expanded markets and development and interest in technological advances. Production was organized in large factories, and large enterprises also grew.

2. The correct answer is 1. A minority within the Republican party, the Radicals drew strength from their clearly defined objectives. They were interested in reforming the South, and ensuring the rights of freedmen was a primary goal.

3. The correct answer is 2. Before this time, immigrants came mostly from northern and western Europe. Immigrants still arrived from this area, but a new wave of immigrants from southern and eastern Europe began appearing in the 1880s. By the next century, large numbers of immigrants were coming from Japan and Mexico, too.

4. The correct answer is 3. This was the closing of Bryan's speech at the convention. It helped him win the presidential nomination for the Democrats. He also became the Populists' choice, with Tom Watson as the vice-presidential nominee. The Democrats chose Arthur Sewall as their vice-presidential candidate.

5. The correct answer is 2. Land was provided to families, according to family size. The act dissolved community-owned tribal land, and went against the way of life of the tribes.

6. The correct answer is 3. Time had to be standardized for rail schedules, so the railroads agreed on these time zones.

7. The correct answer is 1. The Supreme Court ruled that the rights of citizens were the responsibility of the states, and not protected under the Fourteenth Amendment. *Plessy v. Ferguson* and other cases upheld the doctrine of "separate but equal."

8. The correct answer is 1. The AFL was composed of craft unions. Members were skilled workers; women were excluded. The AFL was interested in practical goals like better wages and conditions. It accepted the capitalist system.

9. The correct answer is 1. The IWW espoused socialism and would use violence to achieve its aims.

10. The correct answer is 4. This case involved the Sugar Trust. The Court ruled that domination of manufacturing did not necessarily mean control of trade.

11. The correct answer is 2. Although railroads fought it, the Court upheld the principle of railroad regulation for "the common good."

12. The correct answer is 1. The railroads were instrumental in bringing settlers and supplies to the Great Plains.

13. The correct answer is 3. Johnson was impeached, but not convicted. Congress passed the Tenure of Office Act to limit Johnson's power and to try to protect Secretary of War Stanton.

14. The correct answer is 2. The government encouraged missionaries and teachers to spread the ideals and values of white Americans to the Indians. Tribal life was further diminished under the Dawes Act.

15. The correct answer is 2. Immigrants
    tended to live in their own
    neighborhoods. Living conditions were
    very crowded, and generally unhealthy.

Chapter 6

The Progressive Movement

Responses to the Challenges Brought About by Industrialization and Urbanization

I. Reform In America

A. The Reform Tradition—United States has experienced periodic outbursts of democratic reform protests. Examples:

  1. American Revolution (1776–1781—Treaty signed in 1783)

  2. Abolition movement (c.1820–1861)

  3. Women's rights (1848—Seneca Falls Convention; 1865–1920—Nineteenth Amendment gives women right to vote; c.1960–1970—Betty Friedan's *The Feminine Mystique*, published 1963.)

  4. Civil Service (1865–1891—Pendleton Civil Service Act of 1883)

  5. Disadvantaged: mentally ill (earlier movements in nineteenth century and after WWI) (1970–1990)—concerns about Vietnam veterans; Americans with Disabilities Act of 1990.

B. Pressures for Reform

  1. Effects of developing technologies and their social, ethical, and moral impact.

  2. Struggle for fair standards of business operation and working conditions.

  3. Increasing inequities between wealth and poverty.

  4. Rising power and influence of middle class.

  5. Emergence of communications means that were cheap and socially responsive.

C. Progress: Social and Economic Reform and Consumer Protection

  1. The "muckrakers" and reform: named muckrakers by Theodore Roosevelt. Exposed corruption in society and government; gave public sensationalistic insider views and scandals to read about. Examples:

     a. Magazine writers: Lincoln Steffens's articles on city bosses, collected as *The Shame of the Cities* (1904), originally published in *McClure's; Ida M. Tarbell, on Standard Oil (1904)*.

     b. Novelists: Upton Sinclair, *The Jungle* (1906)—novel about the meat-packing industry.

     c. *The Jungle* spurred passage of a meat-inspection bill that had been sitting in Congress. Congress also passed Pure Food and Drug Act.

     d. Muckraking stories attracted readers, but after a few years, quality of the work declined, and less scrupulous journalists fabricated "news" stories.

     e. Muckraking—investigative journalism still in practice today. Example: coverage of Watergate by Carl Bernstein and Bob Woodward in *Washington Post*. "Watchdog" media can provide a balance to the powers of government and economic forces.

  2. Other areas of concern—rights of ethnic and racial groups under the Constitution; definition of equality has changed over the course of U.S. history.

     a. Social settlement movement—run mostly by middle-class women; live in slum neighborhoods, tried to help poor residents there by improving education, job opportunities, exposure to the arts. Settlement houses generally offered childcare for working mothers, vocational classes, and other activities. Modeled after Toynbee Hall in London. Settlement houses in most major American cities; Jane Addams's Hull House in Chicago.

     b. Women's rights: Leaders in nineteenth century, such as Elizabeth Cady Stanton and Susan B. Anthony spoke more about moral purity of women as reason why they should be permitted to work at social reforming activities and have the right to vote. Stanton believed vote for educated women would help bring "women's influence in public life." After about 1910, feminist movement grew.

Carrie Chapman Catt, American Woman Suffrage Association; Alice Paul, National Woman's Party. Nineteenth Amendment (1920) granted women the right to vote. Paul continued to work for Equal Rights Amendment—has still not been passed as the end of the twentieth century approaches.

c. Progressive Era women involved in other reforms. Birth-control movement—Margaret Sanger wanted to help poor women. Got support from middle class, who wanted to limit own families and limit reproduction of immigrants. Opponents—cited threat to family, and labeled plan immoral. Sanger indicted for breaking obscenity laws, had to flee United States for one year. Women also involved in prohibition and antiprostitution movements. Peace movement during and after WWI—Jane Addams, Florence Kelley, Jeannette Rankin. Rankin was congresswoman from Montana (where women could vote), first woman to sit in House of Representatives—she voted against war in 1917; only member of Congress to do so. Addams became first president of Women's International League for Peace and Freedom. League denounced harsh terms of Versailles Treaty.

d. The black movement and reform: How much to assimilate into white culture, and how to do it? Booker T. Washington, self-help movement, Tuskegee Institute; W. E. B. DuBois, NAACP, "anti-Bookerite." Ida B. Wells, editor of newspaper in Memphis, campaigned against lynching in 1892; was personally threatened, and paper destroyed. Marcus Garvey, black nationalist group, Universal Negro Improvement Association (UNIA) cultivated black pride. His Black Star shipping line helped blacks emigrate to Africa. Black Star went bankrupt; Garvey was deported.

e. B'nai B'rith Anti-Defamation League founded, 1913.

D. Progressivism and Government Action

1. Emerging progressive movement: political reform. Progressive reform—mostly urban middle-class movement; influenced other groups in society.

a. Municipal reform—against older tradition of noninterference by government, need government in more complex times. Urban problems needed to be fixed.

First had to reform corrupt government. 1870–1900: try to get rid of boss system by civil service hiring, keeping watch over public monies and spending; also reforms in housing, labor, poverty relief. After 1900, some cities moved to city-manager and city-commission forms of government and public ownership of utilities. Galveston, Texas—prototype city.

b. Progressive state reform: needed for more sweeping reforms. Looked to governors to bring beyond local level. Robert M. La Follette (governor of Wisconsin—reforms such as direct primaries, regulation of railroad rates, tax reforms. Brought ideas to federal level as U.S. senator. Also developed commissions and agencies such as tax assessments and highway construction.); among other progressive governors, Woodrow Wilson (New Jersey), Theodore Roosevelt (New York).

2. Theodore Roosevelt and the "Square Deal"

a. T. Roosevelt advocated strong and energetic presidency—in the public interest. Able to delegate authority, but very much in charge. Believed complex, industrial society required Hamiltonian rather than Jeffersonian system of government.

b. "Trust-busting": Roosevelt got reputation as trust buster, although did not disapprove of all trusts, only those he considered "bad." Instructed attorney general to go after J. P. Morgan's railroad combination, the Northern Security Company, in 1904. Hepburn Act (1906)—stricter railroad controls imposed by giving ICC more power over railroad rates. Consumer protection: Meat Inspection Act (1906), Pure Food and Drug Act (1906).

c. Labor issues: United Mine Workers called strike (1902). Owners refused to arbitrate, would not recognize union led by John Mitchell Roosevelt; threatened to send in federal troops to operate coal mines. Mine owners agreed to compromise—agreed to shorter hours for miners (a nine-hour day) and higher wages (10 percent wage increase), but did not have to recognize union. Roosevelt called it a "square deal" for everyone. Also showed Roosevelt's belief that president could say when labor demands should be supported or not.

3. Conservation

   a. Roosevelt loved outdoors—concerned about destruction of natural resources through excesses in lumbering, cattle ranching, mining, and drilling for oil. Placed 150 million acres of forest land into federal reserves. In 1908, TR organized National Conservation Conference; after this meeting, many states created conservation commissions.

   b. Federal legislation: enforced National Forest System, added millions of acres to national forests. "Multiple uses" of national forests. National (Newlands) Reclamation Act (1902) put aside money gained from sale of western public lands to use in financing irrigation projects.

   c. John Muir, founder of Sierra Club (1892), wanted to protect wilderness areas; Gifford Pinchot, government's chief forester, wanted to make sure everyone could share in timber, minerals, coal, oil, and water. William Howard Taft—more restrained than Theodore Roosevelt. Taft-Ballinger-Pinchot controversy of 1910: Taft dismissed Pinchot, alienating conservationists.

4. Working Conditions: *Muller v. Oregon* (1908)—Supreme Court upheld Oregon's law limiting women's working hours. *Lochner v. New York* (1905) revoked New York law limiting hours bakers worked. Does judiciary interpret Constitution or shape public policy?

5. Woodrow Wilson and New Freedom

   a. Election of 1912—Taft had angered many reformers; Roosevelt formed third party—Progressive, or Bull Moose, party; Democrats nominated Woodrow Wilson; Socialists nominate Eugene W. Debs. Wilson won election. Wilson—former president of Princeton University and governor of New Jersey.

   b. Wilson's New Freedom—based on ideas of progressive lawyer Louis D. Brandeis. Believed monopolies should be broken; not in favor, as T.R. was, of cooperation between big business and government. Competitions should exist in business, but government should watch over it.

   c. Business Regulation: Couldn't stop corporate mergers, but could regulate. Clayton Anti-Trust Act

(1914)—outlawed price discrimination and interlocking directorates (having same people on boards of "competing" companies). Federal Trade Commission (FTC) investigated and supervised trusts.

d. Underwood Tariff—lowered tariffs to encourage imports. To make up for lost revenues—graduated income tax. Most farmers and factory workers were exempt, as incomes had to be more than $4,000. Tax only 1 percent for incomes of $4,000– $20,000. Highest bracket, $500,000 or more, 7 percent tax.

e. Federal Reserve System established by act in 1913—created twelve Federal Reserve banks; could loan to member banks. By adjusting interest rates, district banks controlled amount of money in circulation. Reserve banks loosened and tightened credit—monetary controls—no longer had to depend on supply of gold.

f. Women's Suffrage Act—Nineteenth Amendment (1920)—gave women right to vote in federal elections.

g. WWI—effect on domestic reforms, also upcoming election, need to please voters: Federal Farm Loan Act (1916)—twelve federal banks lend money to farmers at low interest rates; Adamson Act—eight-hour day for railroad workers plus overtime pay; Keating Owen Act restricted child labor.

II. America Reaching Out

A. The Industrial-Colonial Connection

1. Neomercantilism as an economic/"imperial" policy—Expansion of American industrial system necessitated search for raw materials and new markets—fueled U.S. drive toward overseas expansion

   a. U.S. farmers and factories tied to world markets—belief that surplus must be sold in foreign markets to relieve pressures on domestic market such as overproduction, unemployment, and economic depression.

   b. Expansion of foreign trade required building of bigger navy to protect. Alfred Thayer Mahan's, best seller, *The Influence of Sea Power Upon History* (1890)—great nations need strong navies—United States needed to improve its navy. Congress agreed. Also needed bases, like in Hawaii.

    c. U.S. industry supplies goods cheaper to foreign nations—foreign countries and workers became dependent on U.S. goods, influenced polices here and abroad.

2. Cultural paternalism: racist explanation for expansionism—Josiah Strong, *Our Country* (1885), U.S. "Anglo-Saxon" race should lead the world. Other Social Darwinists agreed in superiority of white Americans over "inferior" races. Missionaries also transform American culture—hope to convert "natives."

3. Tariff controversy: free trade v. protectionism. Protective tariffs—expression of economic nationalism—protect U.S. manufacturing, decrease imports of cheaper foreign goods.

B. Emerging Global Involvement

1. Manifest Destiny and expansion to Pacific Ocean

    a. Perry and the "opening" of Japan: Since 1640, Japan had been closed to foreigners to try to preserve own culture. In 1853, Commodore Perry threatens Japan if it wouldn't negotiate. Japan agreed to open two ports to trade, and later added more. Anti-foreign terrorism in 1860s, but new government in 1867 decided to imitate some aspects of foreign culture, especially building railroads, adopting new technology, and reorganizing army. Copied imperialism of western nations—"opened" Korea, defeated China and took Formosa, and fought Russia over its territory in China.

    b. The China trade: established New England shipping fortunes; brought exposure to Eastern culture. Chinese immigrants arrive in California after gold discovered; immigration picks up after Civil War; peaks at 23,000 in 1872. Exclusion Act (1882) forbids Chinese to come to United States, but this exclusion does not handicap foreign trade with China.

2. Other Pacific overtures

    a. United States and China. Open Door policy—equal opportunity for U.S. trade investments and profits in China, along with other imperialist nations. England opposes. Boxer Rebellion—antiforeign Chinese group besieges legations in Beijing (Peking). United States joins other nations in defeating them—convinces other nations that Open Door was best policy.

b. Acquisition of Hawaii: U.S. traders there since eighteenth century; 1830s, missionaries from New England arrive, stay, and their descendants control property and economics of islands. Gain political power—press for annexation so that Hawaiian sugar would not be classified as foreign under McKinley Tariff. Formally annexed by joint resolution of Congress during Spanish-American War in 1898.

c. Naval Base: Samoa. United States took over in 1878; 1889, divide Samoa between United States, England, and Germany. United States formally annexes in 1899. United States also occupied Midway Island.

3. "Hesitant colonialism": Spanish-American War

a. Monroe Doctrine (1823–1898)—Monroe Doctrine (1823) presented United States as leader in Western Hemisphere. Since that time, United States has tended to take protective and dominant stance toward Latin America. Recurrent intervention by United States has led to tensions and distrust by Latin American countries. Venezuela Crisis of 1895—United States told Great Britain it couldn't interfere there. Anglo-American negotiations settle border dispute.

b. United States empire: United States overseas expansion—same time as European imperialism. Constitutional issues—balancing strategic and economic importance of territories with that country's political preferences.

c. Cuba: seeking independence from Spain—tied to United States economically—United States goes to war after sinking of U.S.S. *Maine* in Havana Harbor. Yellow Journalism—Teller Amendment: passed in Congress, asserted United States would not annex Cuba to United States Platt Amendment (1903): all Cuban treaties had to be approved by United States, and United States had "right to intervene" to maintain and preserve Cuba's independence. Also gave United States a naval base at Guantanamo Bay.

    d. Philippines: Dewey's "New Navy" destroys Spanish fleet in Philippines. Peace Terms (1898)—Cuba gets independence; United States gets Philippines, Puerto Rico, and Guam. Filipinos want independence. Anti-imperialists, against treaty and annexation. Anti-imperialists said that United States should not govern a foreign territory without consent of its inhabitants. Treaty passed 1899, but Bryan continues anti-imperial debate into election of 1900. Philippine Insurrection (1899–1902) led by Aguinaido; costly in terms of lives and money. Racist attitudes toward Filipinos by Americans. Afterward, "Americanization" of Philippines.

    e. Puerto Rico: at first welcomes United States over Spain, but not given freedoms. Foraker Act (1900)—denied Puerto Rico's United States statehood; United States controls government. Puerto Ricans granted U.S. citizenship (1917); 1952, becomes "commonwealth" of United States.

4. Latin American Affairs

    a. Panama Canal: United States aids Panama in gaining independence from Colombia—Roosevelt sends warships to protect isthmus. Panama grants United States long-term rights to canal zone. Canal completed 1914; U.S. industries manufactured most of the technology needed to build it. Anti-American feelings—Congress approves treaties (1978)—Canal Zone reverts to Panamanian control in 2000; United States maintains right to defend Canal Zone after that.

    b. Regarding Caribbean, Roosevelt says, "Speak softly and carry a big stick." Roosevelt Corollary to Monroe Doctrine (1904)—Latin America needs to keep itself in order, or U.S. could take on role of "international police power." Keeping "order" is essential—United States interferes to keep it, assuming Latin America countries unable to do so internally.

    c. Taft and "dollar diplomacy": use of private funds to serve U.S. diplomatic goals and gain profits for American business—used in China and in Latin America.

    d. President Wilson and Mexican Revolution—civil war in Mexico; anti-American—nationalization of United

States–owned properties threatens U.S. interests. Wilson orders troops in several times—orders General Pershing in to find Pancho Villa; seizes Mexican port of Veracruz. Threats of Mexican alliance with Germany—Zimmerman Telegram, Germany proposed that Mexico be its ally against United States if war broke out—leads to Wilson calling for "armed neutrality."

C. Restraint and Involvement: 1914–1920

1. European background to WWI

    a. Nationalistic rivalries and alliance system: 2 Alliances: Triple Alliance made up of Germany, Austria-Hungary, Italy, and the Triple Entente, consisting of Great Britain, France, and Russia. Assassination of Archduke Ferdinand in Sarajevo upset uneasy balance of power. Countries go to war; Turkey joins Germany and Austria-Hungary (Central Powers); Italy and Japan join Britain, France, and Russia (Allies).

    b. Colonialism: European powers (and later United States) dividing up world. Examples: Indochina, colony of France; India, colony of Great Britain; Indonesia, colony of Netherlands. Africa being divided up among European powers. Japan takes Korea and Formosa. Looking for economic gain—raw materials and new markets, but also competition just to have colonies. Imperialism send nations into gaining colonies just so competitors don't get them first.

    c. Importance of sea routes: war at sea supposed to harm enemies' commerce; neutral ships supposed to be permitted to trade with any nation as long as they are not carrying contraband. England's blockade includes mining North Sea, making neutral ships trading with Germany at risk. 1915—Germany declares war zone around British Isles, enemy ships would be sunk, safety of neutral ships could not be guaranteed. Germany's U-boats (*unterseebooten*) were submarines that were fragile sitting targets if exposed. They attacked without warning, destroying ships and leaving sailors to die in the ocean because they did not have room to take extra people on board. United States outraged by Germany's sinking of *Lusitania* (May 1915). Americans saw U-boats as "immoral."

2. United States involvement

   a. Efforts at neutrality and "preparedness"—Wilson's campaign slogan, "He kept us out of War," but he knew it wouldn't take much to go to war—had to be prepared. November 1915, asked Congress to expand army and navy. Roosevelt pushing preparedness, many in Congress antipreparedness. National Defense Act of 1916 passed; Also in 1916, Navy Act and Revenue Act (to help pay for expansion of army and navy—raised taxes on large estates, corporate profits, gains made by munitions manufacturers)

   b. Causes of U.S. entry into war: belief in the anti-German propaganda, Germany's submarine war—violation of freedom of the seas, disruption of commerce—Zimmerman Telegram—making trouble in Mexico; Wilson asks first for "armed neutrality"; Germany resumes destroying all ships around Great Britain, enemy and neutral and sinks U.S. ships; Wilson asks Congress for formal declaration of war. Pacifists were strong; fifty members of House and six Senators voted against war declaration. Wilson also wanted U.S. involvement so he could have more influence in peace settlement.

   c. U.S. role in the war: American convoy system protected ships, defended Atlantic; U.S. destroyers sent to Ireland to assist British. U.S. troops not sent over in large numbers until 1918—helped turn the tide against Germans in France. American participation in the Argonne Forest battle (September, 1918) crucial in pushing German troops back. American deaths in war = 112,432; Americans wounded = 230,074.

   d. U.S. reaction to Russian Revolution: fear and loathing of Germans transferred to Bolsheviks, especially after Lenin's government made peace with Germany, closing eastern front. Wilson sent troops to Siberia in 1918 (without advance notice to Congress), mainly to destroy Bolshevik government, also keep Japan from gaining influence there, protect Russian railroads from Germany. Wilson also sent arms to anti-Bolsheviks, refused to recognize Bolshevik government.

D. Wartime Constitutional Issues

1. Presidential power in wartime and in foreign affairs—Congress has the power to declare war, raise army

and navy, but president is commander-in-chief of army and navy, he can make treaties, but two-thirds of Senate must approve; wartime sometimes compromises human and civil rights in interest of national security.

2. War opposition and patriotism

   a. The draft: Selective Service Act (1917)—registration of all men between ages twenty to thirty (in 1918 made ages 18 to 45). Conscientious objectors and those who would not serve were treated poorly.

   b. Committee on Public Information (CPI) produced propaganda for war effort, set up Loyalty Leagues; superpatriotic groups became vigilantes trying to rid country of "subversives." Anything German was banned or at risk—sauerkraut become "liberty cabbage."

3. Espionage and sedition acts

   a. Espionage Act (1917)—banned "false statements" that might hinder draft and prevented treasonous materials from going through mail.

   b. Sedition Act (1918)—prohibited "disloyal, profane, scurrilous, or abusive" remarks about government, flag, or military uniform to be uttered or printed. Casual remarks could be prosecuted; more than 2,000 Americans were prosecuted under these two acts.

   c. Conviction of Eugene V. Debs: Debs said people had the right to speak out; Espionage Act went against democratic principles. Debs convicted and imprisoned; pardoned and released in 1921.

   d. Attacks on I.W.W.: union seen as being against the government since it stood for crushing capitalism , and I.W.W. officially opposed the war. Also Wobblies members worked in areas crucial to war effort, such as western mines and logging in the Pacific Northwest. Government raided meetings, arrested leaders, deported some. Permitted vigilante terrorism against I.W.W. Finally, 200 indicted under Espionage Act.

   e. *Schenck v. United States* (1919)—Supreme Court upheld Espionage Act—free speech could be limited when a "clear and present danger" existed, such as during a war.

   f. Red Scare, 1918–1919—transference near end of war of hatred of Germans to hatred of Bolsheviks. Labor strikes during 1919 spark Red Scare; fear of foreign conspirators linked to American radicals; formation of Communist Labor party and Communist party of the United States of America both founded 1919; American Legion also founded 1919—preached antiradicalism; Attorney General Palmer creates F.B.I., run by J. Edgar Hoover. F.B.I. jails I.W.W. members, deports Emma Goldman and other alien radicals. Palmer Raids in 1920—violated civil liberties, more than 6,000 arrested; almost 600 deported. Sacco and Vanzetti case in 1920—judge openly hostile because they were Italian and anarchists; convicted due to that, not on evidence of crime.

e. The Search for Peace and Arms Control: 1914–1930

1. The peace movement; Women's International League for Peace and Freedom and other groups had been against war. Women's International League condemned the peace terms. After the war, peace groups attempted to bring about international peace and stability; groups become more popular in 1920s and 1930s. Women's Peace Union wanted a constitutional amendment requiring a national referendum to declare war. Peace groups recounted the costs of WWI; crimes against humanity. Some groups also fought for arms control.

2. The 14 Points: Wilson presented his ideas to Congress in 14 points. Among the points: Germany should be treated fairly in order to prevent resentments that could lead to another war; Germany should not have to pay overly harsh reparations; boundaries of European countries should be defined by the language of the people there; barriers of trade should be removed; "absolute freedom upon the seas," in peace and war; disarmament. Finally, Wilson called for a League of Nations to try to prevent the system of alliances and maybe prevent another war.

3. Versailles Treaty—Paris Peace Conference, palace of Versailles

   a. Wilson's role—1918 elections, Republicans gained control of House and Senate. Wilson refused to take Republicans with him to peace conference; would not listen to Senate Foreign Relations committee. Other members of Big Four—France, England, Italy—want German territory; don't believe in Wilson's ideals.

Clemençeau of France wants only French security. Wilson gives in to them on other points in order to establish League of Nations. During war: allies proclaim moral ideals; postwar: big power rivalries thwart these ideals.

4. League of Nations: Henry Cabot Lodge and U.S. Senate rejection—Most of Senate against treaty, but willing to compromise. Lodge working for defeat, drags out debate; Wilson inflexible. Wilson takes cross-country speaking tour; suffers stroke; back to Washington in isolation. Even healthy, he probably would not have compromised, but in ill health he was not a leader. Senate rejected the treaty.

5. Reparation and war debts: by 1920s, United States is world's leading economic power; leader in world trade. Also shifts from being debtor to creditor nation.

6. Washington Naval Disarmament Conference (Nov. 1921–Feb.1922)—United States plus Great Britain, France, Japan, Italy, China, Portugal, Belgium, and Netherlands meet to discuss limits on naval armaments. Treaties put moratorium on ship construction; establish tonnage ratio: For every 5 tons for United States and Britain, Japan would have 3; France and Italy would have 1.75.

7. Kellogg-Briand Pact (1928): Treaty signed by 62 nations. Agreed to "condemn recourse to war for the solution of international controversies and renounce it as an instrument of national policy." No provision for enforcing it, but showed popular belief that war was barbaric, and popularity of peace movement. American isolationists and pacifists wholly supported pact.

8. World Court: Provision of League of Nations. United States refused to belong to it, although some American jurists served on World Court in Geneva.

Questions

1. The muckrakers were important to the Progressive Movement because they
   1. publicized what they believed were the problems in U.S. society.
   2. opposed all social reform.
   3. wanted to destroy the capitalist system.
   4. were members of the Know-Nothing party.

2. The attempt to remove corruption from government began at the
   1. state level.
   2. federal level.
   3. city level.
   4. regional level.

3. Booker T. Washington's beliefs are best expressed by which of the following?
   1. Blacks should demand total equality in American society.
   2. A select group of intellectual and highly trained African Americans would serve as an example to whites and help uplift other blacks.
   3. Blacks should challenge discriminatory legislation in the courts.
   4. Blacks should work diligently, obtain property, and thus prove themselves to whites.

4. W.E.B. Du Bois's philosophy included which of the following?
   1. The "Talented Ten" would help save the black race by setting an example to whites and motivating other blacks.
   2. Black Americans could best be served by founding more vocational schools for them throughout the country.
   3. He publicly agreed with Booker T. Washington's ideas and helped to carry them out.
   4. African Americans should separate themselves from whites and emigrate to Africa.

5. The Women's International League for Peace and Freedom
   1. ardently endorsed the Treaty of Versailles.
   2. felt the Treaty of Versailles was too generous toward Germany.
   3. supported disarmament for Germany only.
   4. predicted that the peace settlement would lead to the spread of hostility among nations.

6. During the Red Scare of 1919, Attorney General Palmer
   1. staunchly defended the civil rights of accused communists.
   2. defended the actions of the Ku Klux Klan.
   3. violated the rights of many Americans suspected of being communists.
   4. denounced J. Edgar Hoover's tactics.

7. Those in favor of expanding the American empire from the late nineteenth to early twentieth centuries generally believed

1. people of less developed countries could not solve their own problems and should adopt the American model of development.

2. there was no need to expand the navy, since American expansion would be done by peaceful means.

3. American involvement in other countries would occur only when those nations invited the United States to share its technology.

4. when colonies were acquired, the people of those nations must be permitted to shape their own economic and political destinies.

8. Which of the following played a part in initiating the Cuban revolution of 1895?

1. abolition of slavery in Cuba

2. implementing a U.S. tariff on Cuban sugar

3. the beginning of Cuban industrialization

4. an invasion by U.S. forces

9. The Roosevelt Corollary (1904) to the Monroe Doctrine

1. was disparaged by European nations.

2. strictly curbed the place of the United States in the Western Hemisphere.

3. justified direct United States intervention in the affairs of the nations of the Western Hemisphere.

4. was a pretentious declaration that was never applied.

10. In *Schenck v. United States,* the Supreme Court ruled that

1. during wartime, it is constitutional for the the federal government to seize and operate the railroads.

2. it is constitutional for the government during wartime to prohibit the manufacture and sale of distilled liquor.

3. it is constitutional for the government to restrict the First Amendment right to free speech during war.

4. the federal government has the right to compel men to serve in the armed forces during war.

11. Which of the following contributed to the Red Scare following WWI?

1. a series of college protests

2. a series of postwar strikes

3 the dramatic growth of the Communist party

4. the discovery of a conspiracy to overthrow the U.S. government

12. Many of Wilson's critics were opposed to Article 10 of the League charter because

1. it gave up too much of Germany's territory.

2. they disliked Wilson.

3. they sided with Henry Cabot Lodge.

4. they did not believe in the collective security provision.

13. Which is true of the Platt Amendment?

1. It gave Cuba a representative democratic government.

2. It was part of the Americanization of the Philippines.

3. It linked the United States and Cuba in a mutual defense pact.

4. It put a tariff on Cuban sugar.

14. The overiding characteristic of U.S. foreign policy in Latin America at the beginning of the twentieth century was

    1. a desire to establish order in the region.

    2. hesitation to use the "big stick" policy.

    3. a huge investment of U.S. dollars.

    4. a belief that the United States had to save the universe.

15. The Progressive movement

    1. continued the urban reforms of the Populist movement.

    2. consisted mostly of rural members.

    3. had some interests in common with the Populists, but was mainly an urban movement.

    4. had nothing in common with the Populists.

Answers

1. The correct answer is 1. The muckrakers were journalists who investigated and wrote about what they felt were wrongs in U.S. society.

2. The correct answer is 3. Many reformers saw the need for more government in a more complex industrial society, but it was necessary to remove the corrupt politicians first. Progressives attempted to reform city government first to eliminate the boss system.

3. The correct answer is 4. Washington believed in a "separate-but-equal" policy. He believed that the best policy for blacks was to accommodate to whites, but that blacks could help themselves through hard work. In 1881, he founded Tuskeegee Institute, a vocational school in Alabama.

4. The correct answer is 1. DuBois was an anti-Bookerite who did not believe in accommodation. He believed that intellectual leaders, the "Talented Ten" would help save the black race.

5. The correct answer is 4. The League denounced the peace terms, predicting they would "create all over Europe discords and animosities which can only lead to future wars."

6. The correct answer is 3. Palmer was obsessed with the "red menace," and instituted a series of raids which led to the arrest of hundreds and the deportation of over 200, including Emma Goldman. The Palmer raids were a massive violation of civil rights.

7. The correct answer is 1. This has been a persistent belief—that the American way is the right way for every country. For example, in the Philippines, the U.S. government imposed an American-style political system, but also imposed

sedition laws and jailed critics in order to enforce it.

8. The correct answer is 2. The Cuban economy was highly dependent on exports. When the Wilson-Gorman Tariff (1894) was put into effect, it imposed a tariff on Cuban sugar. Formerly, the McKinley tariff permitted Cuban sugar to enter the country duty free. As a result of the new tax, the Cuban economy plunged, and revolution started.

9. The correct answer is 3. Roosevelt was worried about Latin American countries defaulting on loans to European nations. He issued the Corollary to warn Latin America that the United States would intervene if necessary and might assume the role of "an international police power." The United States did intervene in several countries between 1900 and 1917: Cuba, Panama, Nicaragua, the Dominican Republic, Mexico, and Haiti.

10. The correct answer is 3. In 1919, the Supreme Court upheld the Espionage Act in an unanimous decision in *Schenck v. United States,* Justice Oliver Wendell Holmes wrote that if words presented a "clear and present danger" (as in wartime), then the right to free speech could be restricted.

11. The correct answer is 2. More than 3,300 labor strikes occurred in 1919. On May 1, 1919, bombs were sent to some prominent Americans. May Day is the traditional day of celebration for workers around the world. Many believed that anarchists and Bolsheviks were behind the labor strikes, and that they threatened the United States.

12. The correct answer is 4. Most Americans were unwilling to abandon the nation's accepted belief in nonalignment and freedom of choice in international affairs.

They had serious reservations about Article 10—would the United States have to send in troops to ensure collective security? Lodge wanted to add that Congress would have to approve any use of armed forces under Article 10.

13. The correct answer is 3. The Platt Amendment (1903) gave the United States "the right to intervene" in Cuba. The United States had to approve all treaties made by Cuba. The United States also leased a naval base at Guantanamo Bay.

14. The correct answer is 1. Americans believed that order was necessary to guarantee their interests. They were particularly concerned with keeping their economic interests safe and secure. This meant intervening in Latin American affairs, landing marines, pushing Americanization, and practicing dollar diplomacy.

15. The correct answer is 3. The Progressive movement was primarily an urban movement, although it incorporated some of the beliefs held by the Populists. The Progressives drew upon the earlier urban reform movements, seeking social justice and reforms in the legal system, education, and government.

Chapter 7

At Home and Abroad

Prosperity and Depression, 1917–1940

Part I: War Economy and Prosperity:1917–1929

A. War Economy

1. Presidential power in wartime and foreign affairs. The president leads the nation during wartime—power grows. Wilson prepared for war, even before it was declared.

2. During war, economic operations often centralized and concentrated. Labor and armed forces mobilized. Huge bureaucracy develops. Food Administration, Railroad Administration, Fuel Administration, and War Industries Board (WIB) help to regulate WIB, head is Bernard Baruch—oversees all aspects of industrial production and distribution. Federal government and private business became "partners" during war; anti-trust laws suspended, favorable contracts available, and competitive bidding eliminated. Standardization and efficiency are important.

3. Annual expenditures increase 2,500 percent between 1916 and 1919; war expenses exceed $33.5 billion (not counting veterans' benefits, to be paid later). United States goes from being debtor nation to creditor nation after the war.

4. Worldwide connections change as a result of WWI and Russian Revolution. U.S.–Soviet relations damaged due to United States interference in Siberia. Several new states in Central and Eastern Europe were very weak and dependent. Germany full of resentment due to harsh peace terms. This resentment leads to rise of authoritarianism in Germany. War debts hurting many nations.

5. Women take jobs formerly held by men while war is going on. Not that many more women entered workforce, but they changed jobs for wartime industries. Some black women took the domestic positions vacated by white women. After the war, women often forced to leave jobs. Women also worked

as volunteers, making bandages, serving in Red Cross, helping soldiers and refugees. Some women were nurses who served in war zones.

6. Many southern blacks migrate to northern cities to work railroads, steel mills, shipyards, and other industries. Massive migration—approximately half-million African Americans move north. Mostly young men. Face discrimination; race riots in some cities. In the military, blacks placed in segregated units—about 200,000 served overseas.

7. "Normalcy"—term used by President Warren G. Harding. Americans want to forget war years, death and destruction, and unrest and divisions in American society—1920s are mixture of old and new.

B. The Twenties: Business Boom or False Prosperity?

1. Postwar recession—heavy consumer spending, prices went up for two years, then people stopped buying. Exports (including agricultural) and industry slow down because war orders stop. Unemployment grows. Economy improves with growth of electricity, new consumer products, and increased spending.

2. War debt controversy—United States serves as banker for the world after WWI. By late 1920s, Americans stop buying European goods; Europeans cannot buy American goods due to high tariffs; begin to default on war debts. Other countries are bankrupt from war. United States lends money to Germany, Germany pays France and England, France and England pay United States But German economy in poor shape. U.S. could have canceled France and England's debts, and they could have canceled Germany's, but government tied closely to banking interests which were making profits.

3. Avarice and scandal: Teapot Dome. Harding appointed to office many friends who used their positions to engage in fraudulent activities. Most notorious example—Secretary of Interior Albert Fall took bribes in return for leasing government oil reserves at Teapot Dome, Wyoming. Harding dead before scandal revealed in 1923–24.

4. Coolidge prosperity: Coolidge said, "The business of America is business." Coolidge believed that government should interfere as little as possible in national life. Republican elected in 1924; Democratic party split. Keeps

Harding's appointees from business world: Herbert Hoover and Secretary of the Treasury Andrew Mellon. Time of prosperity. Mellon's tax polices favor rich and big business. Melon worked for reductions in corporate and personal taxes. Not everyone shared in prosperity: coal miners, textile workers, many farmers, Native Americans, Hispanics, and blacks not as well off. Most of South lags behind North in income, standard of living.

5. Most farmers did not share in prosperity. Made investments in land and farm machinery based on worldwide demand after war; prices fall after that. Can't repay loans or mortgages. Part of problem was new farming techniques that increased productivity at a time when demand was down. Large commercial farms did well, but small farmers did not. More than 3 million people left farming during 1920s

6. "Big Bull Market": Summer of 1929, values of stocks go crazy—rising prices of stocks do not reflect real value, but price people are willing to pay. Between May 1928 and September 1929, price of stocks rise by 40 percent. Rising prices begin to feed on themselves—companies start putting money into speculation rather than into production. Bubble had to burst.

C. Mass consumption and clash of cultural values

1. Mass consumption

   a. automobile: ownership of cars spreads to all classes and groups in 1920s due to mass production which lowered prices to make them affordable. Changes American culture: women can drive, become more independent; more women in labor force; divorce laws modified; young people escape from watchful parents. Need for improved roads, safety controls, oil companies double prices.

   b. installment buying: 1920s first time large numbers of people borrowing just to buy consumer goods. People buy on installment plan—minimum amount down and low payments every month. Advertising soars to convince people to buy new goods.

   c. real estate boom and suburban development; urbanization continues; 1920 census, first time majority of Americans (51.4 percent) live in urban areas. Migrants from farms, rural southerners, southern blacks. Also growth of Mexicans in western cities; Hispanics in New York. Suburbs develop from those who do not want to live in crowded cities—more prosperous, don't have to deal with big-city problems. Cars and improved roads make this possible.

d. Entertainment: radio—first commercial broadcast in 1920. By mid-1920s people regularly listening to serials such as *Amos 'n' Andy*, and can hear the World Series. In 1924, nominating conventions are broadcast on radio. After 1927, radios begin to appear in cars. Records also appear. Movies popular, by 1929 over 100 million viewers per week. Talking movies—*The Jazz Singer*, first successful full-length talking picture, 1927. Radios, movies, records, advertising contribute to increased nationalization of American culture

2. Constitutional and legal issues

a. Red Scare—labor strikes, fear of immigrants and Bolshevik conspiracies, Palmer Raids—vast infringement on civil rights; Ku Klux Klan—twentieth century KKK begun in 1915 in South, but spread to North and West. In South, mostly anti-Black; in other areas, anti-Jewish, anti-Catholic or anti-immigrants. Klan grew in 1920s—almost 4.5 million members; influence 1924 Democratic primary. 1925, influence declines after revelations of corruption within Klan. Sacco and Vanzetti—arrested for armed robbery in which a guard and paymaster were killed. Convicted and executed in 1927 because they were Italian and anarchists; judge was openly prejudiced; some evidence invented by prosecution.

b. Fearful of large number of "new" immigrants arriving. More racist thinking—Ripley, *Races of Europe* (1899)—divides into Teutonic, Alpine, Mediterranean. Teutons (Britons, Germans, Northern Europeans) were considered best suited to American way of life. Grant, *Passing of the Great Race* (1916), said intermarriage of "new" immigrants with old was destroying bloodlines of Americans. Immigration soars after WWI, new restrictions put into place by Republicans—reduced number of immigrants admitted and put quotas into effect. Numbers of southern and eastern Europeans allowed was very low.

c. Native Americans—forced on to reservations earlier, discriminated against in 1920s. Reformers try to "Americanize"—insensitive to their cultures. U.S. government maintained more control over Indians. In 1924, granted citizenship to all Indians (Dawes Act had made citizens of Indians who accepted land in severalty but not those on reservations.) President Hoover reorganized Bureau of Indian Affairs. New Deal plan: John Collier, American Indian Defense Association, encouraged Indian culture. Indian Reorganization Act (1934)—restored tribal ownership of lands, reversing Dawes Act. New militancy in 1970s—American Indian Movement (AIM) seized hostages at Wounded Knee. 1980, Supreme Court ruled government had to pay Sioux Nation $106 million for Black Hills of South Dakota.

d. Prohibition—a progressive reform, Eighteenth Amendment (1919) and federal law (Volstead Act,1920) prohibited manufacture, sale, and transportation of alcoholic beverages. Prohibition reduced national consumption of alcohol, but prohibitionists' insistence on total abstinence drove moderates to violate the law. More successful in traditional temperance areas, but personal freedom and lax enforcement dooms it. It is difficult to legislate social morality, especially in a culturally diverse society. (For example, colonial New England or earlier temperance movements in nineteenth century.) Smuggling, bootleggers, and bathtub gin prevail. Al Capone and organized crime help supply demand. Prohibition repealed by Twenty-first Amendment (1933), supported by President Franklin D. Roosevelt.

e. Scopes Trial—clash of science and Christian fundamentalism in 1925 over the teaching of evolution in Tennessee schools. Scopes convicted of breaking the law, but pro-evolutionists believed that testimony during the trial (Bryan arguing for the prosecution, and Darrow for the defense) clearly gave them a victory. Darrow cross-examines Bryan, forcing admission that religious dogma could be subject to more than one interpretation.

3. Shifting cultural values

   a. Revolution in morals and manners, fads, flappers, and Freud—clothing styles for men and women of all classes changes to more colorful, casual styles; behavior seen as inappropriate before becomes more acceptable, or at least out in the open—smoking, swearing, talk about sex. Discussions of Freud's theories; people convinced that uninhibited sex lives are necessary. Birth control more openly acceptable. Songs, motion pictures, magazines more openly about sex. The flapper; the "It Girl." More children in school; peer groups become more important. These changes also cause social tensions.

   b. Women's changing roles

     1) After WWI, women continue to move into labor force. Mostly, "women's jobs"—teachers, nurses, secretaries, waitresses, etc. Usually earned less than men. More married women working to help support their families, although most married women, except African American, did not work outside the home.

     2) Nineteenth Amendment—women gain right to vote. Does not result in any dramatic change in political system of United States.

     3) Shepard-Towner (Maternity and Infancy Act) (1921)—funds went to states to set up maternity and pediatric clinics; passed after pressure from women's groups. But pressure from private physicians convinced Congress to rescind it in 1929.

     4) Fewer children; higher divorce rate. Margaret Sanger and birth control movement—returns to United States in 1916, after fleeing prosecution under obscenity laws. Discussion of birth control is controversial—are women violating God's laws? If there are fewer births, will American population get too low? Sanger especially interested in helping poor working-class women. More machines to help with household tasks, but still as much time or more spent on household duties; more pressure to keep everything clean, no servants to help.

   c. The literary scene: the Lost Generation—Ernest Hemingway, Ezra Pound, T. S. Eliot moved to Europe. William Faulkner and Sinclair Lewis attacked racism and irrationality. Against materialism and impersonality of the age—F. Scott Fitzgerald. Edith Wharton wrote of clash between old and new moralities. Antiwar sentiments in John Dos Passos's *Three Soldiers* (1921) and Hemingway's *Farewell to Arms* (1929).

Harlem Renaissance—celebration of modern black culture centered in upper Manhattan. The "New Negro." Eubie Blake; singers Josephine Baker, Florence Mills, Mabel Mercer. Writers: Langston Hughes, Countee Cullen, Claude McKay. Visual artists: Aaron Douglas, James A. Porter, Augusta Savage.

d. The search for heroes; maybe sense of guilt over abandoning traditional values; also, media made many heroes. Sports heroes such as Babe Ruth and Gertrude Ederle (first woman to swim the English Channel in 1926). Movie stars such as Rudolph Valentino. News heroes, such as Charles Lindbergh, first to fly solo over Atlantic to Europe (France).

Part II: The Great Depression

A. Onset of the Depression

1. Weakness in the economy

a. Overproduction/underconsumption—Coal industry, railroads, textiles in decline before 1929, but still there is expansion in consumer goods for a while. Farmers and workers do not purchase as much. By end of 1920s, most increase in wealth goes to the wealthiest 1 percent of the population. Market for consumer goods suffered severely in the monetary contraction of the depression years.

b. Overexpansion of credit (buying stock on margin)—no regulation; people used stock not paid for as collateral to buy more stock. When stocks collapsed, brokers wanted payment, banks put pressure on brokers. Corporations and banks also had been speculating. Many U.S. corporations very shaky; built on unstable foundations. Federal government not regulating banks; Federal Reserve Board pursuing easy credit, helping to keep speculation frenzy going. Everything collapsed, including banks.

2. Stock market crash—worldwide, interdependent nature of banking, international trade, political repercussion. United States—world bankers—United States investing in U.S. stocks in 1920s, not as much money going to Europe; Europeans can't sell to United States due to high tariffs (continued in 1930 by Hawley-Smoot Tariff), so buy less from United States and default on loans. European countries raise tariffs, too; makes international trade worse. Stock market collapse triggers and intensifies economic depression. Rapid spread of Great Depression was evidence of world financial interdependence. Banks tied to stock market or foreign investments are severely weakened. Panics—people trying to get their money from the banks caused some to fold. More than 1,300 banks closed their doors in 1930; 3,700 more closed in next two years.

3. The Hoover Response

   a. Rugged individualism; "trickle down" economics—Hoover elected with belief in American prosperity and the "American system" providing all sorts of new products, such as radios and refrigerators. Widespread feeling that individuals were responsible for own situation; failure was a personal fault. Ups and downs in business cycle were normal. Hoover relied too much on persuasion rather than legal compulsion. Hoover believed that private donations would bring relief—President's Organization on Unemployment Relief (POUR). Hoover would not shift responsibility to federal government. Public works projects: Hoover and Grand Coulee Dams.

   b. Reconstruction Finance Corporation (RFC)—established 1932 to make loans to banks, insurance companies, railroads—idea that money would "trickle down" to people at bottom. Some labeled it the "millionaires" dole.

   c. Hoover stressed balancing federal budget, but by cutting government spending, things got worse.

4. Unemployment soared in 1930s, 13 million unemployed in 1933;so many homeless led to "Hoovervilles"—shantytowns throughout the country; many people severely malnourished. Protests: Farmers' Holiday Association—farm strikes; bonus Expeditionary Force or "Bonus Army"—unemployed veterans and their families march on Washington in support

of bill to give WWI vets immediate bonus instead of waiting until 1945. Ultimately, Bonus Army attacked by U.S. troops led by General Douglas MacArthur.

B. Franklin D. Roosevelt and the New Deal: relief, recovery, reform

　1. The New York prototype

　　a. Roosevelt was elected N.Y. governor in 1928—aid for relief and unemployment—unemployment insurance, direct payments to jobless; N.Y. Temporary Emergency Relief Administration (1931); publicly funded reforestation programs, land reclamation, hydroelectric power to create jobs. La Guardia, mayor of NYC, reformer.

　　b. Eleanor Roosevelt—became more independent; supported equal opportunities for women, African Americans; help the poor. Went on fact-finding missions for her husband.

　2. The New Deal Administration: "New Deal," country needed bold action, and federal power was necessary. The "Brain Trust"—Roosevelt relied on staff of formal and informal advisors, many lawyers and university professors. Idea that "bigness" was okay in economy, just let government regulate them.

　3. Relief of Human Suffering

　　a. Bank "holiday"—Roosevelt declares four-day national bank holiday. Launches First Hundred Days. Emergency Banking Relief Bill—solvent banks to be reopened, others to be reorganized. Prohibited hoarding of gold. First Fireside chat—Roosevelt says banks safe; people start depositing again. Congress passes Federal Deposit Insurance Corporation (FDIC).

　　b. Federal Emergency Relief Administration—head by Harry Hopkins—gave money to the states for them to distribute to poor

　　c. Unemployment—Jobs were important, so many unemployed. Civilian Conservation Corps (CCC)—job corps for young men, 18–25, building bridges, clearing land, etcetera. National Industrial Recovery Act (NIRA) established Public Works Administration—jobs for building roads, public buildings, ships, etcetera. Second New Deal established Works Progress Administration

(WPA): massive public works program for unemployed; also gave work to writers and artists.

4. Recovery for United States economy

   a. National Recovery Administration (NRA): "codes of fair competition" establishd by National Industrial Recovery Act (NIRA)—gave business exemption from antitrust laws; businesses met to draft codes of fair competition—limited production, established prices.

   b. Mortgage relief : Home Owners Loan Corporation (HOLC)—gave Americans low-interest loans to save homes from foreclosures, introduced fixed-rate, long-term mortgages, uniform system of real estate appraisal—"red-lining" kept certain groups out of certain areas. Federal Hoousing Administration (FHA) (1934)—insured mortgages, reduced amount of down payment, favored purchase of new suburban homes.

   c. Agricultural Adjustment Act (AAA, 1933)—direct payments to farmers for reducing production of certain crops. Processing tax used for payment of funds declared unconstitutional. AAA (1938)—continuation of 1933 act, but direct federal payment.

5. Search for effective reform

   a. Banking: Glass-Steagall Act (1932) (FDIC)—passed under Hoover—expanded credit to make loans more available to business and individuals

   b. Stock market: Securities and Exchange Commission (SEC) (1934)—more regulating economy

   c. Social Security—(1935) established unemployment compensation; old-age and survivors' insurance paid for by joint tax paid by employers and employees

   d. Labor

      1) Wagner Act (National Labor Relations Act) (1935)—employees have right to join unions, collective bargaining; created National Labor relations Board to prevent unfair labor practices

      2) Fair Labor Standards Act (1938)—established minimum wage of 40 cents per hour; maximum workweek of 40 hours in enterprises engaged in interstate commerce

6. Popular response

    a. Formation of C.I.O.—Committee for Industrial Organization formed as result of rivalry between craft and industrial unions; expelled by AFL; CIO reorganized in 1938 as Congress of Industrial Organizations

    b. American Liberty League—formed in 1934 by leaders of General Motors, U.S. Steel. DuPont and others against New Deal. Wanted to abolish welfare; believed in self-reliance.

7. Controversial aspects of New Deal

    a. Constitutional issues

        1) Supreme Court and NIRA—*Schechter Poultry Corp. v. United States* (1935)—struck down entire NIRA—commerce clause of Constitution did not give federal government right to regulate intrastate business.

        2) Supreme Court and the AAA—*U.S. v. Butler* (1936)—Court also struck down AAA, ruling that agriculture part of state jurisdiction, not federal.

        3) T.V.A. and R.E.A. attacked as socialism—government should not be producing and distributing electricity. TVA experimented in planned regional interdependence—was passed over the objections of private power.

    b. 1936 election mandate—Roosevelt and Democratic party—landslide victory. "New Deal Coalition"—children of southern and eastern European immigrants, farm migrants to cities, black voters in northern cities, members of labor unions, plus "the Solid South. "

    c. Roosevelt's "court-packing" proposal—trying to get judges sympathetic to New Deal. Court had opposed expanding federal authority. Judiciary Reorganization Bill to add new judges. Conservatives and liberals loudly oppose the bill. Liberals feared that packing the court could be used in the future to curtail liberties. After that, two of the swing-vote justices begin to vote pro–New Deal, and several justices retire, permitting Roosevelt to appoint new justices to the Court.

d. Roosevelt runs for third consecutive term—no president had ever served more than two. Still remained very popular.

e. The Twenty-second Amendment (1951) prohibited a person from serving as president for more than two consecutive terms.

8. The Human Factor

a. FDR was very effective communicator; Fireside chats very effective—first time president had used radio to gain support for programs. Roosevelt also used press conferences. Much of New Deal was psychological, to restore public confidence. Roosevelt dramatized and personalized the office of president, bringing it to center of national attention.

b. Eleanor Roosevelt served as president's eyes and ears. Very active First Lady.

c. Dust Bowl and Okies—maybe one of the worst ecological mistakes in history. The "sod busters" overexpanded and overplowed. When drought hit in early 1930s, plowed land was especially vulnerable. Great dust storms carried dust from the plains to Atlantic Ocean. "Okies" and "Arkies" joined farmers from other states in the South and the plains in a migration to the west coast.

d. The New Deal and Women—Francies Perkins, Secretary of Labor, first woman cabinet officer. Women also appointed as federal appeals judge and ambassadors. More women in workforce, but still discrimination, and lower wages than men received. Many refused to hire married women. Changes did occur after United States entered WWII in 1941 because then it was necessary for women to work in industry.

e. The New Deal and minorities—African Americans were significant component of New Deal coalition; this was switch in political affiliation from Republican party to Democratic. Roosevelt was appealing president to them. New Deal relief programs help many black people who were badly hit by the depression.

1) Black Cabinet or Black Brain Trust—many highly educated African American advisors at White House. Examples: William H. Hastie and Robert C. Weaver in Department of Interior. Mary McLeod Bethune,

director of Division of Negro Affairs of the National Youth Administration. Bethune was first African American woman to head a federal agency. White supporters in New Deal—especially Eleanor Roosevelt.

2) Racism remained, and some New Deal programs worked against African Americans, such as AAA, forced many black tenants and sharecroppers off the land, CCC was racially segregated, FHA would not give mortgages to blacks for houses in white areas, Social Security minimum wages did not include coverage for waiters, janitors, farmers, domestics, cooks, and hospital orderlies—jobs often held by black workers. Roosevelt did not fully support civil rights because he did not want to alienate southern whites. Racism also evident in Scottsboro Trials in 1930s.

f. Mexican Americans—no government programs for them. Many returned to Mexico—some given one-way tickets home.

g. Indian Reorganization Act (1934)—reversal of Dawes Act; restored tribal ownership of land, and did not permit Indian lands to be divided up into individual allotments. Tribes could also obtain loans for economic development and and to establish tribal government. Four million acres of land lost under allotment system were returned to the tribes.

9. Culture of the Great Depression

a. Literary responses: John Steinbeck, *Grapes of Wrath* (1939) and *Tortilla Flat* (1935); Thomas Wolfe, William Faulkner. Margaret Mitchell's best seller, *Gone With the Wind* (1936).

b. Pictorial impact—Walker Evans; Margaret Bourke-White; *Life* magazine.

c. Escaping reality—"golden age of the movies." By 1934, attendance at movies back up—most people could afford. Families, couples on dates, friends went to movies. Greta Garbo, Jean Harlow, Claudette Colbert, Clark Gable, Cary Grant—biggest box-office stars; also Mickey Mouse. Disney's *The Three Little Pigs* released in May

1933; "Who's Afraid of the Big Bad Wolf?" became national hit overnight.

d. WPA—helped to support fine arts—examples: Richard Wright, Jack Conroy, Saul Bellow among authors, paid less than $100 a month.

e. Music—jazz, swing (big bands), and musical comedy all popular. Also, people could listen to music on radio (along with radio shows—soap operas, comedies, dramas, news, and sports)

10. Political extremism

a. Communism—in 1935, declared "Communism is Twentieth Century Americanism." No intention to overthrow U.S. government—worked with other left-wing groups, labor unions, student groups, writer's groups.

b. Socialism: Socialist party candidate Norman Thomas won more votes in 1932 than in 1928, but still small compared to Democratic party. Socialist Upton Sinclair did win 1934 Democratic gubernatorial nomination in California. Left-wing progressive party in Wisconsin re-elected Robert La Follette to Senate in 1934.

c. American demagogues—against New Deal. Father Coughlin, in weekly radio show, became increasingly anti-New Deal, and anti-Semitic; Dr. Francis E. Townsend called for Old-Age Revolving Pensions Plan—claimed it would help elderly and cure the depression; Huey Long elected governor in 1928 in Louisiana, "Share Our Wealth Society," assassinated in 1935.

d. Fascists: European reflections in the United States—evil bankers described by Father Coughlin were Jewish. Fascist groups like Silver Shirts and German-American Bund attacked Jews.

e. Radical alternative political systems that challenged the New Deal failed to gain substantial public support.

Questions

1. The result of the Sacco-Vanzetti case revealed

    1. that political leaders would pursue justice against public pressure for conviction.

    2. that they were clearly guilty of murder.

    3. that the two men were definitely not radicals.

    4. the extent of anti-foreign and anti-radical sentiment in the nation.

2. During the 1920s, a significant factor in changing American lifestyles was

    1. the widespread use of the automobile.

    2. the repeal of prohibition.

    3. less leisure time.

    4. the widespread use of television.

3. U.S. foreign policy during the 1920s

    1. championed the League of Nations.

    2. opposed the Washington Conference on Naval Disarmament.

    3. was generally isolationist.

    4. followed a policy of active involvement in world affairs.

4. Which of the following is one of the main reasons that Prohibition failed?

    1. It was championed by extreme radicals.

    2. Many believed it would destroy capitalism.

    3. Americans were willing to break laws that interfered with their pleasure.

    4. Americans feared its link with organized crime.

5. After the stock market crashed in 1929, how did President Hoover respond?

    1. He demanded that buying stock on the margin end.

    2. He assured the country that the economy was sound.

    3. He closed the banks for two weeks.

    4. He bought $10,000 worth of shares in U.S. steel.

6. For what reason did European nations start to default on repaying their debts to the U.S. in the late 1920s?

    1. American investors stopped loans to the countries and invested in U.S. stocks instead.

    2. Their money was tied up in massive rearmament programs.

    3. They were upset by American isolationist policies.

    4. They were buying stocks in the U.S. stock market instead.

7. President Hoover's attitude toward relief for the jobless and needy

    1. generally supported direct government relief.

    2. supported massive aid to veterans.

    3. stressed private voluntary relief through charities and people helping themselves.

    4. created small business loans through the government.

8. The first woman to serve in a president's cabinet was

    1. Frances Perkins.

    2. Marion Anderson.

    3. Eleanor Roosevelt.

    4. Mary McLeod Bethune.

9. New Deal housing legislation

   1. aided most farmers.

   2. helped to eliminate the nation's housing problem.

   3. favored the purchase of suburban homes.

   4. was concerned only with urban slums.

10. Roosevelt created the strongest opposition to his administration when he

   1. threatened to veto the Social Security Act.

   2. hindered state elections.

   3. advocated a second Agricultural Adjustment Act.

   4. when he attempted to pack the Supreme Court.

11. Movies during the Great Depression

   1. provided entertainment only to the wealthy.

   2. provided Americans with a means of escape from the reality of their lives.

   3. aided Americans in exploring the more serious aspects of their culture.

   4. had little effect on Americans.

12. Which of the following was an outcome of the AAA?

   1. It provided agricultural experts to help farmers.

   2. It helped to revitalize the Tennessee Valley.

   3. It resulted in the removal of many sharecroppers from their land.

   4. It purchased better equipment for farmers.

13. The Share Our Wealth Society was advocated by

   1. Father Coughlin.

   2. Robert La Follette.

   3. Marcus Garvey.

   4. Huey Long.

14. The National Labor Relations (Wagner) Act

   1. granted workers the right to unionize and bargain collectively with management.

   2. established a Social Security Act in which old-age pensions were paid for by employees and employers.

   3. gave the president the right to end strikes that threatened national security.

   4. established unemployment insurance.

15. Which of the following finally ended the Great Depression?

   1. Roosevelt's balanced budget

   2. a new business confidence resulting from New Deal programs

   3. the delayed impact of the second New Deal

   4. massive government spending that accompanied WWII

Answers

1. The correct answer is 4. Sacco and Vanzetti appear to have been convicted because they were Italian immigrants who were also anarchists. The evidence against them was flimsy, and the judge was openly prejudiced toward them.

2. The correct answer is 1. Widespread use of the automobile changed American culture in many ways. Suburban areas could develop because people could drive to the cities. Schools could expand because children could be bused. Trucks could transport goods. Young couples could get away from adult chaperones. Roads were built and improved; petroleum and rubber industries became more important.

3. The correct answer is 3. The United States had rejected the League and many Americans were determined that the United States would never become involved in another European war. However, the United States did remain involved in international affairs, especially in business and commerce.

4. The correct answer is 3. Enforcement was weak in most areas. People smuggled alcohol and produced it in their own homes. Except in areas with a strong temperance history, people easily evaded restrictions and broke the law in order to satisfy their personal quests for freedom.

5. The correct answer is 2. Hoover believed that the economy was strong enough to weather the crash and that it was merely a brief decline.

6 The correct answer is 1. The United States served as the world's banker. U.S. loans went to European countries during the postwar period. In the late 1920s, American investors became more interested in the U.S. stock market.

Europeans could not borrow money or buy U.S. goods due to high tariffs. In turn, they pulled their U.S. investments, raised their own tariffs, and began to default on loans to the United States.

7. The correct answer is 3. Hoover believed that people should help themselves. Charity should come from private agencies, such as the Red Cross, not the government.

8. The correct answer is 1. Perkins was appointed Secretary of Labor by Franklin Roosevelt. Bethune was the first African American woman to head a federal agency. After Marion Anderson, the noted black contralto, was forbidden to sing at Constitution Hall in 1939 by the Daughters of the American Revolution (DAR), First Lady Eleanor Roosevelt arranged for her to perform at the Lincoln Memorial.

9. The correct answer is 3. New Deal housing legislation, such as FHA loans, favored the purchase of suburban homes. HOLC real estate appraisals gave the highest ratings to suburban homes, especially in select neighborhoods where there were no Jews or other "undesirable" groups.

10. The correct answer is 4. Both Liberals and Conservatives denounced his plan to create a court more sympathetic to his New Deal measures.

11. The correct answer is 2. Movies provided a fantasy world for Americans suffering during the Great Depression. Almost everyone could afford the 10–25-cent admission price to enter an ornate movie palace, where one saw short subjects, newsreels, and a cartoon, as well as the featured film. Usually Saturdays included a serial with a cliffhanger, so

that one had to return the next week to see the outcome.

12. The correct answer is 3. Since the AAA encouraged cutbacks in production, many landlords kicked their tenants off the land, and pocketed the money, even though sharecroppers and tenants were supposed to receive some payment, too.

13. The correct answer is 4. Long's plan advocated a guaranteed income for every family. He was a critic of the New Deal, and he probably would have run for president.

14. The correct answer is 1. The Supreme Court had struck down the NIRA, thus eliminating the clause protecting labor unions. The Wagner Act restored this protection.

15. The correct answer is 4. In 1939, unemployment was still at 19 percent. Mobilization for the war in 1941 made unemployment drop to 10 percent, by 1944 it had dropped to 1 percent.

Chapter 8

The United States in an Age of Global Crisis

Responsibility and Cooperation

Part I. Peace in Peril: 1933–1950

A. Isolation and Neutrality

1. Popular disillusionment following WWI contributed to a revived isolationism in U.S. foreign policy. Seeds of WWII sown earlier in the century.

2. Peace and Disarmament: in United States, Fellowship of Reconciliation, The National Council for the Prevention of War, The Women's International League for Peace and Freedom, and the Women's Peace Union became popular in the 1920s and 1930s. Washington Conference (November 1921–February 1922) attempt at decreasing arms race between United States and major European powers and Japan; Five-Power Treaty and Four-Power treaty resulted. Kellogg–Briand Pact (1928) signed by 62 countries condemning war.

3. Nye investigations (1934–1936)—senator from North Dakota investigated munitions industries; said "merchants of death" had maneuvered United States into war in order to gain large profits between 1914 and 1918. The mistakes of 1917 should not be repeated.

4. Neutrality Acts (1935–1937)—U.S. citizens should not sail on ships of countries at war; countries at war had to pay cash for American goods and transport on own ships (cash-and-carry policy); United States would not sell arms or lend money to countries at war. Aim of these acts was to prevent United States from getting caught in another war. Critics said these acts penalized countries that were victims of aggression. FDR could not veto these acts for fear of isolationist backlash. Peak of isolationism was 1937—public

opinion poll revealed 9 percent believed United States should keep out of all foreign wars.

5. Spanish Civil War—1936–1939, Loyalists' republican government against fascist Francisco Franco. Soviet Union backed Loyalists; Germany and Italy backed fascists. France and England stick to concept of nonintervention. Lincoln Battalion, American volunteers fight for Republicans. United States officially neutral. Franco won in 1939.

6. Roosevelt makes "Quarantine" speech (1937) in response to Japan's movement into China, including the bombing of Shanghai. Does not declare it a war in order to permit Chinese to purchase U.S. arms without activating Neutrality Acts.

B. Failure of Peace: Triumph of Aggression

1. Aggressions of Germany, Italy, Japan: 1932–1940

   a. Germany—Hitler came to power, 1933. Stopped paying reparations, began to rearm in 1934. Took over demilitarized Rhineland (1936). Formed Rome-Berlin Axis, an alliance with Italy (1936). In 1938, Germany annexed Austria (the *Anschluss*) and grabbed the Sudetenland of Czechoslovakia. He captured the rest of Czechoslovakia in 1939.

   b. Italy—also rearming; 1935, Italy invaded Ethiopia. United States imposed arms embargo under Neutrality Acts; this hurt Ethiopia, which was quickly defeated by Italy.

   c. Japan—Japan seized Manchuria in 1931. Japan and China at war by 1937—Japan refers to it as "China incident" to appear not to have violated Kellogg-Briand Pact. Bombing of Shanghai. Japanese declaration of "New Order." U.S.–Japanese relations are strained, but don't want to declare war.

2. Appeasement: The Munich Conference (1938)—European nations do not stop Hitler. After his seizure of Sudentenland, France and England decide at Munich Conference to let Hitler have this territory. Believing Hitler will be appeased, English Prime Minister Neville Chamberlain declares, "peace in our time."

3. German attack on Poland (1939)—World War II begins. Germany and Russia sign Nazi-Soviet Pact, secret agreement

to divide eastern Europe between them. German blitzkrieg attack captures Poland. England and France declare war against Germany.

4. Gradual United States involvement

    a. Neutrality Act of 1939—"cash and carry"—sale of arms—attempt to repeal arms embargo.

    b. Roosevelt tries to follow "Good Neighbor" policy of nonmilitary intervention in Latin America. Defense of Western Hemisphere—Declaration of Panama (1939) Latin America warned aggressors to stay away. However, U.S. aids in overthrowing Cuban government by Batista, who remains in charge until overthrown by Castro in 1959. Roosevelt renounces Platt Amendment in 1934.

    c. FDR's Four Freedoms (1941): speech, religion, want, and fear. Lend-Lease Act (1941)—controversial legislation. United States officially neutral, but wants to help England. England broke and being bombed by Germany. Roosevelt says *lend* them the weapons. Churchill asked FDR for fifty old destroyers—FDR traded destroyers for six British naval weapons in Caribbean; British leased bases in Bermuda and Newfoundland. Also sent U.S. Navy to patrol and troops to Greenland to help ensure safety of weapons halfway to England. Later, lend-lease extended to Soviet Union, too.

    d. "Atlantic Charter" conference (1941)—Churchill and Roosevelt meet off coast of Newfoundland. Charter they issue contains aims such as: collective security, disarmament, self-determination, and freedom of seas. January 1, 1942, 26 nations sign in agreement of charter—Declaration of the United Nations.

C. The United States in WWII

1. Pearl Harbor—Germany, Italy, and Japan signed Tripartite Pact, September 1940. Roosevelt places embargo on Japanese, then freezes Japanese assets in United States in July 1941. But Roosevelt wants to avoid war with Japan to concentrate on Germany. U.S. leaders knew that Japan intended war with United States, but did not know about planned attack on Pearl Harbor. Japan wished to destroy U.S. fleet, keep it out of war. Attack was a surprise on December 7, 1941. Attack killed more than 2,400 American servicemen. This surprise attack also produced powerful symbolic impact.

Roosevelt referred to December 7 as "a day which will live in infamy," as he asked Congress to declare war against Japan. Germany and Italy then declared war on United States.

2. War in Europe—debate by Allies over opening second front. Russia suffering the most from Germany's troops, wants U.S.–British to attack in northern Europe to draw Hitler away from eastern front. Churchill against this. Instead, United States and England invade North Africa in 1942; then Italy in summer 1943. Finally, agreement made at meeting of Roosevelt, Churchill, and Stalin in Teheran, Iran (Dec. 1943) to launch Operation Overlord—the invasion of France in 1944. In return, Soviets would help Allies fight Japan after Germany's defeat. Yalta conference (Feb. 1945)—secret agreements by Big Three; later would prove controversial.

a. D-Day—June 6, 1944. Allied troops under command of General Eisenhower land at Normandy. Massive invasion. Another force enters later in south of France. Allied troops able to enter Germany by September; fighting continues—Battle of the Bulge. Russian troops enter Germany through Poland, and American troops meet them in 1945. April 12, 1945, Roosevelt dies; Truman becomes president and commander-in-chief. Hitler commits suicide later that month, and Germany surrenders May 8, 1945.

3. The Home Front

a. mobilizing for war—starts before U.S. entered war. Selective Training and Service Act (1940)—first peacetime draft. 1.2 million draftees summoned for one year service. Industries have to be converted to war production. War Production Board (WPB) created after attack on Pearl Harbor to aid in mobilizing business and make it profitable for them. Antitrust actions suspended if industries were war-related. National War Labor Board (NWLR) to make sure that wages and hours fit government guidelines—under president's wartime powers could seize industries whose owners did not cooperate. "No strike pledge," broken by John L. Lewis's coal strike in 1943. Industries do well in producing war goods; full employment for United States. Taxes go up to help pay. Government bureaucracy increases. Office of

War Mobilization (O.W.M.) to oversee all aspects of mobilization.

b. Rationing—controlled by Office of Price Administration (OPA). Many goods—such as gasoline, sugar, butter, and meat—were rationed.

c. Promoting patriotism—Office of War Information censored the news. Government sold war bonds—helped pay for war, but also part of effort to keep country behind the war effort. Rallies to sell the bonds: movie stars sold them, children bought war stamps at school, employees bought them through payroll deductions. Advertising, movies, radio serials all had war themes.

d. Those who were not in armed forces volunteered with Red Cross, served in civilian defense, planted victory gardens; children collected old rubber, paper, scrap metal.

e. Minorities: much of United States was segregated, including army, where black soldiers usually held menial positions under white officers. Threat of march on Washington in 1941 by African Americans demanding equal rights; Roosevelt refused to desegregate armed forces, but does issue Executive Order 8802—no discrimination in defense industries. Also Committee on Fair Employment Practices to enforce. Many southern blacks continue to move north. Major race riot in Detroit, summer 1943. Mexican Americans also suffered prejudice—in some areas of Southwest, Mexican Americans, along with blacks, could not use public swimming pools or eat in certain restaurants. Reactions against those wearing "zoot suits"—riot in Los Angeles, 1943, servicemen attacked "zoot suiters."

f. Family life—major adjustments had to be made in family life. People moved around; housing shortages, food shortages, many men away at war, many people got married quickly, had children quickly.

g. Role of women: women worked in heavy industries; by 1943 government suggesting its a patriotic duty for women to do so—Rosie the Riveter. Women were paid less than men. Black women found it more difficult to get jobs. After war, may women left their jobs, but many were dismissed, so men could have the jobs. Women also

served in uniform, many as nurses, but others in the army
(WACS) and navy (WAVES), but kept out of combat.

4. The Atomic bomb

   a. The Manhattan Project—organized 1941; centered in Los
      Alamos, NM; secret project to manufacture atomic bomb
      before Germany, but war in Europe was over before
      bomb was tested; many refugee scientists involved.

   b. Decision to use the bomb was up to President Truman.
      Some of the scientists who worked in the Manhattan
      Project opposed using bomb after they saw its power.
      Truman decided to drop bomb on Hiroshima, Japan,
      August 6, 1945; killed 78,000 people outright, and 75,000
      die later—two days before Soviet Union to enter war
      against Japan. United States argues that using bomb
      would save thousands of lives by ending the war and
      prevent Soviet influence in postwar Japan. Bomb dropped
      on Nagasaki, Aug. 9; Japan surrendered five days later.

   c. United States occupation of Japan: United States in
      control of Japan. General Douglas MacArthur was
      director of occupation—wrote democratic constitution,
      destroyed weapons, helped revitalize economy.
      U.S.–Japan sign separate peace in 1951, despite Soviet
      protest; ended occupation, gave Japan sovereignty; gave
      U.S. base on Okinawa. From Japan's empire, United
      States and Soviet Union had divided Korea; United States
      got Marshall Islands, Marianas, and Carolines—islands in
      Pacific; Formosa returned to China.

5. The war's impact on minorities

   a. Incarceration of West Coast Japanese
      Americans—removed to "relocation centers" solely due
      to their ethnic origin. Of 120,000 Japanese Americans
      interned, 77,000 were native-born U.S. citizens (*Nisei*).
      None of them was ever tried for espionage or treason.
      Korematsu v. U.S. (1944)—Supreme Court approved
      removal of Japanese Americans from West Coast. Three
      Justices denounced the decision. In 1982, Commission on
      Wartime Relocation and Internment of Civilians
      recommended compensating those affected by this policy.
      In 1988, Congress approved awarding $20,000 to each
      victim and made a public apology to survivors.

   b. Military remained segregated (see above).

c.   The Holocaust: 6 million Jews killed. During the depression, United States refused to bend immigration laws to help Jews fleeing from Hitler. Ship carrying refugees, the
St. Louis, denied entry first in Havana and then Miami; finally forced to return to Europe. U.S. officials tried to get Latin American countries and Great Britain to take refugees, but they wouldn't; United States didn't, either. Roosevelt refused to bomb concentration camps, although aerial photographs were in existence—thought it would hinder war effort.

d.   Nuremberg war-crimes trial—Nuremberg Tribunal established a precedent that national leaders could be held responsible for "crimes against humanity." Followed by de-Nazification of Germany. Other Nazi criminals tracked down and found in other countries—example, Adolf Eichmann in Argentina. No statute of limitations on crimes committed by Nazis. Current controversy at end of twentieth century over "neutral" countries such as Switzerland profiting from money and goods belonging to Jewish victims of Holocaust. Also, issue of war-crimes trials present in war in Bosnia now.

6.   Demobilization

a.   inflation and strikes—cuts in production cause layoffs of workers; in addition, millions of GIs looking for work in 1945 and 1946. Truman tries to extend New Deal programs. Postwar inflation caused by shortages of consumer goods. Workers also demanding higher wages for fewer hours worked (40 hours compared to average 45 hour workweek during war). Leads to strikes in 1946—coal, automobile, steel, electric, industries, and railroads. United States took over coal mines twice.

b.   Servicemen's Readjustment Act ("GI Bill") of 1944—gave war veterans a chance to go to college by paying tuition and providing living expenses. More than one million veterans enrolled in colleges in 1946—saw it as means of upward mobility.

c.   1946 election—Republicans ran on slogan "Had Enough?" Republican majority in both houses—first time since 1930. Want to dismantle New Deal programs—

Taft-Hartley Labor-Management Relations Act of 1947. Truman vetoes.

d. Truman becomes candidate for organized labor. Wants to expand social services—help everyone have a "Fair Deal." Truman attacks the "do-nothing" Republican Congress. Becomes more popular by spring 1948, but still seems certain to lose presidential election.

e. Election of 1948—Republican Dewey against Truman. Democratic party splits. Left-wing liberals form Progressive party, go with Henry Wallace as candidate; Southerners form " Dixiecrat" or States Rights party— angry at Truman's support of civil rights—their candidate, Strom Thurmond. All political polls show Dewey winning election—Chicago *Tribune* prints front-page headline: "Dewey Defeats Truman." Upset victory—Truman wins election. Polls had stopped interviewing early—did not detect voters switching back to Truman

f. Minorities still face discrimination in housing, employment, education. Truman upset by resurgence of terrorism against blacks, establishes Presidential Committee on Civil Rights. It sends report to Congress—Congress does not act on it. Truman signs executive order banning racial discrimination in armed services, civil service and companies that do business with federal government.

Part II. Peace with Problems: 1945–1960

A. International Peace Efforts

1. Formation of United Nations—agreement made at Yalta on need for United Nations. Conference called in San Francisco in April 1945; fifty nations. General Assembly—every member nation had a seat—could discuss international problems and concerns. Security Council—made up of five permanent members (U.S., Soviet Union, Great Britain, France, China), plus six other nations with two-year terms. Security Council supposed to help maintain peace by imposing sanctions (economic, military, diplomatic) against any nation that threatened peace. U.N. charter also established International Court of Justice and agencies such as International Monetary Fund; World Health Organization;

UN Educational, Scientific, and Cultural Organization
(UNESCO).

2. United Nations's Declaration of Human Rights—adopted
December 10, 1948, largely through vision and persistence of
Eleanor Roosevelt, who was U.S. representative to the United
Nations. She had fought against racism in United States and
was given sense of urgency for a Declaration of Human
Rights by victims of Holocaust. But she and Declaration
were mocked in cold-war atmosphere that followed.

3. Displaced persons: refugee efforts—caught up in partitioning
of Europe and cold-war politics. Creation of state of Israel,
1948, as Jewish homeland. Previously, British had the
colonial mandate for Palestine.

B. Expansion and Containment: Europe

1. Summitry: establishing "spheres of influence"

a. Yalta, Feb. 1945—Roosevelt, Churchill, and Stalin meet
to discuss peace settlement. Secret agreements; some later
controversial. Roosevelt wants Soviet Union's help in
fighting Japan and cooperation in organizing United
Nations. Soviet Union to be given Kuril Islands, southern
part of Sakhalin, railroads and ports in North Korea,
Manchuria, and Outer Mongolia. Germany and city of
Berlin to be divided. Roosevelt and Churchill also give in
to Soviet's demand that it receive eastern half of Poland,
but also say that Poland gets some German territory on its
western border. Also agree to establish United Nations.

b. Potsdam Conference, July 1945—Truman, Stalin, and
Churchill. Truman learned of atomic bomb test; decided
to push his position. Big Three in general agreed on
policies toward Germany—complete disarmament,
dissolution of Nazi institutions and laws. Decided each
nation could decide on reparations from own occupied
zone. Council of Foreign Ministers to solve other peace
issues.

2. The Iron Curtain—in speech by Churchill in 1946, he warned
that Eastern Europe was being cut off by an "iron curtain,"
built by Soviet Union. Called for Anglo-American
partnership to resist the threat.

3. The Truman Doctrine—1947; called for United States to
support Greek government against a rebellion (possibly aided

by Soviets) and to aid Turkey because it was on Soviet border. After much criticism, Senate approved Truman's request—money and military advisors sent to Greece and Turkey. Truman Doctrine established—using massive U.S. aid to support anti-communist regimes.

    a. George F. Kennan's "X" article—advocates "policy of firm containment"—use counterforce to every threat of Soviet encroachment. Required long-term patience on the part of the United States. Eventually, Soviet Union would lose its ideological fervor and change internally. Although criticized, becomes key aspect of cold-war policy.

4. The Marshall Plan—announced June 1947; massive recovery plan for Europe. In place 1948–1951. Soviet Union invited to participate, but refused—didn't want to be under U.S.-administered program. It instituted own recovery programs for Eastern bloc. Plan aided war ravaged nations and also would give U.S. needed markets in Europe. Congress appropriated $13 billion for the program.

5. Berlin Blockade and airlift: Berlin located in Soviet zone of Germany. June 1948, Soviets cut Western access to Berlin. U.S., France, and England had united their German zones, including their zones in Berlin. Truman ordered airlift of food and supplies to Berlin; sent B-29 bombers to Great Britain as message to Soviet Union. Soviets lifted blockade, May 1949, and founded German Democratic Republic (East Germany).

6. Formation of North Atlantic Treaty Organization—NATO formed, April 1949, by United States, Canada, and several western European nations; military alliance to complement the economic one of Marshall Plan, and part of containment policy. First U.S. military alliance with Europe since 1778. Much criticism, but approved by Senate.

7. United States and the Third World: Part of cold-war strategy against Soviet Union, U.S. channeled massive assistance programs toward Third World countries. Four Point Program directed technical assistance in 1950s. More than 90% of U.S. foreign aid went to Third World by 1961.

C. Containment in Asia—United States and wartime allies and enemies in the Pacific were reversed by postwar events.

1. The United States and Japan—separate peace signed by United States and Japan in 1951. United States involved in reconstruction of Japan under General McArthur (see above).

2. The United States and China

    a. United States backed Jiang Jieshi (Chiang Kai-shek) and Nationalists against Mao Tse-tung's (now known as Zedong) communists. Mao proclaimed People's Republic of China in 1949; Jiang fled to island of Formosa.

    b. United States refused to recognize People's Republic until 1979. Truman was waiting to see what would happen; also hesitated to recognize because "China lobby," group of Republican critics, insisted Truman had "lost" China. Truman didn't want to appear to approve of a communist government.

3. USSR tests A-bomb (1949)—United States and Western world's monopoly on atomic bomb gone. Shifts stakes in cold war—Truman orders development of hydrogen bomb. National Security Council produces top-secret document for Truman: NSC-68—urges massive defense spending to fight against Soviet global domination.

4. The "Hot War" in Asia: Korea

    a. United Nations efforts—1950, North Korea's troops cross 38th parallel. Truman sees this as communist threat, similar to Hitler, Mussolini, and Japanese trying to conquer world in WWII. U.N. votes to aid South Korea (Soviet Union was boycotting over U.N.'s refusal to seat People's Republic of China, and did not vote in U.N. decision to assist South Korea). MacArthur is commander of U.S. troops (90% American).

    b. Truman calls this war a "police action." Korean War brings controversy over an undeclared conflict with limited objectives and over civilian control of military decision making. Truman had never asked Congress for declaration of war—he believed he had power as commander-in-chief to send troops.

    c. U.S. air strikes on bridges on Yalu River—border of North Korea and China. November, 1950—Chinese "volunteers" came into war when its appeared North Korea was about to be extinguished as a sovereign nation. China warning United States off. MacArthur wanted massive strike on China. Both sides ready to negotiate by 1951—back at 38th parallel. MacArthur denounced concept of limited war (no nuclear weapons; confined to one place); publicly stated that China should be attacked. Truman fired MacArthur for insubordination in April 1951. Truman almost impeached after firing.

d. Armistice talks began 1951, but not signed until 1953, under President Eisenhower. Big trouble point was over prisoners of war (POWs). United States frustrated with limited war that Americans had not won.

D. The cold war at home

1. Truman and government loyalty checks—March 1947, all government employees ordered to sign loyalty oaths, stating they were not members of Communist party or other groups believed to be disloyal to U.S. government.

2. The Smith Act and the House Un-American Activities Committee (HUAC)—Smith Act of 1940 made it illegal to advocate or teach about overthrowing the government. *Dennis v. United States* (1951) upheld Smith Act in conviction of eleven communist leaders. HUAC intent on rooting out communists; investigates motion picture industry in 1947. Some refuse to testify under oath; Hollywood Ten cited for contempt and sent to prison. Others were blacklisted and could not get jobs at studios.

3. Alger Hiss case (1950)—Hiss had been Assistant Secretary of State; accused by Whittaker Chambers of being Soviet spy. Both men's stories had contradictions, but Hiss eventually convicted of perjury (for lying under oath about not knowing Chambers and passing documents to him for Soviets.) Dean Acheson and Truman had supported Hiss. Case occurred same time as Russian testing of A-bomb and China declaring People's Republic. Democrats discredited. Investigation of Hiss case led by Congressman Richard Nixon—says communism is real threat to U.S.—helps build his career.

4. Robert Oppenheimer—physicist; had directed Manhattan Project at Los Alamos. President Eisenhower suspended his security clearance in 1953 because he lied about a conversation he had with a friend in 1943 about Soviet interest in atomic secrets, and he opposed development of H-bomb.

5. McCarthyism

   a. Senatorial inquisition—McCarthy was demagogue who gained power due to the anticommunist hysteria. Claimed to have a list of 205 "known" communists in State Department. Republicans win control of Senate in 1952; McCarthy's power grows. He becomes head of Permanent Investigations Subcommittee.

   b. The Army-McCarthy hearings (1954)—McCarthy starts investigating army security. Army complains that McCarthy is going too far; Senate investigates. Hearings televised; brings downfall of McCarthy. Senate condemns him. McCarthy never produced any definitive evidence that any federal employee was a communist.

6. Cold-war period in United States—time when there are tensions between patriotic loyalty and the right to dissent. Intensified during times of crisis or stress in foreign policy. Other examples: post-WWI "red scare," Alien and Sedition Acts in 1798. These were times when civil rights became threatened—need for balance between government and the individual.

Questions

1. Between 1933 and 1937, the Congress of the United States responded to developments in Europe by

   1. sending troops to Spain.

   2. sending arms to England.

   3. passing a series of neutrality acts.

   4. providing aid to Ethiopia after Italy attacked there.

2. Roosevelt's plan to aid England after his reelection in 1940 was to

   1. ask Congress to declare war.

   2. call for the United Nations to send in troops against Germany.

   3. maintain strict neutrality.

   4. promote the Lend-Lease Act in order to help the British war effort.

3. After the Japanese attack on Pearl Harbor

   1. Japanese Americans were forced to move into "relocation centers."

   2. the United States restricted the rights of Japanese Americans, German Americans, and Italian Americans, because Germany and Italy were allies of Japan.

   3. the United States bombed Hiroshima six months later.

   4. the United States carefully protected Japanese Americans from angry crowds and made sure that their civil rights were not violated.

4. After WWII was over, most American women

   1. were expected to leave their wartime employment and return to their traditional role in the home.

   2. fought to keep the opportunities acquired during the war.

   3. found that they had many new opportunities for equal treatment in the workplace.

   4. turned their energies toward winning the right to vote.

5. Which of the following was part of the agreements made at the Yalta Conference?

   1. Truman would order the atomic bombing of Japan.

   2. The Soviet Union would declare war on Japan after Germany was defeated.

   3. Poland would become part of the Soviet Union.

   4. China would be recognized as a major World power.

6. U.S. reaction to Nazi persecution of the Jews resulted in

   1. immediate easing of immigration restrictions to allow victims of persecution to enter the United States

   2. little direct action until after the war.

   3. bombing raids on Nazi concentration camps.

   4. U.S. assistance through the International Red Cross.

7. The GI Bill of Rights

   1. provided educational benefits to veterans.

   2. guaranteed employment for returning veterans.

   3. provided that military personnel would not be discriminated against based on race.

   4. provided that military personnel would not be discriminated against based on sexual orientation.

8. The first atomic bomb was dropped

   1. by the Soviet Union on the city of Hiroshima.
   2. by the United States on the city of Hiroshima.
   3. by the United States on Tokyo.
   4. by a joint Allied effort on multiple targets in Japan.

9. Truman's containment policy

   1. was not supported by Congress.
   2. made relations between the United States and Soviet Union stronger.
   3. became the basis for American foreign policy in the post-WWII period.
   4. had been designed by Franklin Roosevelt.

10. After the Communists won control of China in 1949

    1. many Republicans accused Truman of "losing" China to the communists.
    2. the United States recognized the new government.
    3. the United States repudiated the leadership of Jiang Jieshi.
    4. troops under the leadership of General MacArthur attacked Mao's army.

11. The purpose of the Marshall Plan was to

    1. assist South Korea.
    2. hasten the economic recovery of Europe.
    3. hasten the economic recovery of Japan.
    4. remove Soviet influence in Greece and Turkey.

12. One of the political consequences of the Korean War was

    1. that it strengthened support for the Democratic party in 1952.

    2. to increase the powers of Congress over foreign policy.
    3. to increase the powers of the president in determining foreign policy.
    4. to increase bipartisan support for the use of atomic weapons.

13. Truman contributed to the anti-communist fear by

    1. order investigations into the loyalty of federal employees.
    2. publicly accusing Alger Hiss of spying for the Soviet government.
    3. ordering investigations of the military.
    4. claiming that all liberal Democrats were communists or communist sympathizers.

14. What led to Senator Joseph McCarthy's downfall?

    1. He accused fellow senators of being communists.
    2. He publicly stated that President Eisenhower was a communist sympathizer.
    3. He took on the U.S. Army in front of millions of viewers in televised hearings.
    4. the discovery that he had belonged to the Communist party as a young man.

15. After the Soviet Union tested an atomic bomb, the United States

    1. threatened to attack the Soviets' nuclear laboratories.
    2. was happy to have an ally with atomic power.
    3. asked the U.N. to regulate the development of nuclear research.
    4. authorized the development of the hydrogen bomb.

Answers

1. The correct answer is 3. Congress and most Americans did not want to be involved in a world war again. The neutrality acts prohibited arms shipments to nations at war and advised U.S. citizens not to travel on ships of countries at war.

2. The correct answer is 4. In 1940, Americans were still hesitant about entering another war. However, the country was preparing for war. Roosevelt wanted to give England more help, and so he invented "lend-lease." This plan enabled the English to "borrow" military equipment. The Lend-Lease Act also meant the United States was not maintaining neutrality any longer.

3. The correct answer is 1. Approximately 110,00 Japanese Americans were evacuated, mostly from the West Coast. They were not a threat to the nation, but their physical features made them stand out more than those of German and Italian ancestry. The largest population of Japanese Americans, those in Hawaii, were not forced to evacuate. The 442nd Infantry Combat Team was made up entirely of *nisei* (Japanese born in the United States). It became the most decorated unit in the military.

4. The correct answer is 1. After the war, many women quickly left their jobs. Although some left by choice, many were dismissed. Ideas about gender roles did not really change.

5. The correct answer is 2. There was much diplomatic give-and-take at this conference, with each of the Big Three getting something it wanted. Since this was before the atomic bomb was created

and tested, Roosevelt was eager for Soviet help in the war with Japan.

6. The correct answer is 2. The United States refused to ease restrictions early in the war. Although later possessing aerial photographs of concentration camps, U.S. officials declined to bomb them, arguing it would detract from the war effort. The War Refugee Board was not created until 1944.

7. The correct answer is 1. The Servicemen's Readjustment Act of 1944 (GI Bill of Rights) provided tuition payments and living expenses for veterans. More than one million veterans enrolled in colleges in 1946.

8. The correct answer is 2. The United States was the first country to develop the atomic bomb. The first atomic bomb was dropped on Hiroshima.

9. The correct answer is 3. Containment became the basis for American foreign policy. The Truman Doctrine was the first major application of containment policy when Truman warned of the threat the Soviet Union posed in Greece and Turkey. This was a major step in the cold war.

10. The correct answer is 1. Most Americans failed to understand the support Mao had in China or the intricacies of the long internal dispute there. In the cold-war atmosphere, the issue of China caused staunch anti-communists to blame the United States for losing China to the communists. China was perceived as being a puppet of the Soviets.

11. The correct answer is 2. The United States financed a massive recovery plan for Europe known as the Marshall Plan (1947–1949). The Soviet Union refused to participate in a U.S.–dominated plan,

and instituted its own recovery plan for Eastern Europe.

12. The correct answer is 3. Congress had deferred to Truman throughout the war. He had never asked Congress to declare war. Instead, he used his power as commander-in-chief to send troops overseas.

13. The correct answer is 1. In 1947, Truman ordered that federal employees be investigated. In 1950, the government began discharging employees who were suspected of being "security risks"—homosexuals, debtors, alcoholics—people who could be blackmailed. These people could not defend themselves, and for the most part, there was no evidence that they were disloyal to the government. They were victims of the anti-communist hysteria of the times.

14. The correct answer is 3. McCarthy's wild accusations against the army were displayed along with his drunken rantings in front of millions of television viewers. His abusive behavior finally prompted Joseph Welch, counsel for the army, to declare, "Have you no sense of decency, sir?" Spectators burst into applause.

15. The correct answer is 4. After learning that the Soviets had secretly tested an atomic bomb, Americans were anxious that their monopoly on nuclear weapons was gone. Truman authorized the development of the hydrogen superbomb in 1950.

Chapter 9

A World in Uncertain Times: 1950–Present

Part I. Toward a Postindustrial World: Living in a Global Age

A. Within the United States: all of the following changes slowly altered the country between 1950 and the present. But, in terms of historical time, the transition has been extremely rapid.

1. Changing the energy sources: toward nuclear power

2. Changing materials (plastic; light materials)

3. Changing technology (computers; the Internet)

4. Changing corporate structures (multinational corporations)

5. Changing nature of employment (agriculture to industry to service)

B. In the World

1. Agriculture: traditional patterns and "green" revolutions

2. Manufacturing: developing and developed nations

3. World population growth: hunger and control

4. Environmental concerns

5. Emerging power relationships: East/West; North/South; haves/have-nots; developed/developing nations

Part II: Containment and Consensus: 1945–1960

A. Postwar Events: In Europe and Asia, 1945–1952 : The period after WWII saw significant shifts in traditional balance-of-power relationships, with the United States and the Soviet Union emerging as rival power bases. Republicans campaign in 1952 on "KC2"—Korea, communism, and corruption

B. Eisenhower Foreign Policies

1. The end of the Korean War—Eisenhower elected with campaign promise that he would go to Korea. Armistice signed July 1953. Boundary between North and South Korea set near 38th parallel, where it was before the war. Americans frustrated by the limited war and failure to achieve victory; helped to elect Eisenhower in 1952. MacArthur had asserted that there is no "substitute for victory."

2. John Foster Dulles, Secretary of State; trusted and relied upon by Eisenhower; staunch anti-communist; saw struggle against communism in religious, "good versus evil" terms.

   a. massive retaliation: Eisenhower administration phrase for nuclear annihilation of Soviet Union or People's Republic of China if they took aggressive actions—wasn't believed by communist adversaries—was United States going to nuclear war whenever its allies were threatened?

   b. deterrence: that the United States could make such a threat was thought to be a deterrent to hostile Soviet movements

   c. brinkmanship: if there was a crisis, the United States would not back down, even if the nation was on the brink of war. Domino theory would be used as a justification for Vietnam intervention.

   d. domino theory: if United States did not help small nations, they could fall like dominoes to threat of communism. This led to increased covert action by Central Intelligence Agency (CIA) in Third World countries.

3. The H-Bomb—United States tested first one in 1952. In 1954, United States detonated largest H-bomb—destroyed island of Bikini in Pacific. Fallout sickened crew of Japanese fishing boat and killed one sailor. International protests.

   a. Eisenhower becomes concerned about arms race. In 1953, "atoms for peace"—fissionable materials should be given to U.N. for industrial projects.

   b. "open skies"—proposed that aerial surveillance should be made of U.S. and Soviet military sites so that there would be no surprise attacks. Soviets refused, wanted no aerial or even ground inspections, felt this was espionage.

4. Uprisings in Hungary and Poland—1955, testing Soviet government of Khrushchev. Soviet troops and tanks crush rebellion in Budapest. Eisenhower cannot really do anything without causing another world war.

5. Summits and U-2—Summit planned for Paris, 1960, to discuss problems between U.S./West Germany and Soviet/East Germany and city of Berlin. Shortly before the summit, CIA pilot Francis Gary Powers is shot down over Soviet Union; had been taking photographs of Soviet military installations from U-2 spy plane. Eisenhower first claimed it was an off-course weather plane. United States refused to apologize; Soviets walk out of summit. Khrushchev withdraws his invitation to Eisenhower to visit USSR.

6. China policy: islands of Jinmen (Quemoy) and Mazu (Matsu) were used by Jiang as bases for attacking mainland. China fights back in 1954, and Eisenhower decides to defend the islands. Formosa Resolution (1955)—Congress says president can deploy forces to defend Formosa and nearby islands. 1957, United States put nuclear missiles on Formosa. China develops nuclear bomb capacity in 1964.

7. Establishment of Southeast Asia Treaty Organization (SEATO)—Fall 1954, United States, France, Britain, Australia, New Zealand, the Philippines, Thailand, and Pakistan form organization—partly to protect southern part of Vietnam. In 1954, Eisenhower refused to send troops or use air power to rescue French forces trapped by Vietnamese communist soldiers at Dien Bien Phu.

8. Eisenhower Interventions
   a. Suez crisis—1956; United States retracted its offer to help finance Aswan Dam project in Egypt. Nasser then nationalized the British-owned Suez Canal to use the money from it to finance the project. France and England conspire with Israel to invade Suez—oil went through Suez canal to get to West. Eisenhower feared Nasser would turn to Soviets for help; also upset that invasion had shifted attention from Soviet invasion of Hungary. Allies had not consulted United States prior to invasion. Eisenhower demanded that they pull the troops from Suez. Result: Egypt kept canal; Soviets helped build Aswan Dam; Nasser became Third World hero for fighting Western imperialism.

    b. Lebanon—Eisenhower sends troops to Lebanon, 1958. Part of Eisenhower Doctrine: United States would intervene in Middle East if any government asked for assistance, fearing a communist takeover.

  9. Sputnik and space missile race: Soviets launched first intercontinental ballistic missile (ICBM) and then sent Sputnik, first artificial satellite, into space in 1957. Americans nervous that Russians ahead in rocket technology. United States soon develops ICBMs and other weapons. National Aeronautics and Space Administration (NASA) created in 1958. American schools begin to stress the study of science and math in classrooms across the nation. In Latin America, Cuba would become a communist state under the control of Fidel Castro. United States severed diplomatic relations with Cuba, 1961.

C. Domestic Politics and Constitutional Issues

  1. The Eisenhower Peace—Eisenhower's slogan, "It's Time for a Change. " He promises to end Korean War. "Modern Republicanism" or "dynamic conservatism" is what Eisenhower calls his approach to government. He wants to keep some of the programs instituted by New Deal, but wants to reduce the growth of the federal government. He especially wants to reduce spending and balance the budget. Very business oriented; willing to risk unemployment in order to keep inflation under control. But policy actually leads to decline in growth, and recessions, during Eisenhower's presidency.

  2. Civil Rights

    a. Jackie Robinson—broke color line; became first African American man to play in major-league baseball; Brooklyn Dodgers, 1947.

    b. *Brown v. Topeka Board of Education* (1954)—reversed "separate but equal" doctrine of *Plessy v. Ferguson* as applied to public schools. Eisenhower disagreed, but carried out the law; desegregated Washington, D.C. schools. In 1955, the Court ordered the states to desegregate "with all deliberate speed." Eisenhower thought that equality could not be obtained by government edict.

   c.   Little Rock, AR: confrontation over school desegregation, 1957. Gov. Faubus of Arkansas posts National Guard to keep black students from entering Central High School. Federal court orders them to leave; black students enter to taunts of white students; black students leave. Eisenhower reluctantly sends 1000 paratroopers to Little Rock and puts 10,000 National Guardsmen under federal control. Black students able to enter the school with military protection.

   d.   Rosa Parks and Montgomery, AL, bus boycott; Dec. 1955; Rosa Parks, a black seamstress and member of NAACP, refused to move to back of a bus in Montgomery, Alabama. African Americans were supposed to sit at the back of the bus and give up seats to white riders, if asked. Black leaders decided to lead boycott of buses; leader is Martin Luther King, Jr. He believed in nonviolence and peaceful protests.

   e.   Supreme Court declares Alabama's Jim Crow laws unconstitutional in 1956. Civil Rights Act of 1957— creates U.S. commission on civil rights. Not very effective.

   f.   Sit-ins: four black college students sit at lunch counter in Greensboro, North Carolina. Lunch counter did not serve African Americans, but they refused to move. Nonviolent sit-in movement begins. Martin Luther King, Jr., arrested at a sit-in in Atlanta. Sent to prison. Senator John F. Kennedy gains his release. In November, black vote goes to Kennedy during presidential election. "Freedom Riders" integrated groups, go to South in buses to try to integrate transportation system there. (1961)

D. The People

1. Prosperity and conservatism

   a.   Postwar consumption: United States began time of prosperity after war—economic prosperity continued to grow through 1950s and 1960s; people also had larger paychecks and more money to spend. From 1945–1960, GNP grew by 250%. Need for homes and schools spurred by baby boom. In turn, this led to construction of stores, offices, factories, airports, and other buildings—much building done in suburbs. This meant demand grew for automobiles.

    b. Baby boom—natural for births to increase immediately after war, but huge birth rate continued through 1950s, did not start to decline until 1961; still more than four million births per year through 1964. Before war, birth rate had been declining; baby boom reversed the trend. This meant that homes and schools had to be built; many products became geared toward families. Later goods and services aimed at "baby boomers."

    c. GI Bill—government pays for college education of veterans. More than one million enrolled in 1946.

    d. Television—1946: only 8,000 privately owned T.V. sets; 4 million by 1950. Ed Sullivan; mid-1950s westerns and quiz shows, and quiz-show scandal (contestants receiving answers before the show). Less socializing outside the home at movies and dance clubs. Invention of "TV dinners." More conformity—news announcers speak "standard American English" with little regional variations; national businesses get known; people see same entertainment, programs tend to portray white, middle-class suburban life as American norm.

2. Migration and immigration

    a. Suburbanization: Levittowns—first Levittown, NY; followed by Levittowns in NJ and PA: assembly-line "tract" housing; huge development of rows and rows of nearly identical houses in treeless lots; built very quickly. Ideals of conformity; family togetherness.

    b. Cities: declining—many young couples looking for housing could not find it in the cities. Suburban housing was built quickly and was affordable. Many white Americans fled to suburbs to avoid integrated urban neighborhoods. As suburbs developed, cities declined. By 1960, about one-third of U.S. population lived in the suburbs. People were doing their shopping and activities in the suburbs. Cities become more populated with people who could not afford to move, like migrants from the South (African American and poor whites from southern Appalachia region) and immigrants.

    c. Growing numbers of immigrants from Mexico, Dominican Republic, Colombia, Ecuador, and Cuba. Puerto Rican population in New York City increased from

70,000 in 1940s to 600,000 in 1960s. Most of these immigrants lived in cities.

Part III: Decade of Change: 1960s

A. The Kennedy Years

1. The New Frontier: dreams and promises—John F. Kennedy narrowly elected over Richard M. Nixon—gets 49.9 percent of popular vote.

   a. Domestic policy initiatives stalled in Congress—Congress controlled by conservative coalition of Republicans and southern Democrats. Did not want to pass his programs—federal aid to education defeated; feared Kennedy would give aid to parochial schools. Kennedy did not press very hard for civil rights measures; wanted to appease conservative members of Congress. Also took on U.S. Steel over price increase; strained relationship with business community.

   b. Civil rights actions

      1) James Meredith—1962; Kennedy sends U.S. marshals to protect James Meredith, first African American to attend University of Mississippi. Mob violence; many wounded, two killed. Kennedy orders army troops onto campus.

      2) "Letter from Birmingham Jail" (1963)—Martin Luther King Jr. arrested after boycotts and marches in Birmingham, Alabama, that he had organized with the Southern Christian Leadership Conference (SCLC). King wrote this famous letter in response to an "open letter" written by several white clergymen. In it, he responded to their points and explained the philosophy of nonviolent protest and the goals of the civil rights movement.

      3) Assassination of Medgar Evers—NAACP official murdered in his own driveway in Mississippi, 1963.

      4) March on Washington, August 1963. Kennedy had asked Congress to prohibit segregation in public accommodation in June. Martin Luther King Jr. "I have a dream" speech. More than 250,000 people gathered at Lincoln Memorial.

2. Rights of disabled citizens

   a. Background—historically, disabled were considered to be defective; nineteenth century, development of more humane treatment; also large institutions.

   b. Development of educational programs. Gallaudet College established, 1865. Some public school programs developed between 1850 and 1950. Education of Handicapped Act passed in 1966. New York State repealed legislation excluding the "feeble-minded" from schools in 1985.

   c. WWI—Smith-Sears Vocational Rehabilitation Act of 1910; Vocational Rehabilitation Act of 1920; Social Security Act of 1935. Assistance for disabled veterans expanded to all people with disabilities.

   d. WWII—Conscription—no visible handicaps made apparent. Return to institutions after war.

   e. Kennedy administration, 1961–1963: more awareness and change in attitudes: President's Council on Mental Retardation; Special Olympics. Kennedy brought national awareness to needs and abilities of disabled; connected to sister with special needs.

   f. Litigation and legislation in 1960s and 1970s—parents and advocates used legal system to bring about change. Examples: *PARC v. Penn*; *Mills v. Board of Education*. Rehabilitation Act of 1973 ; Education for All Handicapped Children Act (1971).

   g. Dependence to Independence: 1977 sit-in by disabled adults; activism by disabled veterans.

3. Action in foreign policies

   a. Latin America

      1) Bay of Pigs invasion: Cuba signed trade agreement with Soviet Union in 1960. Eisenhower broke diplomatic ties with Cuba and planned invasion to topple government before he left office. Kennedy authorized invasion at Bay of Pigs, 1961. Had ordered that no Americans be directly involved so it would appear to be Cuban affair, but first man ashore was CIA agent, and Cubans did not revolt. Raid was fiasco. Kennedy did not permit U.S. air power to be used during the invasion.

2) Cuban missile crisis: result of U.S. hostility, Bay of Pigs, and later plans. Cuba and Soviet Union agreed to install nuclear missiles in Cuba as deterrent to U.S. "brinksmanship. " United States responded with naval blockade of Cuba, B-52 bombers with nuclear bombs patrolling the skies. Finally, United States and Soviet Union agreed: missiles would be withdrawn if United States promised not to attack Cuba and accepted its sovereignty. Kennedy privately promised to withdraw Jupiter missiles aimed at U.S.S.R from Turkey. The two nations came close to nuclear war. Led to creation of a telephone "hot line" between White House and Kremlin.

3) Alliance for Progress: created in 1961 to stimulate economic development in Latin America; program did not succeed since much of aid was misused by Latin American leaders.

b. Vienna Summit/Berlin Wall: summit after Bay of Pigs. Khrushchev upstages Kennedy, who returns home in anger. Soviet Union resumes nuclear testing in atmosphere and orders border between East and West Germany secured. Many had been defecting from East Germany to West. Khruschev has wall built in Berlin, October 1962, to divide East and West Berlin.

c. Peace Corps: volunteer service sent into Third World nations; included teachers, agriculturalists, and health care workers. Purpose also to align these countries with United States.

d. Launching race to the moon: part of Kennedy's New Frontier program. 1962—launched massive effort of space program—goal to overtake Soviet Union, which was first country to orbit an artificial satellite and first to have a human space traveler. United States sent John Glenn to orbit the Earth in 1962. Kennedy vowed to have man on moon by 1970. Neal Armstrong stepped on moon's surface in July 1969.

e. Nuclear Test Ban—Limited Test Ban Treaty with Soviet Union (1963)—banned nuclear testing in atmosphere, outer space, and under water, but arms race actually accelerated during Kennedy's administration.

    f.   Assassination in Dallas: Kennedy assassinated November 22, 1963, in Dallas. Warren Commission later found Lee Harvey Oswald acted alone in the slaying, but many Americans still not convinced, and conspiracy theories abound. Nation was stunned by the assassination. Kennedy had not accomplished very much, but had given nation hope. Lyndon Johnson, his vice president, became president and continued Kennedy programs.

B. Johnson and the Great Society

    1.   Expanding on the Kennedy social program—-Great Society programs continued philosophy of New Frontier and the New Deal.

        a.   War on Poverty—In 1960, close to 40 million Americans considered "poor"; $1 billion appropriation in 1964 to begin War on Poverty. Expands in 1965 and 1966 to include Job Corps; Project Head Start; Upward Bound; Legal Services for the Poor; Volunteers in Service to America (VISTA), a domestic Peace Corps program to help poor in United States; and Model Cities program.

        b.   Federal aid to education: besides Head Start (for low-income preschoolers) and Upward Bound (for low-income high schoolers who wanted to go to college); Elementary and Secondary Education Act (provided general federal aid to education for first time); Higher Education Act.

    2.   Moon landing—United States lands first men on moon in 1969, *Apollo 11*. Neal Armstrong and Buzz Aldron become first two men to step onto the moon's surface.

    3.   Continued demands for equality: civil rights movement

        a.   Legislative impact

            1)   Truman and civil rights—1946, executive order established president's committee on Civil Rights. Committee's report, called to secure these rights, sets out goals for civil rights agenda for next twenty years. Truman signs two executive orders in 1948: "fair employment" in federal government, and desegregation of armed forces.

            2)   *Brown v. Board of Education* (1954)—reversed "separate but equal" policy in education.

3) Civil rights Acts of 1957—created U.S. Commission on Civil Rights. Civil Rights Acts of 1964—prohibited discrimination on the of race, color, religion, sex, or national origin, both in public accommodations and employment.

4) Voting Rights Act, 1965—gave attorney general right to supervise voter registration of minority residents. Increased black registration in South: 1960, 29 percent of black population registered; in 1969, almost two- thirds of black population registered.

5) Twentieth Amendment (1964)—eliminated the use of a poll tax to deny people the right to vote.

6) Warren Court—Supreme Court led by Earl Warren—considered by many to be one of two most influential Chief Justices in U.S. history (other was John Marshall). Handed down liberal rulings in school desegregation cases of 1950s and throughout 1960s. *Baker v. Carr*, "one person, one vote," required some state legislatures to be reapportioned. Other rulings prohibited school prayer and Bible readings in public schools. Court upheld Civil Rights Act of 1964 and Voting Rights Act of 1965. *Miranda v. Arizona* (1966)—police have to inform suspects of their rights and that anything they say may be used against them.

b. Black protest, pride and power

1) N.A.A.C.P. (National Association for the Advancement of Colored People)—membership grew in 1940s; Legal Defense Fund under Thurgood Marshall (became first African American Supreme Court Justice in 1967) in 1930s trying to overturn *Plessy v. Ferguson*—won admission for African American students to attend professional and graduate schools at several state universities.

2) S.N.C.C. (Student Nonviolent Coordinating Committee)—inspired by sit-in movement; black college students organized SNCC)—practiced nonviolent protest.

3) S.C.L.C. (Southern Christian Leadership Conference)—Martin Luther King Jr. became

president in 1957; participated in sit-ins and other nonviolent civil rights protests.

4) C.O.R.E. (Congress of Racial Equality)—organized in 1942; began first Freedom Ride in May 1961—trying to test segregation laws, group of black and white riders on bus from Washington, D.C., into the South. They were attacked and bus was burned at Anniston, Alabama. Second Freedom Riders bus went to Montgomery, and riders were again beaten.

5) Black Muslims and Malcolm X: sect favored separation from white society and promoted black pride. Malcolm X became leader of Black Muslims; assassinated by other Black Muslims in 1965.

6) Civil Unrest: August 1965; riot in Watts, black ghetto area of Los Angeles. Sparked by police brutality, but also upsets about lack of jobs and opportunities. Other race riots in U.S. cities between 1966 and 1968. National Commission on Civil Disorders, chaired by Otto Kerner, Governor of Illinois, 1968—report said United States would rapidly become two separate nations, of suburban whites and urban blacks.

7) Assassinations: 1968—Martin Luther King Jr. assassinated by James Earl Ray in Memphis. Set off riots in many areas, which in turn produced white backlash (e.g., Governor Spiro Agnew in Baltimore and Mayor Richard Daley in Chicago.) Robert Kennedy assassinated in Los Angeles by Sirhan Sirhan after winning California primary to run for president.

4. Demands for equality: women

a. Subject of women trying to gain rights goes back to colonial period—married women's rights limited, women could not attend professional schools; Seneca Falls Convention, etcetera.

b. The modern women's movement

1) *The Feminine Mystique*, by Betty Friedan (1963).

2) President's Commission on the Status of Women (1963)—chaired by Eleanor Roosevelt. Issued report stating that barriers to women's full participation in society needed to be removed. Gender equality

provisions of Civil Rights Act of 1964 not being enforced.

   3) NOW—National Organization for Women—founded in 1966 to fight for equal rights for women; used lobbying and tested cases in courts.

   4) Title IX of the Educational Amendments of 1972: female athletes at college granted same financial support as male athletes.

  c. Issues

   1) Shifting roles and images—many moving away from 1950s model-housewife image.

   2) Goal of trying to gain equal job opportunities and equal pay for equal work.

   3) Equal Rights Amendment (ERA)—Congress approved in 1972, but not ratified by states.

   4) *Roe v. Wade* (1971)—Legalized abortion. Decision continues to remain controversial.

5. Rising consciousness of Hispanic Americans—Cesar Chavez and Farm Workers Union led strike against growers in California in 1965. Large numbers of Mexican Americans cross border in 1960s; Hispanics made up fastest growing minority in United States by 1970s, but did not have large share of political power. Many living in poverty.

6. American Indian Protests

  a. Occupation of Alcatraz Island in 1969, until 1971, by group of Indians—argued they were entitled to possession of unused federal lands, according to 1868 Sioux treaty.

  b. Wounded Knee—members of American Indian Movement (AIM) seized hostages at Wounded Knee. After seventy-one days, government agreed to examine treaty rights of Oglala Sioux.

  c. New York State Treaty violations: Kinzua-Allegany, Seneca land loss; Seaway-Akwesasne and Caughnawaga Mohawk land loss; Power Authority—Tuscarora land loss.

Part IV : The Limits of Power: Turmoil at Home and Abroad, 1965–1972

A. Vietnam: Sacrifice and Turmoil

1. French-Indo-Chinese War: Indochina (Vietnam, Cambodia, Laos) colony of France. During WWII, Japan occupied. Vietnamese nationalists led by Ho Chi Minh; he had joined French Communist party as means of gaining independence for Vietnam. Looked at United States as revolutionary model and based his declaration of independence on that of United States French and Vietnam at war in 1946.

2. U.S. involvement: United States not really interested until Chinese communists win in China. Truman in 1950 supports French puppet government and agrees to send weapons and military advisors to French. French losing to Vietminh. Eisenhower cautious about getting involved in war after Korea, but worries about "domino theory." French become weary of war, enter into peace talks (United States involved, too). Geneva Accords (1954) signed by France and Ho's Democratic Republic of Vietnam—divides Vietnam at 17th parallel—Ho in North. Supposed to be temporary line. United States supports government of Ngo Dinh Diem in South Vietnam; refuses to allow national elections, fearing Ho would win. Diem receives over $1 billion in U.S. aid, mostly military. Diem's government repressive and corrupt. In 1960, Vietcong form in South to fight against Diem's government.

3. Kennedy does not want to back down in Vietnam after Bay of Pigs and Berlin Wall. Orders more military personnel to Vietnam and more money to Diem's government. Finally, through CIA, United States helps South Vietnamese in a coup against Diem, who is captured and killed.

4. Johnson—gains wide power to conduct war through Tonkin Gulf Resolution (1964). Johnson creates "credibility gap" in 1964 campaign, promising he will not send American troops to Asia. First U.S. ground troops arrive in Vietnam, April 1965. He sees it as essentially declaration of war. More U.S. troops sent in, and war escalates. Vietnamese fight a guerrilla war—U.S. technology not effective. War drags on; morale of troops very poor.

5. Student protests at home

   a. Antiwar protests—In 1965, "teach-ins" began at universities, and March on Washington protested war. Secretary of Defense Robert McNamara resigned. Protests continued through Johnson's administration and into Nixon's war in Cambodia.

   b. Political radicals: many students protesting against war and conditions in United States Free Speech movement begins at Berkeley. Students for a Democratic Society (SDS)—led by Tom Hayden and Al Haber; started in Port Huron, Michigan. In Port Huron Statement they denounced racism, poverty in America, and cold war.

   c. Counterculture—Timothy Leary; "turn on, tune in, drop out," Haight-Ashbury "flower children"; hippies, communes.

6. President Johnson—announces reduction in bombing of Vietnam and states he will not run for reelection in 1968. Tet offensive in January 1969 proves war not over.

   a. Democratic Convention of 1968: war protesters attacked by Chicago police. Americans watch on TV. Hubert H. Humphrey nominated as Democratic candidate—loses election to Nixon by slim margin. (Third-party candidate, George Wallace, a conservative segregationist, won nearly 10 million votes.)

   b. War drew money away from Great Society programs. Public disillusioned by Vietnam experience. Inflation results. Abuse of executive power—continues into Nixon's presidency with secret bombing of Cambodia. Leads to War Powers Act (1973)—president must consult Congress before sending troops into foreign wars (could send troops for no more than 60 days without congressional approval). President has an additional 31 days to withdraw troops. All presidents have ignored these restrictions.

Part V: The Trend Toward Conservatism, 1972–1985

A. Nixon as President, 1969–1974

  1. Domestic policies and events

    a. Dismantling the Great Society: During Nixon's first term, Congress still retains Democratic majority who pursue liberal agenda. Nixon really not interested in domestic affairs; feels president's chief duty is foreign relations.

b. Economy in bad shape—inflation (partly caused by Johnson's deficit spending to finance both Vietnam War and Great Society). By 1971, United States suffering from "stagflation"—economic recession (stagnation) and inflation. Nixon's New Federalism (1972), a revenue-sharing program. Funds shifted from federal government to states.

c. Environment—Nixon opposed to environmental movement, which had been growing since 1960s. First Earth Day celebrated in 1970. Nixon reluctantly signs Clean Air Act (1970), Clean Water Act (1972), and Pesticide Control Act (1972). Also creates Environmental Protection Agency (EPA) (1970).

d. Reshaping Supreme Court—Earl Warren retires; Nixon replaces him with conservative Warren Burger. Later appoints more conservative members to court. Senate rejects two of Nixon's nominees to the Court—both southern judges. Still, Court never becomes as conservative as Nixon wanted it to be.

e. Pentagon Papers: *New York Times* started publishing top-secret report by Pentagon on Vietnam War. *Pentagon Papers* (Daniel Ellsbert) reveal that presidents had lied to American public about the war.

f. American Indians (see above)

2. Nixon's internationalism

a. Henry Kissinger and *realpolitik*

1) Withdrawal from Vietnam and Cambodia—Kissinger and North Vietnamese sign cease-fire agreement in 1973. War erupts again: Fall of Saigon, 1975. South Vietnamese government collapses.

2) Nixon Doctrine: United States would help nations that help themselves—"Vietnamization"—built up South Vietnamese troops to replace U.S. military.

3) Détente (means relaxation of tensions): part of Nixon-Kissinger strategy to promote a global balance of power. Too dangerous to have showdown between superpowers with nuclear weapons—better to keep things balanced. Strategic Arms Limitations Talks

(SALT) produced SALT treaty in 1972 between United States and Soviet Union that limited antiballistic missle (ABM) systems, and five-year freeze on number of offensive nuclear missiles for each side.

4) China: American table-tennis team invited to China. Kissinger then flew to Beijing in secret and arranged for Nixon to make a trip to China in 1972. This opened dialogue between United States and China—official diplomatic recognition came in 1979.

3. The "Imperial Presidency" in trouble

a. Resignation of Spiro Agnew—pleads "no contest" to income-tax evasion and charges that he had accepted bribes while serving as governor of Maryland. Resigns October 1973. Gerald Ford becomes new vice president.

b. Watergate: June 17, 1972, five men arrested for trying to place eavesdropping equipment in Watergate apartment complex in Washington, D.C.—Democratic Party headquarters. Part of "dirty tricks" campaign of Nixon. "Burglars" worked for the Committee to Reelect the President (CREEP). Nixon ordered bribe money for the men to hush them up. Two of the men talk. Informant known as "Deep Throat" talks to *Washington Post* reporters Carl Bernstein and Bob Woodward, who later wrote a full account of events in *All the President's Men*. Senate Committee headed by Sam Ervin uncovers illegal activities of Nixon White House. The "Imperial Presidency" that thought it was above the law— confirmed in tapes Nixon kept of Oval Office conversations.

c. House of Representatives Judiciary Committee recommends that Nixon be impeached.

d. Nixon resigned August 9, 1974—he announced it on national television.

B. The Ford and Carter Presidencies

1. Ford became president after Nixon resigned. He appointed Nelson Rockefeller as his vice-president. Both appointed under provisions of Twenty-Fifth Amendment. Neither was elected. First time such an event had occurred in American history.

2. Domestic Policies

   a. Ford immediately pardons Nixon. Also gives amnesty to draft dodgers.

   b. Oil crisis—occurs after October 1973 Middle East War ("Yom Kippur War"). Shifting energy priorities. United States dependent on oil, a nonrenewable source of energy. OPEC and oil crisis—Americans have to wait in huge lines to get gas for their cars and pay much more for it. Looking at nuclear energy as an energy source.

   c. Inflation—Ford's plan called WIN! (Whip Inflation Now). Says Americans should not buy expensive products and stop asking for higher wages in order to beat inflation. Plan ridiculed. Ford then tightened money supply—result was worst recession since 1937.

   d. Recession hits auto industry—Americans buying foreign compact cars instead of large American gas guzzlers. Thousands of workers laid off at General Motors in Detroit. Recession spreads to other industries because auto companies not buying rubber, steel, and other products.

   e. Cities also in trouble due to energy crisis, inflation, recession, and people moving to suburbs and Sunbelt. New York City almost bankrupt by 1975. Congress approved loan guarantees to save the city.

   f. Environmental concerns—Three Mile Island reactor core overheats—fears of nuclear disaster—100,000 people evacuated from area. Also fears of acid rain, toxic waste.

3. Foreign Policies

   a. Oil Crisis: Organization of Petroleum Exporting Countries (OPEC) placed embargo on oil to United States in 1973 to try to pressure United States into pro-Arab position. Embargo lifted in 1974, but OPEC raised oil prices several times in 1970s.

   b. Helsinki Accords—specified European security arrangements and emphasized basic human rights. Ford also continued SALT.

   c. Afghanistan invasion by Soviet Union in December 1979 affected SALT II. Carter refused to present the agreement to the Senate, and United States boycotted 1980 Olympics in Moscow. Also imposed a grain embargo.

d. Panama Canal treaties—Carter fought to have Senate pass treaties returning Panama Canal to Panama by year 2000. Panamanian resentment had been growing over United States presence there. Treaties passed by margin of one vote.

e. Camp David Accords: Carter invited Anwar el-Sadat of Egypt and Menachem Begin of Israel to negotiate at Camp David. Peace treaty signed March 1978. Egypt agreed to recognize Israel and establish normal diplomatic relations; Israel agreed to withdraw from occupied Sinai peninsula.

f. Iranian hostage crisis, 1979–1981—In 1979, Fundamentalist Islamic regime headed by Ayatollah Khomeini drove shah of Iran from power. Carter then permitted shah to come to United States for medical treatment. In retaliation, Iranian students seized the American embassy in Teheran and took 53 American hostages. They were held captive for over a year, 444 days. Carter broke diplomatic relations with Iran, but could not get hostages released. Finally, he authorized commando raid; did not succeed—eight American soldiers died. Confidence in Carter's leadership plummeted. Americans believed Carter caused the problem; elected Reagan in 1980. Hostages released day Carter leaves office.

C. The "New " Federalism

1. "Reaganomics"—Reagan's plan for economic recovery. To reduce budget, he initiated series of cuts in domestic programs such as Medicare, Medicaid, food stamps, and urban aid. Supply-side economics consisted of giving tax cuts to the wealthy and to corporations to stimulate the economy. Said this would result in new plants, jobs, and products; prosperity would "trickle down" to middle class and poor. By late 1982, economy was in a deep recession. Also, federal deficit increased substantially.

2. Reagan opposed to federal environmental, health, and safety regulations. According to his philosophy, they diminished business profits and deterred economic growth because American goods became too expensive and could not then compete on world market. He appointed people who shared his objections to these policies to regulate them. Critics of

Reagan believed his policies could lead to environmental or nuclear disasters. Reagan vetoed a Clean Water Act.

3. Social issues: Economic conservatives joined by evangelical Christians in 1970s and 1980s. Jerry Falwell founded Moral Majority in 1979. Reagan supported prayer in public schools. Abortion: "Prolife" movement developed after *Roe v. Wade* (1973)—Rep. Henry Hyde introduced legislation to cut Medicaid funds for abortions. Supreme Court upheld Hyde Amendment in 1980. Many feminists organized to protest conservative policies of Reagan; many outraged over his insensitivity to children's welfare, characterized by cuts in food stamps and school meals.

4. Minority status—Reagan worked against civil rights: attempted to dismantle affirmative-action programs, and only supported extension to Voting Rights Act of 1965 under duress. Approved tax exemptions for whites-only Christian schools. This was overturned by Supreme Court. Worked against Civil Rights Commission.

D. New Approaches to Old Problems

1. Farmers—many had incurred huge debts; also suffered due to low prices for agricultural products; droughts and floods occurred. In 1980s, many farmers forced to sell their farms and goods to pay debts.

2. U.S. society increasingly polarized between haves and have-nots in 1980s. Rich got richer, poor got poorer. As many poor people in United States as in 1964, when Johnson declared his war on poverty, but more poor were children living with one parent. Gaps also widened between whites and blacks, Hispanics, and Native Americans.

3. "New" immigrants—many from Indochina, Mexico, Latin America, and Caribbean. Immigration reform—especially aimed at controlling illegal immigration. But record numbers continued to arrive from Mexico.

4. Elderly—politicians began to pay more attention to elderly and issues of concern to them. Growing numbers of elderly meant their support was important to politicians.

E. Renewed United States Power Image

1. Central America and the Caribbean: Reagan believed Soviet Union (and Cuba) was instigating rebellions. El

Salvador—country involved in civil war. United States sent military assistance to support Salvadoran government. Saw this as preventing communism from gaining there. Nicaragua—CIA trained counterrevolutionaries called contras. Used bases in Honduras and Costa Rica. In 1986, learned that CIA Director William Casey, national security affairs advisor John M. Poindexter, and an aide, Oliver North, covertly sold weapons to Iran and diverted profits to support contras. Scandal known as "Irangate" or "Contragate." Scandal tainted Reagan's reputation—he seemed either incompetent if he had no knowledge of the matter, or dishonest if he did.

2. Middle East—United States became involved in Lebanon; U.S. Marines served as peace keeping force. Reagan pulled marines out after 240 killed by bombing of a marine barracks.

3. South Africa—United States imposed economic sanctions on South Africa in 1986 due to its apartheid policy. Many U.S. companies withdrew from South Africa.

F. United States–Soviet Relations

1. Gorbachev and soviet relations—New Soviet leader Mikhail Gorbachev and new system of *glasnost* ("openness"). Cold war winds down as Soviets decide that reductions in military spending would allow more spending on reforms. Soviet Union pulls troops from Afghanistan and makes changes elsewhere. Reagan and "Gorby" sign treaty in 1987 eliminating many missiles in each country. Leads to changes in Eastern Europe, too.

2. "Star Wars" and arms limitations—Reagan begins largest peacetime arms buildup in American history—increased federal debt. Reagan advances Strategic Defense Initiative System, an antimissile defense system in outer space. Critics call it "Star Wars." By late 1990s research continued on SDI, but on modest basis.

3. Chernobyl—nuclear plant in Soviet Union had terrible accident in 1986. Contaminated area with significant levels of radioactivity; ensuing years show devastating effects on people (high cancer rates), livestock, and land.

Part VI: To the Present

A. Presidency of George Bush

1. Wins election in 1988, although Democrats had regained Congress in 1986.

2. Inherits problems from Reagan, including federal debt. But Bush, who had once ridiculed Reagan's policies as "voodoo economics," now supports them. But economy gets worse.

3. Collapse of communism

    a. Poland—elects noncommunist government in 1989.

    b. Berlin Wall comes down in 1989, and in 1990 East and West Germany reunited.

    c. Soviet Union comes apart: 1990—Lithuania, Latvia, Estonia declare independence. Soviet Union became separate states of Russia, Ukraine, Uzbekistan, and many others. Gorbachev loses power.

4. Tiananmen Square Massacre—In 1989, Chinese government slaughtered unarmed students protesting in Tiananmen Square in Beijing, crushing pro-democracy movement.

5. Panama—December 1989, Bush sent troops into Panama, succeeds in toppling Manuel Noriega from power.

6. Persian Gulf War—Kuwait invaded by Iraq in August 1990. Bush secured U.N. approval for boycott of all foreign trade with Iraq. Iraq did not back down, and its leader, Saddam Hussein, became more defiant, annexing Kuwait. In January 1991, American-led forces started air attack—Americans watched on television. Americans then won ground assault in about 100 hours—Bush's popularity rose. Enthusiasm died down when Hussein remained in power, and it was revealed that the United States had been pursuing relations with him up until he invaded Kuwait. Also, environmental disaster from burning of Kuwaiti oil wells by retreating Iraqi soldiers. Many U.S. soldiers returned home with "Gulf war syndrome," possibly caused by chemical warfare.

7. Somalia—Operation Restore Hope. Somalia was ravaged by famines. United States was sending relief, but warring local clans and bandits kept it from arriving. After gaining U.N. approval, Bush sent U.S. troops to Somalia to make sure humanitarian aid got there. But when U.S. troops were killed,

U.S. public opinion turned against the operation. U.N. peacekeeping force replaced U.S. troops in 1993.

8. North American Free Trade Agreement (NAFTA)—1992 agreement among United States, Canada, and Mexico—envisioned tariff-free trade within nations of North America. Critics said U.S. workers would lose jobs as corporations moved to Mexico. However, by 1997 it was apparent that as many jobs were created by NAFTA as were lost.

9. American-Japanese relations—trade deficit was in Japan's favor, as Japanese goods flooded American markets. Some championed campaign of "Buy American." American-Japanese relations remain strained.

10. Bush's domestic policies: economy got worse during Bush's administration; unemployment grew; federal debt grew; federal bailout of failed savings and loans increased federal debt in 1992. Bush seemed passive—no clear solution to problems; did not believe government should interfere. Social problems that began in 1980s—prevalence of "crack" cocaine and other drugs; AIDs; poverty, especially of children—continued in 1990s, but increasingly also affected middle class.

   a. Pledged to be "the environment president": Worked against environmental regulations in belief that they slowed economic growth. Pledged to be "the education president": pushed program in which government would issue vouchers that parents could use to pay tuition at private schools.

   b. Clarence Thomas nomination: Bush nominated conservative black, Clarence Thomas, to Supreme Court in 1991. Anita Hill accused Thomas of sexual harassment; testified before all-male Senate Judiciary committee. Senate confirmed Thomas, but many women upset by testimony and reactions of Republican senators to it.

   c. Riots in Los Angeles: April 1992, riots erupted when California jury acquitted four white police officers charged with beating African American motorist, Rodney King. Forty-four people died; 2,000 injured.

   d. Americans with Disabilities Act (ADA) of 1990: prohibited job discrimination against blind, deaf, mentally retarded, physically impaired, and those who were HIV-positive or who had cancer. Also required "reasonable accommodations" for disabled, such as wheelchair ramps.

    e. Congressional scandals: House bank covered bad checks of Representatives; savings and loans scandals; members of Congress received free jet flights and money from lobbyists. Public opinions of Congress as an institution was negative.

    f. Pardon of Iran-Contra figures: Bush pardoned those accused of felony charges of lying to Congress and obstructing justice right before he left office (Oliver North).

B. Presidency of Bill Clinton

    1. Election of 1992: Bush, Clinton, and third-party candidate, Ross Perot. Clinton became first "baby boomer" president. Believed in liberal tradition, but wanted to move Democratic party more to center.

    2. First goal was to fix economy: His plan sent to Congress in February 1993 called for higher taxes for middle class and 10 percent surtax on those with incomes over $250,000, as well as energy and corporate taxes. Also proposed to cut defense budget. Congress killed some of his plans, and many Americans protested the taxes. First Lady Hillary Rodham Clinton's health care reforms not successful.

    3. Clinton lost popularity as critics charged him with being indecisive. Signed "motor voter" and family-leave bills; campaign finance reform bill; international agreement protecting rare and endangered species (reversing Bush's anti-conservation and anti-environment policies).

    4. Nevertheless, Clinton defeated Republican Robert Dole in 1996 presidential election.

    5. Clinton's tenure as president helped by a thriving economy. A very strong "bull" stock market, low interest rates, inflation, and low unemployment were all economic "positives."

Questions:

1. In *Brown v. Board of Education*, the Supreme Court ruled
   1. racially segregated public educational facilities were unconstitutional.
   2. that school prayer should be permitted in the schools.
   3. that segregation in the schools was permissible, "separate but equal."
   4. that schools must make facilities handicapped-accessible.

2. An important development in Greensboro, North Carolina, in February 1960 was
   1. Martin Luther King Jr. was assassinated.
   2. the Freedom Ride campaign began.
   3. James Meredith became the first black student at the university.
   4. four black students began the sit-in movement.

3. In the 1960 presidential campaign, Vice President Nixon
   1. was heavily endorsed by Eisenhower.
   2. accused Kennedy of being a communist sympathizer.
   3. came across as surly and with a five-o'clock shadow on television debates, while Kennedy came across as self-assured.
   4. used the media to great advantage.

4. The 1961 Bay of Pigs invasion
   1. demonstrated that the Cuban people wished to be rid of Castro.
   2. was based on the U.S. assumption that the Cuban people would rise up against Castro.
   3. was skillfully planned and executed.
   4. did not involve the CIA.

5. One of Carter's responses to the 1970 Soviet invasion of Afghanistan was
   1. to divert shipments of grain from U.S.S.R. to the rebels in Afghanistan.
   2. to initiate a boycott of the 1980 Summer Olympics in Moscow.
   3. to continue negotiations of SALT II.
   4. to begin production of "Star Wars" weapons.

6. The United States and the Soviet Union both wanted relationships with Third World nations because
   1. these nations were technologically advanced.
   2. they had stable political systems.
   3. they possessed strategic raw materials.
   4. they had productive industrial systems.

7. When Ho Chi Minh declared independence in Vietnam in 1945, he used phrases from
   1. *The Communist Manifesto*.
   2. the *American Declaration of Independence*.
   3. Tom Paine's *Common Sense*.
   4. the French Constitution.

8. The United States supported the French in Indochina because
   1. of a desire to contain communism.
   2. of a belief that the country belonged to France.
   3. of a belief that most Vietnamese wanted the French to remain.
   4. Kennedy promised the French that the United States would help.

9. The Tonkin Gulf Resolution

1. gave President Johnson great latitude to increase U.S. presence in Vietnam.

2. gave President Kennedy great latitude to increase U.S. presence in Vietnam.

3. called for the creation of a coalition government uniting North and South Vietnam.

4. kept secret bombings of Cambodia from the American people.

10. The Civil Rights Act of 1964

1. guaranteed educational opportunities to all.

2. guaranteed equal pay for equal work.

3. prohibited discrimination in employment based on race, color, religion, sex, or national origin.

4. upheld *Plessy v. Ferguson*.

11. Richard Nixon's resignation from the presidency was caused by which of the following?

1. American anger over the war in Vietnam

2. the Supreme Court's order to release the unedited Watergate tapes

3. his ill health

4. testimony by Spiro Agnew that Nixon ordered the Watergate burglary

12. Which of the following made the Ford administration different from any other in U.S. history?

1. Congress gained unprecedented power.

2. more people voted than ever before in a national election.

3. neither the president nor the vice-president had been elected to office.

4. the vice president was a member of the Communist party.

13. By the 1970s, which ethnic group was the fastest-growing minority in America?

1. Hispanic Americans

2. American Indians

3. Asian Americans

4. African Americans

14. The Persian Gulf war was caused by

1. Israel's invasion of Syria.

2. Saudi Arabia's invasion of Iraq.

3. Iraq's invasion of Kuwait.

4. Iran's invasion of Iraq.

15. After his inauguration in 1993, President Clinton

1. passed a comprehensive health-care plan.

2. quickly reversed the policy on homosexuals in the armed services.

3. persuaded Congress to pass an economic-stimulus package.

4. none of the above.

Answers

1. The correct answer is 1. In 1954, the Warren Court overturned the "separate but equal" ruling of *Plessy v. Ferguson*.

2. The correct answer is 4. The student from North Carolina Agricultural and Technical College in Greensboro sat at a department store lunch counter that did not serve African Americans. They refused to move. Sit-in movement spread, joined by Martin Luther King; part of nonviolent protest.

3. The correct answer is 3. Kennedy came across as self-assured in the televised debate. Nixon appeared surly and uncomfortable. He was not well made up, and appeared with a five-o'clock shadow. TV debates helped Kennedy's campaign.

4. The correct answer is 2. The Bay of Pigs invasion was poorly planned and based on the assumption that Cubans would rise up against Castro. Despite Kennedy's orders, the first person to land was a CIA agent. Castro retained his popularity, and the United States looked foolish.

5. The correct answer is 2. Carter shelved SALT-II, suspended grain shipments to the Soviet Union, and asked for an international boycott of the 1980 Summer Olympics.

6. The correct answer is 3. Many of these nations possessed raw material such as oil and tin. They also were magnets for foreign investment by American companies. Part of the cold war strategy was to have Third World nations allied with the superpowers.

7. The correct answer is 2. Ho Chi Minh admired the United States. He equated his quest to gain independence for Vietnam with that of the American colonies fighting for independence.

8. The correct answer is 1. The United States looked at Vietnam through the cold war beliefs that communism was evil and must be contained. U.S. officials looked at Ho as more of a communist than a nationalist. After China was won by the communists, it appeared that Vietnam had to be kept from communism.

9. The correct answer is 1. In this resolution, Congress gave Johnson wide powers to conduct the war. He considered it a declaration of war.

10. The correct answer is 3. President Johnson, a Southerner, made civil rights a priority.

11. The correct answer is 2. The House Judiciary Committee voted to impeach Nixon, and he knew the tapes would condemn him.

12. The correct answer is 3. Ford was appointed by Nixon to replace Agnew as vice president. After Nixon's resignation, Ford became president and appointed Rockefeller as vice president.

13. The correct answer is 1. This was due to immigration and a high birth rate. However, they lacked proportionate political power.

14. The correct answer is 3. Iraq was eager to control Kuwait's oil industry, and invaded in August 1990. U.S. Operation Desert Storm began in January 1991.

15. The correct answer is 4. President Clinton was elected on his promises to change things, but critics accused him of "waffling" on many issues.

Part III

Sample Exams and Answers

Sample Regents Exam #1

Directions (1–47): For each statement or question, write on the separate answer sheet the *number* of the word or expression that, of those given, best completes the statement or answers the question.

1 Which feature of government was developed most fully during the colonial era?
1 separation of church and state
2 an independent court system
3 universal suffrage
4 representative assemblies

2 In writing the Declaration of Independence, Thomas Jefferson based his argument for American independence on the idea that
1 people have natural rights as human beings
2 the British refused to import colonial raw materials
3 monarchy was evil by nature
4 Britain was too far away to rule the Colonies effectively

3 The most essential feature of democratic government is
1 a bicameral legislature
2 a free and open election process
3 a written constitution
4 separate branches of government

4 "We should consider we are providing a constitution for future generations of Americans, and not merely for the particular circumstances of the moment."

— Delegate at the Constitutional Convention of 1787

The writers of the Constitution best reflected this idea when they provided that
1 Senators should be elected directly by the people
2 three-fifths of the slaves should be counted as part of the total population
3 Congress shall make all laws necessary and proper to carry out its constitutional powers
4 political parties should be established to represent various viewpoints

5 In the late 1780's, some key states were persuaded to ratify the Constitution by the promise that provision would be made for
1 low taxes
2 a bill of rights
3 a national court system
4 national assumption of state debts

Four statements dealing with the formation of a new government are given below. Base your answers to questions 6 and 7 on these statements and on your knowledge of social studies.

Statement A: Each person must be able to voice his or her concerns on all issues that involve this new nation and bear the responsibility for the decisions made.

Statement B: The power of this new nation must rest in a strong, stable group that makes important decisions with the approval, but not the participation, of all.

Statement C: There must be several governments within one nation to ensure adequate voice and responsibility to all.

Statement D: Individuals must not allow their freedoms to be swallowed by an all-powerful government.

6 Which statement best shows the desire for safeguards such as those in the Bill of Rights?
(1) A   (3) C
(2) B   (4) D

7 Which statement best represents the ideas of federalism?
(1) A   (3) C
(2) B   (4) D

8 The constitutional power to regulate commerce allows the Federal Government to exercise control over
1 post offices and post roads
2 interstate trade
3 international relations
4 the value of money

9 The significance of the Supreme Court case of *Marbury* v. *Madison* is that
1 a Federal law was declared unconstitutional
2 the principle of States rights was greatly strengthened
3 the separate but equal principle was established
4 the constitutionality of the National Bank was upheld

10 At the beginning of the Civil War, President Abraham Lincoln maintained that the war was being fought to
1 uphold national honor
2 prevent foreign involvement
3 free all slaves
4 preserve the Union

This discussion of constitutional amendments took place just after the Civil War. Base your answers to questions 11 through 13 on this discussion and on your knowledge of social studies.

Speaker A: Some slaves were freed after the Emancipation Proclamation; others were freed by an amendment to the Constitution. We all know that free men may vote, and we do not need further amendments to tell us that.

Speaker B: If we pass these amendments, we still do not ensure the rights of the freed people. In states where white people traditionally have run the government, freed people will find it difficult to exercise their rights.

Speaker C: As a member of the Republican Party, I want to see these amendments adopted to ensure the voting strength of our party in the South.

Speaker D: These amendments must be passed. The passage of these amendments will guarantee equal rights with no further governmental action required.

11 The constitutional amendments under discussion are the
1 first and second
2 fifth and tenth
3 fourteenth and fifteenth
4 twenty-first and twenty-second

12 Speaker *C* assumed that the Republican Party could count on the votes of the
1 former slaves
2 Western farmers
3 urban factory workers
4 former Confederate soldiers

13 Which speaker describes most clearly the political situation that actually occurred after Reconstruction?
(1) *A*   (3) *C*
(2) *B*   (4) *D*

14 One effect of monopolies on the United States economy is that they have tended to
1 reduce business competition
2 keep prices low
3 give consumers a greater choice in purchasing goods and services
4 lead to a greater variety in the price for a particular product or service

15 Immigrants to the United States during the early 1900's had an advantage over the immigrants of today in that most of the earlier immigrants
1 were familiar with the English language
2 had higher levels of education
3 found that jobs for unskilled laborers were more widely available
4 were able to buy land on the frontier

16 The passage of the immigration acts of 1921 and 1924 indicated that the United States wished to
1 restrict the flow of immigrants
2 continue the immigration policies followed during most of the 19th century
3 encourage cultural diversity
4 play a larger role in international affairs

17 Trustbusting, the suffragettes, and the Pure Food and Drug Act are associated with the
1 New Deal
2 Progressive Era
3 return to "normalcy"
4 Great Society

Base your answers to questions 18 and 19 on the cartoon below and on your knowledge of social studies.

THROWING DOWN THE LADDER BY WHICH THEY ROSE.

— Thomas Nast, 1870

18 According to this 1870 cartoon, which statement about the time period is accurate?
1 Chinese laborers were welcomed to the United States with open arms.
2 The Know-Nothing Party was formed to help gain rights for minorities.
3 Very few Chinese were interested in coming to the United States.
4 A movement existed in the United States to prevent the immigration of Chinese.

19 At the time this cartoon was published, the majority of immigrants to the United States were coming from
1 Africa   3 Asia
2 Europe   4 South America

20 Jane Addams, Lillian Wald, and Jacob Riis are best known as
1 social reformers
2 leaders of industry
3 congressional leaders
4 inventors

21 In the late 1800's, which reason led the United States to give greater attention to the world beyond its borders?
1 fear of revolution in Latin America
2 fear of Russian expansion in Alaska
3 interest in finding places to settle surplus population
4 interest in obtaining markets for surplus goods

22 The women's rights movement in the early 20th century focused its efforts primarily on securing
1 a cabinet position for a woman
2 reform of prisons
3 civil rights for all minorities
4 suffrage for women

23 The decision of the Supreme Court in the 1896 *Plessy* v. *Ferguson* case is important because it
1 upheld the legality of sharecropping
2 denounced the violence of the Ku Klux Klan
3 approved separate but equal facilities for black Americans
4 declared slavery to be illegal

24 Which was a major problem faced by United States farmers in both the 1890's and the 1920's?
1 lagging technology
2 lack of tariff protection
3 overproduction of basic staples
4 inflationary currency

25 Which is the most valid generalization to be drawn from the study of Prohibition in the United States?
1 Social attitudes can make laws difficult to enforce.
2 Increased taxes affect consumer spending.
3 Morality can be legislated successfully.
4 People will sacrifice willingly for the common good.

26 In the United States, one of the basic causes of the Great Depression that began in 1929 was the
1 lack of available credit
2 abundance of purchasing power of farmers
3 low protective tariffs of the 1920's
4 overexpansion of industrial production

27 During President Franklin D. Roosevelt's first two terms, the strongest opposition to his New Deal policies came from
1 big business
2 labor union members
3 the poor
4 Western farmers

28 One major result of President Franklin D. Roosevelt's New Deal policy was that it
1 weakened the power of the chief executive
2 strengthened the policy of laissez faire
3 increased the power of the Federal Government
4 expanded the importance of States rights

29 A major reason for United States neutrality in the 1930's was the nation's
1 belief in the domino theory
2 disillusionment resulting from World War I
3 strong approval of political conditions in Europe
4 military and naval superiority

30 Which action is often viewed as the most serious attempt to undermine the independence of the judiciary?
1 appointment of conservative Supreme Court Justices by President Ronald Reagan
2 President Franklin D. Roosevelt's plan to reorganize the Supreme Court
3 appointment of Supreme Court Justices to unlimited terms of office
4 periodic increases in the salaries of Supreme Court Justices

31 The careers of Theodore Roosevelt and Franklin D. Roosevelt were similar because each man
1 was an outstanding military leader before becoming President
2 led the cause for international peace, but involved the United States in a war
3 succeeded to the Presidency upon the death of the previous President
4 believed in a strong Presidency and acted accordingly

32 Which statement is accurate concerning the forced relocation of Japanese Americans during World War II?
1 President Franklin D. Roosevelt authorized the action as a military necessity.
2 Few of those relocated were actually United States citizens.
3 Widespread Japanese American disloyalty and sabotage preceded the forced relocation.
4 The Japanese American experience was similar to what happened to German Americans at this time.

33 The purpose of the Marshall Plan was to provide Europe with
1 defensive military weapons
2 economic aid
3 cultural exchange programs
4 political alliances

34 Following the end of World War II, United States foreign policy changed significantly in that the United States
1 assumed a more isolationist stance
2 began to rely on appeasement to reduce world tensions
3 perceived the containment of communist expansion as a major goal
4 concentrated most heavily on events within the Western Hemisphere

35 One important result of the Red Scare of the 1920's and the McCarthy Era of the 1950's was the realization that
1 large numbers of Soviet agents had infiltrated high levels of the Federal Government
2 fears of subversion can lead to the erosion of constitutional liberties
3 communism gains influence in times of economic prosperity
4 loyalty oaths by government employees prevent espionage

36 As economic slowdowns have occurred in the United States, blacks have frequently found that
1 gains made through equal employment laws can be lost
2 racism has decreased
3 affirmative action has hurt them
4 their job opportunities are not affected by business cycles

Base your answers to questions 37 and 38 on the graph below and on your knowledge of social studies.

Persons Aged 65 and Over as a Percent of Total United States Population

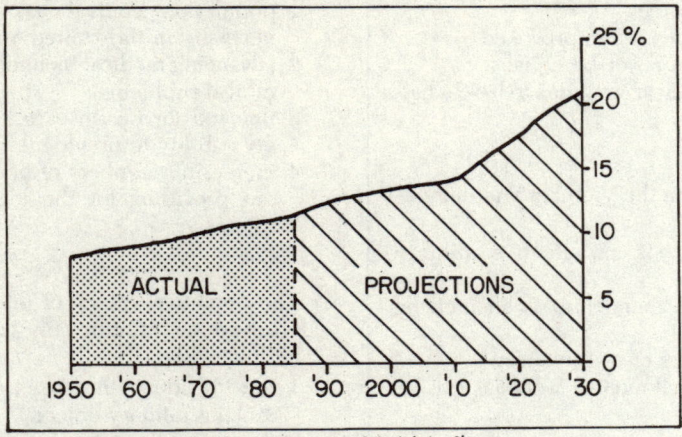

U.S. Census Bureau and Social Security Administration

37 Which statement can best be supported by the data in the graph?
1 The birth rate increased steadily between 1950 and 1980.
2 While the percentage of elderly is increasing, the total population is actually decreasing.
3 Policies concerning the elderly will have to be reviewed and revised.
4 Voters under age 30 will have proportionately more political power during the next 40 years.

38 If the projection in the graph holds true, a probable consequence will be a decrease in the percentage of
1 marriages ending in divorce
2 individuals living alone
3 Americans below the poverty level
4 full-time workers

39 The relationship between the automobile and the development of suburbs is most similar to the relationship between
1 television and increased uniformity of United States culture
2 skyscrapers and the decline of commuter railroads
3 political parties and the growth of big business
4 nuclear power plants and rising oil prices

40 As United States involvement in world affairs has increased, the power of the Presidency has also increased because
1 congressional leaders have been unwilling to divert their attention from domestic issues
2 according to custom and tradition, Congress does not discuss foreign policy issues
3 the Senate has consistently failed to check the President's power by refusing to ratify treaties
4 the Constitution gives primary responsibility for foreign relations to the President

41 Both the New Deal and the Great Society shared the idea that
1 foreign trade should be cut to a minimum
2 the Federal Government should meet the economic and social needs of the less fortunate
3 taxes should be raised to stimulate consumer spending
4 key industries should be nationalized

42 Frequently the United Nations has not been able to resolve international disputes because
1 there are too many countries represented at the United Nations
2 lack of funds has seriously curtailed peacekeeping efforts
3 the most powerful countries are not members of the United Nations
4 the most powerful members often disagree on fundamental issues

43 The concept of balance of power is based on the assumption that
1 nations will not start wars when faced with equal or superior forces
2 nations will fight only when provoked
3 blocs of nations can never be equal
4 all nations need nuclear weapons to have a balance of power

44 United States actions in the Vietnam War demonstrated that
1 the domino theory is an effective military tactic
2 military policy in a democracy is affected by popular opinion
3 advanced technology ensures victory
4 limited use of tactical nuclear weapons can be successful

45 The muckrakers of the Progressive Era and the investigative reporters of the 1970's and 1980's are similar in that both
1 sought to document corruption in United States life
2 advocated fewer government controls on the economy
3 tried to increase the spirit of patriotism
4 called for expanded aid to economically less developed nations

46 Issues related to living wills, legal definitions of death, and death-with-dignity have increased in recent years because
1 population control has become a critical necessity in the United States
2 advancing medical technology has created new ethical problems
3 demand for health care has outstripped society's ability to provide it
4 increasing numbers of people are dying without providing for the legal transfer of their estates

47 The executive branch of the United States Government has traditionally gained power during periods when
1 the Presidency has been occupied by a high-ranking military officer
2 the Republican Party was in the majority in Congress and the President was a Democrat
3 there has been a serious domestic or international problem facing the United States
4 the Supreme Court and Congress have been in conflict over constitutional issues

Answers to the following questions are to be written on paper provided by the school.

Students Please Note:

In developing your answers to Parts II and III, be sure to

(1) include specific factual information and evidence whenever possible
(2) keep to the questions asked; do not go off on tangents
(3) avoid overgeneralizations or sweeping statements without sufficient proof; do not overstate your case
(4) keep these general definitions in mind:

   (a) <u>discuss</u> means "to make observations about something using facts, reasoning, and argument; to present in some detail"
   (b) <u>describe</u> means "to illustrate something in words or tell about it"
   (c) <u>show</u> means "to point out; to set forth clearly a position or idea by stating it and giving data which support it"
   (d) <u>explain</u> means "to make plain or understandable; to give reasons for or causes of; to show the logical development or relationships of"

Part II

ANSWER ONE QUESTION FROM THIS PART.   [15]

1 In reference to the Declaration of Independence and the United States Constitution, it has been said that 1776 gave us liberty, but 1787 gave us order.

   a Discuss the extent to which you agree with the statement above. In your discussion, include *three* specific points of evidence that support your position.   [9]

   b Discuss how either liberty or order was fostered by the adoption of the Bill of Rights in 1791. Cite *two* specific references to the Bill of Rights to support your position.   [6]

2 Listed below are goals that the United States Government has pursued to further the growth of democracy.

Goals

To guarantee liberty and freedom to *all* citizens
To protect the rights of minorities
To meet the changing needs of society
To encourage greater participation in the political process

Select *three* of the goals listed. For *each* one chosen, discuss a specific occasion in United States history when the United States Government sought to achieve that goal through legislative action, executive action, or judicial decision. In your answer, show how the Government's action addressed a specific need and furthered the growth of democracy in United States society.   [5,5,5]

Part III

ANSWER TWO QUESTIONS FROM THIS PART.   [30]

3 The growth of industry in 19th-century United States had a major impact on the aspects of society that are listed below.

Aspects of Society

> Role of women
> Urbanization
> Rise of organized labor
> Government involvement in the economy
> Status of the farmer

Select *three* of the aspects of society listed. Using specific examples, show how the growth of industry in the 19th century had a major impact on *each* of the *three* aspects.   [5,5,5]

4 Leadership is an essential ingredient for the success of any movement in history. Listed below are leaders paired with the movements they led.

Leaders/Movements

> John C. Calhoun/States rights
> Elizabeth Cady Stanton/Women's rights
> Frederick Douglass/Abolitionism
> Samuel Gompers/Organized labor
> William Jennings Bryan/Populism
> Theodore Roosevelt/Progressivism
> Eleanor Roosevelt/Human rights
> Martin Luther King, Jr./Civil rights
> Ralph Nader/Consumerism

Select *three* of the pairs listed above. For *each* pair selected, evaluate the success of the leader and movement by discussing:

- The role of the leader in the movement
- Tactics used by the movement
- The effect of the leader and the movement on United States history   [5,5,5]

5 Some of the major goals of United States foreign policy are listed below.

Goals

To foster foreign trade and United States economic interests
To provide for the military security of the United States
To promote the spread of the democratic ideals and values of the United States

a Select *two* of the goals listed and for *each* one chosen:

- Describe an action taken by the United States Government at any time before the end of World War II (1945) to achieve the goal
- Describe an action taken by the United States Government since the end of World War II (1945) to achieve the goal   [12]

b Discuss one way in which life in the United States has been significantly influenced by *one* of the actions described in answer to *a*.   [3]

6 In the United States, geographic differences have contributed to the development of specific regions, each with its own needs and concerns. Listed below are three geographic regions.

Regions

Northeast
South
West

a For *each* region listed, explain the impact of specific geographic factors on the economic and historic development of the region.   [12]

b Show how technological development has lessened the influence of geographic factors on the United States.   [3]

7 Listed below are issues confronting United States society.

Issues

Students with AIDS attending public schools
Media censorship
Environmental protection
The homeless
Prayer in public schools

Select *three* of the issues listed and for *each* one chosen:

- Discuss a controversy related to the issue
- Identify *one* specific argument on each side of the controversy
- Discuss *one* specific action through which the government has attempted to deal with the issue   [5,5,5]

Sample Regents Exam #1—Answers

1. The correct answer is 4. Representative assemblies were the most common feature of the prerevolutionary War colonies.

2. The correct answer is 1. The Declaration states: "We hold these truths to be self-evident, that all Men are created equal, that they are endowed by their Creator with certain unalienable rights."

3. The correct answer is 2. A democracy is based upon a government selected by the people through a free and open election. Note that Great Britain does not have a written Constitution and actually "fuses" the legislative and executive branches. The state of Nebraska has only a unicameral state legislature.

4. The correct answer is 3. The "elastic clause" is one of the main components that makes the Constitution a living document. Senators were originally elected by state legislatures. Parties were not a concern of the convention. The decision on slavery was an "expedient compromise."

5. The correct answer is 2. When it came time for the states to ratify the Constitution, the lack of any bill of rights was the primary sticking point. This was the issue that many anti-federalists raised—the absence of a Bill of Rights in the Constitution—in opposing ratification.

6. The correct answer is 4. The Bill of Rights deals with protecting individual freedoms.

7. The correct answer is 2. The ideas of federalism call for a strong central government.

8. The correct answer is 2. Commerce deals with trade, i.e., interstate trade. This would differ from intrastate trade, which would fall under the jurisdiction of the state.

9. The correct answer is 1. In the case, the Supreme Court upheld the idea that the Supreme Court may declare unconstitutional any law or provision of a law contrary to the Constitution. This is known as the power of judicial review.

10. The correct answer is 4. This was Lincoln's primary objective. Hence, the "House Divided" speech.

11. The correct answer is 3. These amendments dealt with representative apportionment, equality before the law, and the right to vote.

12. The correct answer is 1. These amendments were designed to ensure the newly freed slaves would have the right to vote. They voted predominantly Republican.

13. The correct answer is 2. These amendments were designed to ensure the newly freed slaves would have the right to vote. However, Southern whites found several ways to prevent this from happening, i.e., poll tax, literacy test, etcetera.

14. The correct answer is 1. The concept of monopoly is to reduce or eliminate competition. The other options are all results of competition.

15. The correct answer is 3. The immigrants coming in the 1900s were primarily from southern and eastern Europe as well as Asia. They did not speak English, they were from the lower classes, and by 1900 the frontier was closed. This leaves only number 3 as a possible answer.

16. The correct answer is 1. Both of these acts placed tighter restrictions on immigration.

17. The correct answer is 2. All three of these items occurred during the Progressive Era of 1901–1921.

18. The correct answer is 4. The wall is designed to keep the Chinese out of the country.

19. The correct answer is 3. This is the reason that Asians were targeted the hardest by antiforeign or nativist groups.

20. The correct answer is 1. These were all social reformers who worked to ease the plight of the urban poor.

21. The correct answer is 4. This is what led us to become involved in China and Japan, as well as other areas. Russia was an ally at the time, we had no surplus population, and the Latin American revolutions occurred primarily in the early 1800s.

22. The correct answer is 4. Women did not gain the right to vote (suffrage) until 1920.

23. The correct answer is 3. *Plessy v. Ferguson* established the "separate but equal" doctrine. This doctrine would not be overturned until the 1954 *Brown* decision.

24. The correct answer is 3. In both instances there was surplus production, which eventually led to declining demand and price.

25. The correct answer is 1. It is *very difficult* to legislate social morality. Resistance to prohibition eventually led to repeal of the Eighteenth Amendment in 1933. Prohibition proved 3 and 4 were untrue. Answer 2 has nothing to do with Prohibition. Because it was nearly impossible to enforce, 1 is the best choice.

26. The correct answer is 4. Once there was a surplus, there was more than demand. As this happens, labor is let go to reduce expenditures. More people unemployed means even less demand, more people are fired, etcetera.

27. The correct answer is 1. The New Deal completed the transition from laissez faire to regulated capitalism. As such, it greatly affected the role of government in business. The poor and labor union members became the "backbone" of FDR's political support.

28. The correct answer is 3. The federal government greatly expanded its role in society. The full extent of federal activity is revealed best by the listing of New Deal laws and agencies.

29. The correct answer is 2. Congress passed several neutrality acts during this period, hoping that neutrality would prevent the economic and emotional entanglements that, many believed, had involved the United States in World War I.

30. The correct answer is 2. FDR's court-packing plan (adding pro-FDR justices to the Court) would have placed the power of the Supreme Court at the mercy of the executive branch. The plan engendered substantial political opposition. Supreme Court justices do serve for life.

31. The correct answer is 4. Both men used the presidency as an office of moral and political leadership.

32. The correct answer is 1. Responding to pressure, FDR issued Executive Order 9066, which authorized the relocation of Japanese Americans. Many *were* citizens who had not shown any disloyalty before relocation. German Americans were not placed in relocation centers.

33. The correct answer is 2. The Marshall Plan was officially known as the European Recovery Program which involved providing economic assistance to war-torn Europe. The United States sent $12 billion in aid to Western Europe.

34. The correct answer is 3. This is best evidenced by the numerous alliances we joined: NATO, CENTO, SEATO.

35. The correct answer is 2. This is the most logical choice; 1 cannot be correct because the numbers were minimal at best; 3 and 4 state the exact opposite of reality.

36. The correct answer is 1. Racism generally increases, affirmative action had benefited them, and everyone's job opportunities are affected by business cycles. Equal employment laws may get them a job, but if the business is suffering, they risk losing the job, like everyone else.

37. The correct answer is 3; 1 and 2 cannot be proven by the data presented; 4 states the exact opposite of what the graph indicates. This leaves only 3 as a viable option.

38. The correct answer is 4. The first three answers cannot be proven one way or another with the data given. Answer 4 is logical if we can assume people will retire at the age of 65.

39. The correct answer is 2. The relationship is that of mode of transportation and centralization of people.

40. The correct answer is 4. The president determines and carries out foreign policy. This authority derives from the constitutional powers to receive ambassadors, to command the armed forces, to negotiate treaties, to appoint major foreign affairs officials, etcetera.

41. The correct answer is 2. Both programs were geared toward welfare legislation.

42. The correct answer is 4. Ideological differences between the most powerful members, such as the United States and Soviet Union, often led to disputes due to conflicting political, military, and economic interests.

43. The correct answer is 1. This is best evidenced by the concept of mutual deterrence. Why start a war, knowing that "victory" is unlikely?

44. The correct answer is 2. Societal displeasure and unrest over Vietnam greatly affected military policy. At the same time, the domino theory has been proven to be unfounded; the United States did not win, even though it was technologically superior; and, nuclear weapons were not used.

45. The correct answer is 1. The muckrakers documented corruption in industry, and the investigative reporters of the 1970s and 1980s documented corruption in politics and industry.

46. The correct answer is 2. Population is increasing, but it is not yet a critical concern in the United States; 3 and 4 are true, but are not the cause of the issue presented. This leaves answer 2 as the best possible option.

47. The correct answer is 3. This is best evidenced by looking at FDR and the Great Depression, FDR and WWII, Wilson and WWI, Lincoln and the Civil War, etcetera.

Essay Questions

(Note: Answers provided are not all inclusive. These are suggested responses and should be used as a guide for the type of answers that would be acceptable.)

Part II

Question 1a

Liberty in 1776, Order in 1787—In 1776 the colonists asserted their liberty with the Declaration of Independence. This independence was confirmed with the colonial victory in the American Revolution. However, due to the ineffectiveness of the Articles of Confederation, there was no real sense of order in the new country. At best, this was a loose confederation of states with no executive head or leadership. In 1787, the delegates adopted the United States Constitution. With its strong federal government, and visible executive, legislative, and judicial branches, a sense of order had been achieved. This new-found order was best evidenced by the putting down of the Whiskey Rebellion, which was an attempt to undermine this new order.

Question 1b

Bill of Rights: Liberty and Order—It could be argued that either liberty or order was fostered by the adoption of the Bill of Rights in 1791. Liberty is evidenced by the freedoms guaranteed under various amendments such as: freedom of the press, religion, assembly, and speech in the First Amendment; freedom from excessive bail, fines, or cruel and unusual punishment in the Eighth Amendment; and, the reserved rights expressed in the Tenth Amendment. Order can be evidenced by the following examples: the militia and right to bear arms in the Second Amendment; aspects of law and order defined in the Fourth and Fifth Amendments; and the aspects of the criminal justice system outlined in the Sixth and Seventh Amendments.

Question 2

To Guarantee Liberty and Freedom to all Citizens—The Emancipation Proclamation freed the Negroes in the rebellious Southern states. The Thirteenth Amendment banned slavery in the United States, thus freeing millions of former slaves. The Snyder Indian Citizenship Act granted full citizenship to all Native Americans who had not yet acquired citizenship. The Fifteenth Amendment assured newly freed slaves their right to vote, thus increasing the size of the electorate. The Nineteenth Amendment gave women the right to vote, concluding the suffragates' fight, and, in effect, doubling the size of the American electorate.

To Protect the Rights of Minorities—The Civil Rights Act of 1864 sought to weaken the Black Codes and gave blacks equal rights to those of whites and authorized the use of federal troops for its enforcement. The 1972 Higher Education Act prohibited public colleges and universities from discriminating against women in school admission policies. The Civil Rights Act of 1964 prohibited discrimination based on race in voting requirements, public facilities, employment, and public accommodations. The Civil Rights Act of 1991 expanded the rights of workers in cases of job discrimination.

To Meet the Changing Needs of Society—Many times throughout the history of the United States, the government has acted to meet the changing needs of society in order to further the growth of democracy. Three ways in which this can be illustrated would include: compulsory education laws; Franklin D. Roosevelt and the New Deal; and, Lyndon B. Johnson and the Great Society. The founding fathers were products of the enlightenment. As such, they realized the importance of education to ensure an informed electorate. To that end, legislation was enacted to mandate compulsory education. When the United States entered into its greatest depression, Roosevelt sought to ease the burden of the lower and middle classes through actions such as the bank holiday, "fireside chats," "hundred days," and press conferences. In the 1960s, Johnson asserted that humanity then possessed the capacity to eradicate poverty and racial injustice, dispel ignorance, and, in general, permit people to enjoy a life of freedom and prosperity. To that end, the 89th Congress responded favorably to Johnson's requests for far-reaching legislation. Some examples of this legislation would include: Civil Rights Act of 1964, Economic Opportunity Act of 1964, Voting Rights Act of 1965, Medicare Act of 1965, and Civil Rights Act of 1968.

To Encourage Greater Participation in the Political Process—As the United States has grown and matured, so has the size of the electorate. In 1776, the electorate was limited to white Anglo-Saxon Protestant males over the age of twenty-five. Since then, many changes have been made to expand the size of the electorate. The Fifteenth Amendment stated the right to vote could not be denied on account of race, color, or previous condition of servitude. The Nineteenth Amendment gave women the right to vote. The Twenty-fourth Amendment did away with any form of poll tax requirement in order to vote. The Twenty-sixth Amendment extended the right to vote to those Americans between the ages of eighteen and twenty-one. Along with extending the franchise to more elements within society, participation has also been increased by allowing the electorate to become involved more directly in the political process. A prime example of this would be the Seventeenth Amendment which allowed for the direct election of Senators.

Part III

Question 3

Role of Women—Industrialization had a tremendous impact on the role of women. One of the key aspects of industrialization was that machines replaced manpower. As a result, both women and children could be effectively utilized in the factories at a fraction of the wages. This led to an overall increase in the number of women in the workplace. At the same time, as women found work outside the home, they were able to become economically independent of male relatives. Once women became accustomed to having a life other than that of a housewife and mother, many women sought more to their lives. This was best accomplished through education. By the late nineteenth century, young girls had available a secondary-level education preparing them for citizenship as well as an occupation or admission to

institutions of higher learning. Once women broke the educational barriers, it was just a matter of time before they would begin entering the professions. Ironically, as women became better educated and more aware of their position in society, many women began to demand a political voice. Yet, it was their contributions in World War I that gained them the right to vote, not the logical arguments they had been presenting.

Urbanization —In the early phases of the industrial revolution, water power was used to drive the machinery. Once the steam engine was perfected, the factories could be located in the urban areas rather than in the rural areas, where the water power was to be found. This led to the migration of workers to the cities to work in the factories. These workers added to existing city populations or created new cities. Because urban dwellers needed food, clothing, entertainment, and professional services, still more people came to the cities. At the same time an influx of rural farmers to the cities as a result of declining agricultural prices and the increased mechanization and growth of commercial farming. Added to this, there were the waves of immigrants entering the United States that began to settle predominantly in the cities following the final settlement of the frontier.

Rise of Organized Labor—With the factory system, workers became dependent for their livelihood upon factory owners. Over time, workers desired to improve labor conditions: safer working conditions, higher pay, shorter hours, etcetera. The workers quickly realized that individual bargaining with the employer did not accomplish any improvements. In most cases, the employer simply fired the employee, and work continued as usual. The workers finally came to realize that they would be in a stronger position by bargaining collectively. Some early attempts at uniting to improve conditions would include: Uriah S. Stephens and the Knights of Labor; Samuel Gompers and the American Federation of Labor (A.F.L.); and John L. Lewis and the Congress of Industrial Organizations (C.I.O.).

Government Involvement in the Economy—In the initial phases of the Industrial Revolution the government had adopted a laissez faire attitude toward business and the economy. However, as a result of the effects of the Industrial Revolution, the government steadily became increasingly involved with the economy. The three main areas the government became involved with were business regulation, labor, and consumer protection. Some examples of the government becoming directly involved with business practices would include: the

Sherman Antitrust Act (1890); the Clayton Antitrust Act (1914); and the Federal Trade Commission Act (1914). As for the government becoming involved with labor and labor-management relations, one could look at: Department of Labor (1913); Adamson Act (1916); the Norris–LaGuardia Act (1932); and the Wagner National Labor Relations Act (1935). When it comes to consumer protection, the best examples would be: the Pure Food and Drug Act (1906); Food, Drug, and Cosmetic Act (1938); and the Federal Deposit Insurance Corporation (FDIC).

Status of the Farmer—An area hit extremely hard by the Industrial Revolution was agriculture. The four main areas in which farmers were hurt the worst were; low agricultural prices, insufficient and expensive credit, high rates charged by others, and high industrial prices. In the latter part of the nineteenth century, the demand for agricultural produce fell and prices declined. Farmers also had to contend with increased competition in world markets. Since farmers were considered bad risks, banks were reluctant to give them loans. When loans were made, farmers were charged excessive interest rates, up to 25 percent a year. As a result of monopolies, especially railroad monopolies, farmers endured poor service and exorbitant rates. Finally, while farmers received low agricultural prices, they paid dearly for manufactured goods. Again, this was in part due to the growth of business monopoly, which curtailed domestic competition. To combat these problems farmers began to form coops, such as the Grange, to work together and become more active in state politics.

Question 4

John C. Calhoun and States' Rights—As the Vicepresident of the United States and as a senator from South Carolina, Calhoun served as a champion for states' rights. When the Tariff of Abominations was passed in 1828, Calhoun responded by secretly writing the *South Carolina Exposition and Protest*. In this, he stated that state conventions had the power to declare laws of Congress unconstitutional, which would then make them null and void (policy of nullification). As a last resort, a state could terminate its compact with the other states and secede from the Union. When a new tariff was passed in 1832 South Carolina passed the Ordinance of Nullification. Andrew Jackson's response to this was a request to use military force against South Carolina. Henry Clay introduced a Compromise Tariff that averted the military action and demonstrated that democracy could work to resolve sectional differences.

However, it did nothing to resolve the more basic issues of states rights and nullification.

Elizabeth Cady Stanton and Women's Rights—Along with Lucretia Mott, Elizabeth Stanton issued the call for, and directed, the first women's rights convention, held in 1848 at Seneca Falls, New York. Stanton served as an organizer, a speaker, and a focal point for the movement. The primary tactics used by Stanton were demonstrations, rallies, petitions, and speeches. As a result of her efforts and those of others, women slowly began to achieve equality. In 1848, in New York, legislation was passed that allowed the property of a wife at the time of marriage to remain under her control. In 1860, New York enacted further laws giving women the right to sue and be sued, to control their own wages and personal property, and to exercise joint guardianship of minor children. In 1869, the territory of Wyoming granted women the right to vote. In 1920, the Nineteenth Amendment was passed giving all women the right to vote (suffrage).

Frederick Douglass and Abolitionism—Frederick Douglass served as both a spokesman and as an example. Douglass was an escaped slave who was able to tell firsthand about the evils of slavery. In his autobiography, *Narrative of the Life of Frederick Douglass*, he gives testimony to the harsh treatment and inhuman existence associated with slavery. The primary tactics of the abolitionists ranged from voicing their concerns to breaking laws. The primary examples of illegal tactics would include violating the fugitive slave laws and the creation and implementation of the Underground Railroad. It is difficult to ascertain the impact of the abolitionists as to whether they were successful or not. Whereas it is true the slaves were all freed and slavery was abolished, this was more out of military necessity than anything else.

Samuel Gompers and Organized Labor—In 1881 Samuel Gompers organized the American Federation of Labor. The A.F. of L. shunned political crusades and emphasized "bread and butter" unionism, and the furthering of the economic well being of its members. Unlike the Knights of Labor, the A.F. of L. admitted mostly skilled workers and organized workers into separate craft unions. By combining workers with the same economic interests, the A.F. of L. could serve its members more effectively. Some of the tactics used by organized labor included: strikes, walkouts, and collective bargaining. Initially, the unions faced strong opposition from both management and government. However, over time the unions were able to exert greater pressure on management with the assistance of government. The strength and effectiveness of unions has been most recently demonstrated by the United Parcel Service workers.

William Jennings Bryan and Populism—When farmers and silver interests gained control of the Democratic convention of 1896, they selected Bryan as the Democratic candidate for president. He also won the populist nomination. The Populist, or people's, party advocated free and unlimited coinage of silver, a graduated income tax, government ownership of the communication and transportation industries, the secret ballot, and the direct election of senators. In order to a achieve a famer-labor alliance, they also endorsed pro-labor planks, shorter working hours, and restrictions on immigration. Bryan lost the election, but a number of the Populist goals would be realized later in the Progressive movement.

Theodore Roosevelt and Progressivism—Progressivism was a movement to improve American life by expanding democracy and achieving economic and social justice. As the governor of New York, and later as the president of the United States, and a Progressive, Roosevelt was able to direct the actions of the Progressive movement at both the state and federal levels. Roosevelt considered himself morally bound as president to further the interests of the people. The Progressive movement ushered in numerous changes within the country at both the local and federal levels. At the local level some examples would include: direct primaries, secret ballots, corrupt practices laws, initiative and referendum, recall, child labor laws, factory inspection laws, etcetera. At the federal level new legislation was passed relating to: women's suffrage; direct election of senators; federal regulation of railroads, industrial combinations, and banks, federal income tax; and consumer protection laws. The Progressive movement promoted the belief that the government had the responsibility to act for the people's welfare; marked the transition from laissez faire to government regulation of the economy; and demonstrated the ability of our democratic institutions to meet problems arising out of urbanization and industrialization.

Eleanor Roosevelt and Human Rights—In her roles as the First Lady and as the U.S. delegate to the United Nations, Eleanor Roosevelt served as a spokeswoman and champion for human rights. Being heavily connected to, and involved with, politics, Eleanor was extremely influential in assuring the passage of human rights legislation.

When she learned of what she deemed violations of human rights by the Daughters of the American Revolution, Eleanor disassociated herself from this organization. As chairman of the U.N. Commission on Human Rights (1946–51), she helped draft and secure adoption of the Universal Declaration of Human Rights (1948).

Martin Luther King, Jr., and Civil Rights—King had many roles as a leader in the civil rights movement. He was an organizer, a spokesman, the head of the Southern Christian Leadership Conference, and a martyr. His "I have a dream" speech will always be remembered and treasured as a monument to man. King advocated nonviolence to achieve equality. This manifested itself in peaceful marches and demonstrations, sit-ins, and ride-ins. Though the struggle was hard and not without its costs, in the end legislation was passed to assure equality for all Americans. President Johnson said, "The fury of bigots and bullies served to strengthen the will of the American people that justice be done." In 1964 he secured passage of the comprehensive Civil Rights Act of 1964.

Ralph Nader and Consumerism—Ralph Nader is a lawyer and consumer advocate. He gained national attention in the mid 1960s, when he published *Unsafe at Any Speed*, which led to the National Traffic and Motor Vehicle Safety Act of 1966. Other issues of corporate ethics and human safety to which he has drawn attention include environmental pollution; the danger of atomic energy plants; health hazards in food, medicine, and occupations; fraud; and the secrecy and immunities of large companies. His main tactics for protecting consumers has been research, investigation, and political lobbying. As a result of the work of his team of researchers, Nader's Raiders, several pieces of legislation have been passed. However, many critics accuse Nader of being biased against big business and government which they claim prejudice his findings.

Question 5
5a—To Foster Foreign Trade and United States Economic Interests Prior to the End of World War II—Following Great Britain's example, and in order to compete globally, many nations including the United States, adopted the policy of imperialism. This entailed the United States's obtaining raw materials and markets in foreign countries. Three prime examples of this would be the United States involvement with China and the Open Door Policy; sending Commodore Perry to Japan to open that region up to foreign trade, and the support of the Panamanian

Revolution in order to ensure the construction and access to the Panama Canal to expedite trade between the Atlantic and Pacific oceans.

5a—To Foster Foreign Trade and United States Economic Interests Following the End of World War II—In the years following World War II, the global marketplace had become a reality. At this point it became critical that the United States be able to compete with other major economic powers. To assist in this, the United States took several actions to increase accessibility to foreign markets. One example of this would be President Nixon reestablishing diplomatic and economic relations with China in 1972. More recent examples of U.S. actions would include pressuring Japan to open its markets to U.S. goods; and NAFTA (North American Free Trade Agreement), which created a three-way trade pact linking Mexico, Canada, and the United States.

5a—To Provide for the Military Security of the United States Prior to the End of World War II—There are numerous examples one could use to address this issue, from the acquisition of Florida from Spain in 1819 to the creation of an atomic bomb in 1945. One should examine common themes when dealing with this question. Three themes that become readily apparent are the acquisition of territory, military conflict, and legislation. When dealing with the acquisition of territory, one could examine the idea of obtaining strategic locations such as the Philippines, or border areas such as Florida. For military conflict, the most obvious examples would be American participation in both world wars. This was deemed critical to American security, because in both instances, if the autocratic or dictatorial powers should prevail, the only thing separating the United States from these powers would have been the Atlantic Ocean. When looking at legislation that was designed to provide for the military security of the United States, the best example would be the Monroe Doctrine, which was implemented to cut off foreign intervention in the Western Hemisphere.

5a—To Provide for the Military Security of the United States Following the End of World War II—After the conclusion of World War II, the United States became involved in a different kind of warfare, the cold war. In order to ensure the security of the United States, it was deemed necessary to prevent the spread of communism. This led to the United States's first attempting to gain the support of Western European nations through the European Recovery Program (Marshall Plan). This was followed by forming numerous

alliances in an attempt to hem in the Soviet Union: North Atlantic Treaty Organization (NATO), Southeast Asia Treaty Organization (SEATO), and Central Treaty Organization (CENTO). The United States also adopted new official policies regarding the spread of communism: containment and massive retaliation. Along with economic and military assistance, these policies also involved the United States's becoming involved in military conflicts, the most notable being in Korea and Vietnam. With the introduction of weapons of mass destruction, and in an effort to maintain technological and military superiority, the Soviet Union and the United States began a nuclear arms race. The same concept also led President Reagan to endorse the Star Wars program.

5a—To Promote the Spread of Democratic Ideals and Values of the United States Prior to the End of World War II—There are three main themes that can be identified that deal with this concept: the spreading of democracy within the continent (Manifest Destiny), elevating the status of other cultures (White Man's Burden), and global connectivity. As the country began to grow, many people believed that this was essential in order to spread democracy and democratic ideals across the continent. Once we had spread these ideal across the span of our own continent, Americans believed they should share these ideas with indigenous persons of other continents, albeit this was usually done by force, and whether the indigenous persons wanted these ideals thrust upon them or not. An example of this would be the formation of the Weimer Republic in Germany after the conclusion of World War I. The other way the United States has attempted to spread its ideals and values has been by cooperating with organizations such as the League of Nations and signing numerous international pacts during the period between World War I and World War II.

5a—To Promote the Spread of Democratic Ideals and Values of the United States Following the End of World War II—Following World War II the United States not only emerged as a world power, but also accepted the role and responsibility of being one of the major superpowers. As a result, the United States actively sought to promote democracy and democratic ideals around the world in competition with the Soviet Union and the spread of communism. This involved the formation and joining of the United Nations; initiating the European Recovery Program (Marshall Plan), adopting the Truman Doctrine, and active military involvement in areas such as Korea and Vietnam. At the same time, the United States also embarked on peaceful ventures to promote American values such as the Food for Peace Program, Peace Corps, Alliance for Progress, and the Caribbean Basin Initiative. Whether the actions were hostile or peaceful in nature, the end result was to be the same—the further spread of democracy and democratic ideals at the expense of communism and communist ideals.

5b—Influence on American Life—Regardless of which item one examines, the influence is relatively similar. In all instances the influence on Americans has been a greater involvement in foreign affairs. Washington had encouraged Americans to avoid foreign entanglements in his Farewell Address. However, as the country began to grow this became an increasingly more difficult task to accomplish. The main reason for this was the competitive nature of the global marketplace and national interests. Whether the United States was competing with the British for raw materials and foreign markets, or with the former Soviet Union for global power, the results were the same—greater involvement in foreign affairs. The greatest influence this has had on the life of Americans is that we have emerged as a world power. This gives us certain benefits, such as a high standard of living, but it also comes at a price. We must periodically sacrifice our young men and women in global conflicts in order to preserve our way of life as well as our position in the world.

Question 6

6a—Northeast—Because the Northeast has minimal arable land and short growing seasons, the region became primarily industrial rather than agricultural. As a result of this industrial base—the need for raw materials, the need for access to foreign markets, and the presence of numerous good harbors—the region also became heavily involved in international trade. Typically, industrial-based regions also have large urban areas. Once the frontier had been closed, many immigrants would migrate to these urban areas, providing an ample supply of labor. As a result, slavery was unprofitable in the Northeast. As the cities grew in size, a greater demand was created for foodstuffs. The Western region had an abundance of foodstuffs, but was in need of manufactured goods. This led to an interdependent relationship between the two regions based on the profitable exchange of foodstuffs for manufactured goods. To facilitate this exchange railroads were built, linking the two regions. Now that they were

linked physically and economically, this led to a political linkage as well.

6a—South—Because the South had an abundant amount of arable land, the region became primarily agricultural rather than industrial. However, agriculture does not necessitate large urban centers. As a result, there was minimal labor available. This led to the need to utilize slave labor in order to maximize the economic potential of the region. Due to the numerous good harbors available, the South would also be heavily involved in international trade, but for different reasons than the Northeast. In the South the primary purposes of international trade would be to find markets for the abundant cotton crops.

6a—West—The vast open areas of the West were ideal for the farming of both crops and animals. There was also an abundance of natural resources. Whereas farming required minimal human presence and vast areas of land, the population would be predominantly rural. At the same time, the need for labor to obtain the raw materials available would lead to the influx of immigrants to work in the mines and lumber mills. This immigrant labor force would also be utilized to construct the railroads that would be built to link the West with the Northeast to facilitate the mutually profitable exchange of foodstuffs for manufactured goods.

6b- Impact of Technology—There are four main areas that can be addressed within this category: transportation, communications, power, and urbanization. With the construction of the railroads, materials could be taken to where the people were instead of the people having to be where the resources were located. This would also speed up the delivery time as well as maximize the amount of material that could be moved at one time, ideally lowering the costs of transporting the goods. At the same time, the railroads facilitated the movement of people to the West in larger numbers. Communications cut the distances between regions. With the pony express, the telegraph, and later the telephone, people could now communicate at a much faster pace. This would in effect cut down on geographic barriers to communication. When factories were first built, they had to be erected near swift running rivers that could be used as a power source. Once the steam engine had been perfected, the location of the factory became independent of the power source—that is, the factories could now operate in any area. This led to the movement of the factories to the urban regions where labor was more abundant. The problem with the urban areas was that they grew horizontally. The larger the area became, the more distance one had to travel within the city. Once skyscrapers and the safety elevator had been invented, this changed. Then cities began to experience vertical growth rather than horizontal growth.

Question 7

Students with AIDS Attending Public Schools— Out of fear and paranoia many people feel that allowing a student with AIDS to attend a public school unjustly jeopardizes the physical safety of the other children. At the same time, the parents of the child with AIDS believe that their child should not be denied a basic education because of the child's illness. They argue that you would not ban a child with polio or one whose hearing impaired. Furthermore, the disease cannot be transmitted via casual contact. Therefore, the child should be given the same opportunities. In 1990, the U.S. government passed the Americans with Disabilities Act (ADA). This law bars discrimination against people who carry the virus that causes AIDS and against people with AIDS.

Media Censorship—A recent controversy surrounding media censorship involves the right of the press to cover criminal trials. The press argues that the people have the right to know and that the press is covered under the First Amendment. Others argue that press coverage could potentially deny the defendant his or her constitutional right to due process of law. In 1966 the U.S. Supreme Court handed down a ruling involving this issue. The media coverage of Dr. Sam Sheppard's arrest for the murder of his wife was extensive. The brutal nature of the crime, the relationship between the victim and the accused, and the social position of the accused all helped to fuel the public's interest in the trial. Sheppard argued that this media coverage prevented him from receiving a fair trial. The Supreme Court agreed with him and reversed the decision of the lower court. This was justified by the Court through the "Roman Holiday" atmosphere of the trial in which the judge "failed to minimize the prejudicial impact of massive publicity." The Sheppard decision allowed the use of the "gag" order to limit pretrial publicity.

Environmental Protection—There are several key issues that could be examined when dealing with environmental protection: fluorocarbons, effect on the ozone layer, nuclear hazards from waste materials and from fall-out such as at Chernobyl, destruction of the rainforests, and the utilization of harmful chemicals such as pesticides. In examining the issue involving pesticides, proponents argue that this is the most effective method to kill large amounts of insects. However, evidence clearly indicates that the use of certain pesticides definitely harms the environment. When this has happened, the government has banned the use of those pesticides. Three such pesticides that have been banned are DDT, aldrin, and dieldrin.

The Homeless—Given the economic prosperity of the United States and its role as the leading world power, how is it possible that certain elements of society do not have access to the most fundamentally basic need of a roof over their heads? Many Americans argue that this is a basic human right, and all efforts should be made to provide all Americans with a home. Others argue that one should have to work for one's possessions, even a home. The government favors the position that a home is a basic human right. As such, it has taken great strives to ensure that all people have this basic necessity. Former President Carter has spearheaded an organization that builds homes for the homeless. At the same time, legislation has been passed to provide for low-income housing projects, as well as rent control.

Prayer in Public Schools—In order to prevent our country from becoming a theocracy (government ruled by religious leaders), the founding fathers were very specific in providing for the separation of church and state. During the past century this led to many controversies—from teaching the theory of evolution in school, to the use of prayer in school. Some Americans argue that prayer equates to morality and students should learn morality. Others argue that prayer in school violates the separation of church and state; and morals are something that should be taught at home by the parents. This has led to much debate in the courts. The Supreme Court in *Abington v. Schempp* (1963) struck down as unconstitutional state laws that required public schools to begin each day with a recitation of verses from the Bible. The Court held that even though children could be excused from these religious ceremonies if they obtained written permission from their parents, the state violated the constitutional mandate that the government may not establish a religion. In *Wallace v. Jaffree* (1985), the Court struck down an Alabama law that required public schools to begin each day with a moment of silent prayer or meditation. The Supreme Court held in *Lee v. Weisman* (1992) that public schools may not allow prayers during graduation ceremonies.

Sample Regents Exam #2

Part I (55 credits)

Answer all 48 questions in this part.

Directions (1–48): For each statement or question, write on the separate answer sheet the *number* of the word or expression that, of those given, best completes the statement or answers the question.

1 "The only representatives of the people of these colonies are persons chosen therein by themselves; and that no taxes ever have been, or can be constitutionally imposed on them but by their respective legislatures."

— Statement by the Stamp Act Congress, 1765

What is a valid conclusion that can be drawn from this quotation?

1 The colonial legislatures should be appointed by the English King with the consent of Parliament.
2 Only the colonists' elected representatives should have the power to levy taxes.
3 The English King should have the right to tax the colonists.
4 The colonists should be opposed to all taxation.

2 The authors of the Articles of Confederation established a decentralized political system mainly to

1 cancel state debts incurred during the Revolutionary War
2 assist the southern states in their efforts to gain a manufacturing base
3 promote the common goal of national sovereignty
4 prevent the abuses of power that had existed under British rule

3 Senate ratification of treaties negotiated by the President is required by the United States Constitution as a way of

1 maintaining United States prestige in international affairs
2 preventing Federal abuse of State power
3 implementing the principle of checks and balances
4 expanding the authority of the executive branch

4 The United States Constitution requires that a census be taken every ten years to reapportion

1 membership in the House of Representatives
2 the number of delegates to national nominating conventions
3 Federal aid to localities
4 agricultural subsidies

5 In the United States Congress, differences between Senate and House of Representatives versions of a bill are usually resolved by accepting the version that is

1 preferred by a majority of the State legislatures
2 supported by the Supreme Court
3 preferred by the House in which the bill originated
4 agreed to by a joint conference committee of both Houses

6 "The privilege of the writ of habeas corpus shall not be suspended, unless when in cases of rebellion or invasion the public safety may require it."

This provision is evidence that the writers of the United States Constitution

1 wanted the President to have unlimited power during wartime
2 wanted to balance individual liberty with the needs of the nation
3 did not trust the common people to obey the laws
4 expected the American people to oppose most government policies

7 In the United States, activities such as Cabinet meetings and political party conventions are best described as

1 examples of direct democracy
2 responsibilities of the executive branch
3 features of the unwritten constitution
4 requirements of the system of checks and balances

Base your answer to question 8 on the cartoon below and on your knowledge of social studies.

8 The most commonly proposed solution to the problem shown in the cartoon is to

1 establish poll taxes
2 have candidates finance their own campaigns
3 eliminate primaries from the election system
4 use public funds to pay for political campaigns

9 Actions and policies of the Government under President George Washington generally resulted in the

1 establishment of strong political ties with other nations
2 liberation of many enslaved persons
3 failure to create a sound financial program for the country
4 strengthening of the Federal Government

10 "By the 1850's, the Constitution, originally framed as an instrument of national unity, had become a source of sectional discord."

This quotation suggests that

1 vast differences of opinion existed over the issue of States rights
2 the Federal Government had become more interested in foreign affairs than in domestic problems
3 the Constitution had no provisions for governing new territories
4 the Southern States continued to import slaves

11 Early in his Presidency, Abraham Lincoln declared that his primary goal as President was to

1 enforce the Emancipation Proclamation
2 preserve the Union
3 end slavery throughout the entire country
4 encourage sectionalism

12 In their plans for Reconstruction, both President Abraham Lincoln and President Andrew Johnson sought to

1 punish the South for starting the Civil War
2 force the Southern States to pay reparations to the Federal Government
3 allow the Southern States to reenter the nation as quickly as possible
4 establish the Republican Party as the only political party in the South

13 The poll tax, the literacy test, and the actions of the Ku Klux Klan were all attempts to limit the effectiveness of

1 the 14th and 15th amendments
2 the Supreme Court's decision in *Brown* v. *Board of Education*
3 civil rights legislation passed in all states after the Civil War
4 immigration laws such as the Gentleman's Agreement and the Chinese Exclusion Act

14 According to the theory of laissez faire, the economy functions best when the government

1 subsidizes business so that it can compete worldwide
2 regulates businesses for the good of the majority
3 owns major industries
4 does not interfere in business

15 Businesses formed trusts, pools, and holding companies mainly to

1 increase profits by eliminating competition
2 offer a wide range of goods and services to consumers
3 provide employment opportunities for minorities
4 protect the interests of workers

16 The Rockefeller Foundation, Carnegie Hall, and the Morgan Library illustrate various ways that entrepreneurs and their descendants have

1 suppressed the growth of labor unions
2 supported philanthropic activities to benefit society
3 applied scientific discoveries to industry
4 attempted to undermine the United States economic system

17 The major reason the United States placed few restrictions on immigration during the 1800's was that

1 few Europeans wished to give up their economic security
2 little opposition to immigration existed
3 the growing economy needed a steady supply of cheap labor
4 most immigrants spoke English and thus needed little or no education

18 The American Federation of Labor became the first long-lasting, successful labor union in the United States mainly because it

1 refused to participate in strikes against employers
2 concentrated on organizing workers in industries in the South
3 formed its own political party and elected many prolabor public officials
4 fought for the rights of skilled workers

19 In the late 1800's, the goal of the Federal Government's policy toward Native American Indians was to

1 destroy tribal bonds and thus weaken their traditional cultural values
2 grant them full citizenship and due process
3 give their tribal groups authority over their own affairs
4 increase the land holdings of western tribes

20 W.E.B. Du Bois believed that African Americans should attempt to gain equality in the United States by

1 setting up a separate nation within the United States
2 entering vocational training programs in separate schools
3 demanding full and immediate participation in American society
4 taking over the leadership of the two major political parties

21 In the United States during the late 19th century, much of the prejudice expressed toward immigrants was based on the belief that they would

1 cause overcrowding in farm areas
2 refuse to become citizens
3 support the enemies of the United States in wartime
4 fail to assimilate into American society

22 During the late 19th and early 20th centuries, United States policy toward Latin America was most strongly characterized by

1 friendship and trust
2 intervention and paternalism
3 tolerance and humanitarianism
4 indifference and neglect

23 A major purpose of the Federal Reserve System is to

1 deal with the trade deficit through tariffs and quotas
2 control the minimum wage
3 establish the Federal budget
4 regulate interest rates and the money supply

24 A major goal of reformers during the Progressive Era was to

1 end segregation in the South
2 correct the abuses of big business
3 limit immigration from Latin America
4 enact high tariffs to help domestic industry grow

25 "We are to be an instrument in the hands of God to see that liberty is made secure for mankind."

— President Woodrow Wilson

President Wilson tried to carry out the idea expressed in this quotation by

1 protesting the sinking of the *Lusitania*
2 proposing a program of civil rights for minorities in American society
3 urging the Allies to adopt the Fourteen Points
4 taking control of territories conquered in World War I

26 In stating the principle of a "clear and present danger" in *Schenck* v. *United States*, the Supreme Court established that

1 constitutional rights are not absolute
2 the Constitution guarantees the right to privacy
3 Congress can pass a law to eliminate any part of the Bill of Rights
4 all individual rights are eliminated during wartime

27 In the 1920's, the Immigration Act of 1924 and the Sacco-Vanzetti trial were typical of the

1 rejection of traditional customs and beliefs
2 acceptance of cultural differences
3 increase in nativism and intolerance
4 support of humanitarian causes

28 The economic boom and the financial speculation of the 1920's were caused in part by

1 installment buying and an unregulated stock market
2 the expansion of civil rights to women and minorities
3 the mobilization of the economy for war
4 increased government restrictions on big business

29 The popularity of escapist novels and movies during the Great Depression is evidence that

1 the Great Depression was not really a time of economic distress
2 popular culture is shaped by economic and social conditions
3 American society did not try to solve the problems of the Great Depression
4 the greatest employment opportunities for the average person in the 1930's were in the field of entertainment

30 The power of labor unions increased during the New Deal mainly because

1 a new spirit of cooperation existed between employers and government
2 a shortage of skilled and unskilled laborers developed
3 management changed its attitude toward organized labor
4 Federal legislation guaranteed labor's right to organize and bargain collectively

31 An immediate result of the Supreme Court decisions in *Schechter Poultry Corporation* v. *United States* (1935) and *United States* v. *Butler* (1936) was that

1 some aspects of the New Deal were declared unconstitutional
2 State governments took over relief agencies
3 Congress was forced to abandon efforts to improve the economy
4 the constitutional authority of the President was greatly expanded

32 The United States became involved in World War II primarily because

1 Germany refused to pay its debts from World War I
2 European democracies supported United States policies toward Germany and Japan
3 President Franklin D. Roosevelt did not enforce the Neutrality Acts
4 Germany and Japan achieved important military successes in Europe and Asia

Base your answer to question 33 on the cartoon below and on your knowledge of social studies.

THE INGENIOUS QUARTERBACK!

33 This cartoon portrays President Franklin D. Roosevelt's attempt to

  1 continue life terms for Supreme Court Justices
  2 increase Presidential influence on the Supreme Court
  3 prevent Congress from interfering with the Federal Court system
  4 strengthen the independence of the Supreme Court

34 In the United States during World War II, the role of women changed as they

  1 were drafted and assigned military roles equal to those held by men
  2 continued to work outside the home only in jobs traditionally performed by women
  3 made major contributions to the war effort by taking jobs in factories
  4 achieved positions of leadership in most major industries

35 After World War II, the United States occupied Japan, joined the North Atlantic Treaty Organization (NATO), and helped organize the United Nations. These actions show that the United States was

  1 concerned solely with rebuilding Europe
  2 taking on greater global responsibility
  3 expanding its imperialistic empire
  4 returning to its policy of neutrality

Base your answer to question 36 on the graph below and on your knowledge of social studies.

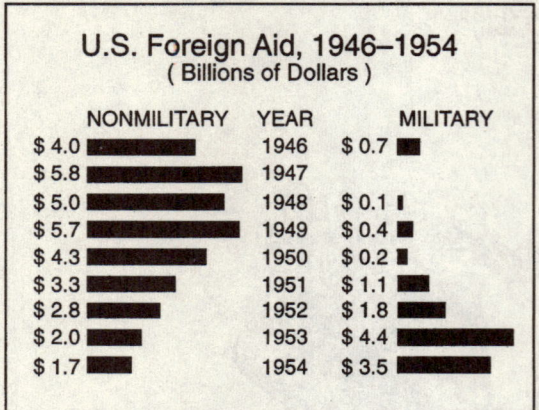

U.S. Foreign Aid, 1946–1954
(Billions of Dollars)

NONMILITARY	YEAR	MILITARY
$ 4.0	1946	$ 0.7
$ 5.8	1947	
$ 5.0	1948	$ 0.1
$ 5.7	1949	$ 0.4
$ 4.3	1950	$ 0.2
$ 3.3	1951	$ 1.1
$ 2.8	1952	$ 1.8
$ 2.0	1953	$ 4.4
$ 1.7	1954	$ 3.5

36 Which United States program is most likely reflected in the amounts of nonmilitary foreign aid given from 1947 to 1950?

1 Peace Corps
2 Marshall Plan
3 Alliance for Progress
4 Lend Lease

37 Which is a valid conclusion based on United States involvement in the Korean War?

1 The policy of containment was applied in Asia as well as in Europe.
2 United Nations economic sanctions are more effective than military action.
3 The American people will support United States participation in any war, whether declared or undeclared.
4 United States cooperation with a wartime ally ends when the war ends.

38 Which statement about public education in the United States is most accurate?

1 The Federal Government controls but does not fund education.
2 The problems that affect other segments of American society seldom affect education.
3 Education is largely controlled and financed by state governments and local communities.
4 High school enrollments have decreased over the last 100 years.

39 "Those of us who shout the loudest about Americanism in making character assassinations are all too frequently those who, by our own words and acts, ignore some of the basic principles of Americanism."

— Senator Margaret Chase Smith, 1950

This criticism of Senator Joseph McCarthy and his supporters suggests that

1 Senator McCarthy did not do enough to protect the nation from a Communist conspiracy
2 the tactics of Senator McCarthy were necessary to protect the basic principles of democracy
3 free speech must be limited in times of national crisis
4 Senator McCarthy was a greater threat to the nation than Communist sympathizers were

40 The Great Society programs of the 1960's used the power of the Federal Government to bring about

1 an all-volunteer military
2 antipoverty reforms
3 deregulation of business
4 reduced defense spending

41 A major long-term effect of the Vietnam War has been

1 an end to communist governments in Asia
2 a change in United States foreign policy from containment to imperialism
3 a reluctance to commit United States troops for extended military action abroad
4 a continued boycott of trade with Asia

42 The Camp David accords negotiated during President Jimmy Carter's administration were an attempt to

1 decrease United States control of the Panama Canal
2 encourage the use of solar and other nonpolluting energy sources
3 end inflationary oil prices
4 establish peace in the Middle East

43 According to the supply-side economics principles promoted by President Ronald Reagan, economic growth would occur when

1 corporate business taxes were reduced
2 business was regulated by antitrust legislation
3 unemployment benefits were increased
4 investment in capital goods was decreased

44 The rulings of the Supreme Court in *Dred Scott* v. *Sanford* (1857), *Plessy* v. *Ferguson* (1896), and *Korematsu* v. *United States* (1944) all demonstrate that the Supreme Court has

1 continued to extend voting rights to minorities
2 protected itself from internal dissent
3 sometimes failed to protect the rights of minorities
4 often imposed restrictions on free speech during wartime

45 Which characteristic of the American frontier continues to be an important part of life in the United States today?

1 widespread support for the Populist Party
2 necessity for families to have many children
3 a predominantly agricultural and mining economy
4 significant opportunities for social and economic mobility

46 The main purpose of a progressive income tax is to

1 base tax rates on a person's ability to pay
2 increase government spending on welfare programs
3 tax everyone at the same percentage rate
4 ensure a balanced budget

Base your answers to questions 47 and 48 on the statements below and on your knowledge of social studies.

Speaker A: We must take action even if we are not sure it will work. To do nothing to stop them would be a repeat of the Munich mistake.

Speaker B: We must recognize the increasing interdependence of nations and join the United Nations.

Speaker C: Stopping the spread of communism can and must take several forms. We must be willing to do whatever is necessary.

Speaker D: Involvement in European affairs would be a mistake. We should not jeopardize our peace and prosperity over issues that Europe's ambitions and rivalries control.

47 Which speaker best describes the basic foreign policy of the United States until the late 1800's?

(1) *A*   (3) *C*
(2) *B*   (4) *D*

48 The "Munich mistake" mentioned by speaker *A* refers to a policy of

1 interdependence   3 balance of power
2 appeasement   4 collective security

Answers to the following questions are to be written on paper provided by the school.

Students Please Note:

In developing your answers to Parts II and III, be sure to

(1) include specific factual information and evidence whenever possible
(2) keep to the questions asked; do not go off on tangents
(3) avoid overgeneralizations or sweeping statements without sufficient proof; do not overstate your case
(4) keep these general definitions in mind:

    (a) <u>discuss</u> means "to make observations about something using facts, reasoning, and argument; to present in some detail"
    (b) <u>describe</u> means "to illustrate something in words or tell about it"
    (c) <u>show</u> means "to point out; to set forth clearly a position or idea by stating it and giving data which support it"
    (d) <u>explain</u> means "to make plain or understandable; to give reasons for or causes of; to show the logical development or relationships of"

Part II

ANSWER ONE QUESTION FROM THIS PART.　　[15]

1 The United States democratic system includes certain features that are intended to protect against the abuse of power by government and public officials.

Protective Features

Judicial review
Impeachment process
Freedom of expression
Protection against unreasonable searches
Equal protection under the law
Rights of the accused

Choose *three* of the features listed and for *each* one chosen:
* Explain how the feature is intended to protect against abuse of governmental power
* Discuss a specific situation in United States history in which the feature was used to protect against an abuse of governmental power [Use a different historical situation for each feature discussed.]
* Discuss the extent to which the feature was successful in protecting against abuse of governmental power in that situation　　[5,5,5]

2 Different groups have played a role in influencing policies and shaping legislation in the United States.

Influential Groups

Representatives of foreign nations
Lobbyists
Media
Political action committees
Political parties
Unions

Choose *three* of the groups listed and for *each* one chosen:
- Identify a specific group and show how that group attempted to influence a specific governmental policy or to shape legislation
- Discuss the extent to which the attempt was successful   [5,5,5]

Part III

ANSWER TWO QUESTIONS FROM THIS PART.   [30]

3 At different times in the history of the United States, Presidents have taken various foreign policy actions.

Presidential Foreign Policy Actions

George Washington warns against "entangling alliances" in Farewell Address. (1796)
James Monroe announces the Monroe Doctrine. (1823)
Theodore Roosevelt supports the independence of Panama from Colombia. (1903)
Franklin D. Roosevelt asks Congress for a declaration of war. (1941)
John F. Kennedy orders a blockade of Cuba. (1962)
Ronald Reagan begins a major military buildup. (early 1980's)
Bill Clinton sends United States forces to Bosnia. (1995)

Choose *three* of the foreign policy actions listed and for *each* one chosen:
- Describe a circumstance that motivated the Presidential foreign policy action
- Explain a goal of the United States in taking that action
- Discuss an impact of that action   [5,5,5]

4 Since colonial times, various methods of protest have been used to bring about change.

Methods of Protest

Boycott
Civil disobedience
Demonstration/protest march
Petition
Rebellion
Sit-in
Strike

a Choose *three* of the methods listed and for *each* one chosen, describe a specific historical situation in which that method of protest was used to bring about change and explain why that method was used. [Use a different historical situation for each method.]   [4,4,4]
b For *one* of the methods of protest chosen in answer to part *a*, discuss the extent to which that method was successful in bringing about change.   [3]

5 Certain actions have aroused controversy in American society. Some of these controversial actions are listed below.

Controversial Actions

Proposal of the Virginia Plan (one-house federal legislature) at the
    Constitutional Convention (1787)
Election of Abraham Lincoln to the Presidency (1860)
Annexation of the Philippines by the United States (1898)
Proposal of United States membership in the League of Nations by President
    Woodrow Wilson (1919)
Ratification of the Prohibition amendment (1919)
Proposal of New Deal legislation by President Franklin D. Roosevelt (1933)
Decision concerning abortion in *Roe* v. *Wade* by the Supreme Court (1973)

Choose *three* of the controversial actions listed and for *each* one chosen:
- Discuss *one* argument given by supporters and *one* argument given by opponents of the action
- Discuss *one* result of the action   [5,5,5]

6 Certain issues concern American society today. Some of these issues are listed below.

Issues of Concern to Americans

Changing family patterns
Crime
Health care reform
Homelessness
Immigration
Technological change

Choose *three* of the issues listed and for *each* one chosen:
- Discuss *two* reasons the issue concerns Americans today
- Describe a specific proposal that has been suggested to deal with the issue   [5,5,5]

7 Songs sometimes describe the experiences and problems of various groups. Excerpts from some songs are given below. Choose *three* of the excerpts and for *each* one chosen:

- Identify the group described in the song and describe a problem suggested by the song
- Show how a specific political or economic policy of government attempted to deal with the problem   [5,5,5]

"HARD TIMES" SONGS

Excerpt 1 —
> The farmer is the man, the farmer is the man
> Lives on credit 'til the fall
> With the interest rate so high, it's a wonder he don't die
> For the mortgage man's the one who gets it all.
>
> — Anonymous

Excerpt 2 —
> O it's all in the past you can say
> But it's still going on here today
> The Government now wants the Iroquois land
> That of the Seneca and the Cheyenne
> It's here and it's now you must help us, dear man
> Now that the Buffalo's gone.
>
> — Buffy Sainte-Marie

Excerpt 3 —
> It is we who dug the ditches, built the cities where they trade
> Blasted mines and built the workshops, endless miles of railroad laid
> Now we stand outcast and starving 'mid the wonders we have made,
> But the union makes us strong. . .
>
> — Ralph Chaplin
> (adapted)

Excerpt 4 —
> Bumpy wagons moving through the days and nights
> They've been travelin' far in search of women's rights
> Not much comfort or supporters but within this country's borders
> They won't quit 'til they've won all of the fights.
>
> — Eileen Abrams

Excerpt 5 —
> Too old to work, too old to work
> When you're too old to work and you're too young to die
> Who will take care of you, how'll you get by
> When you're too old to work and you're too young to die?
>
> — Joe Glazer

Sample Regents Exam #2—Answers

1. The correct answer is 2. This was the basis of "taxation without representation." The colonists are arguing that they can be taxed only by their own colonial legislatures.

2. The correct answer is 4. The fundamental reason for a decentralized political system is to decentralize power. The colonists equated centralization of power with abuse and corruption.

3. The correct answer is 3. The president has the authority to make treaties, but they must be ratified by the Senate. This is an example of the "checks and balances" system; i.e., the power of one branch checks or restrains the power of another branch.

4. The correct answer is 1. This is in keeping with Article 1, Section 2, of the U.S. Constitution. The census records which states have gained or lost population. Hence, some states will gain or lose representatives in the House.

5. The correct answer is 4. Committees are used to resolve the differences. If the differences were not resolved it would pass one house but fail in the other regardless of which version was used. Furthermore, both versions must be identical before submission to the president.

6. The correct answer is 2. The condition for suspension of this civil liberty is clearly defined as a threat to the nation. Rebellion or invasion would be clear examples of such a threat.

7. The correct answer is 3. Cabinet meetings and political party conventions are best described as features of the unwritten constitution because they developed through custom and usage. They were not mentioned specifically in the U.S. Constitution.

8. The correct answer is 4. Under the current system, public money subsidizes the election campaigns of incumbents but not of challengers. The only way the challengers acquire any funding is to win the primaries. This is detrimental to true democracy.

9. The correct answer is 4. This is evidenced by his use of force to put down the Whiskey Rebellion, his endorsement of Hamilton's financial plan, and usage of the elastic clause.

10. The correct answer is 1. Sectional discord revolved around the issues of states' rights. The importation of slaves had ended in 1808. The federal government was not more interested in foreign than domestic affairs. Choice 3 is not relevant since there were provisions.

11. The correct answer is 2. Lincoln stated that his primary objective was to preserve the Union; hence the "House Divided" speech; and the Civil War which was fought not to free the slaves, put to preserve the Union.

12. The correct answer is 3. Lincoln had proposed the 10 Percent Plan for readmission to enable the healing process to begin as quickly as possible. Johnson attempted to carry out this plan after Lincoln's assassination.

13. The correct answer is 1. These items were all attempts to get around the Fourteenth and Fifteenth Amendments, which were designed to protect the rights of the newly freed slaves. Choice 3 would possibly be correct, but the condition of "all states" makes it invalid. Eventually, poll taxes and literary tests were abolished, but not until the 1960s.

14. The correct answer is 4. Laissez faire means "hands off". The idea is that under laissez faire, the government will keep its "hands off" industry.

15. The correct answer is 1. The major purpose of trusts, pools, and holding companies was to create a monopoly on a service or product by elimination of the competition.

16. The correct answer is 2. These are all examples of philanthropic projects that were initiated by the individuals they were named after.

17. The correct answer is 3. During the period of industrialization, management needed increasing numbers of cheap labor. Immigrants provided the source for this abundant labor pool.

18. The correct answer is 4. By admitting most skilled workers, the AFL could strike with greater hope of success than could the unskilled members of the Knights.

19. The correct answer is 1. This is the only possible answer. Choice 2 did not occur until 1924, with the Snyder Indian Citizenship Act; Choices 3 and 4 in 1934 with the Wheeler-Howard Indian Reorganization Act.

20. The correct answer is 3. W. E. B. Du Bois strongly opposed Booker T. Washington's

policies of vocational training and gradualism. He believed that African Americans should demand full equality, to be obtained immediately.

21. The correct answer is 4. In the late nineteenth century the majority of immigrants were coming from southern and eastern Europe, as well as Asia. Once in America they formed their own ethnic communities within the larger cities. As a result, they were less inclined to assimilate into American society.

22. The correct answer is 2. This is clearly evidenced by such items as involvement in Panama, Dollar Diplomacy, Roosevelt Corollary to Monroe Doctrine, etcetera.

23. The correct answer is 4. The Federal Reserve system is designed to regulate interest rates and the money supply to help combat the effects of inflation and recession.

24. The correct answer is 2. Progressives were forward looking, they did not want to return to an agrarian-based economy; they simply wanted to correct the abuses associated with the current industrial-based economy, such as monopolies and worker exploitation.

25. The correct answer is 3. Wilson's Fourteen Points were designed to ensure a lasting peace globally.

26. The correct answer is 1. Justice Holmes held that "free speech would not protect a man falsely shouting 'fire' in a theater and causing a panic." This indicated that there were limits to constitutional rights. However, this specific case dealt with a wartime incident; choice 4 would not be valid because it says all individual liberties are eliminated.

27. The correct answer is 3. These actions by nativists were clear examples of multicultural intolerance and nativism on the rise. The United States was isolated (not concerned with fighting a war overseas), its government supportive of businesses and not interested in expansion of civil rights for women and minorities.

28. The correct answer is 1. The false economy of the 1920s was the result of installment buying and an unregulated stock market.

29. The correct answer is 2. When people are depressed or unhappy with their condition they attempt to escape via novels, movies, radio, etcetera. This is also evidenced by the popularity of films following WWI.

30. The correct answer is 4. One of the New Deal legislative acts was to protect the right of the workers to organize and bargain collectively. The other three items would all be false statements.

31. The correct answer is 1. The Court said that the codes were illegal since they were laws not enacted by Congress. A prime example was the declaring of the NIRA as unconstitutional.

32. The correct answer is 4. If Germany succeeded in Europe, this would have posed a threat to our national security. At the same time, Japan's victory at Pearl Harbor created an environment in the United States that endorsed entering the war.

33. The correct answer is 2. This was part of FDR's court-packing plan to increase presidential influence over the Supreme Court and circumvent the system of checks and balances.

34. The correct answer is 3. As men went to war, workers were needed in factories. Women filled this role to assist in the war effort. A prime example here would be Rosie the Riveter.

35. The correct answer is 2. Following WWII, the United States was now one of the major global powers. Unlike in earlier wars, the United States now accepted its role and responsibility as a world power.

36. The correct answer is 2. The time period indicated covers the time span where the United States attempted to help western European nations recover following the destruction of WWII. This was known as the Marshall Plan. Lend-lease was in 1940, and the Peace Corps and Alliances for Progress were operative in the early 1960s.

37. The correct answer is 1. This was one of the first examples of containment applied in Asia. The other answers have all been proven incorrect during the last fifty years: 2, in Iran; 3, in Vietnam; 4, the Marshall Plan.

38. The correct answer is 3. This is the only viable answer. Schools are financed and controlled by state and local agencies. The federal government does help fund education, problems in society do affect schools, and enrollment has increased along with the population.

39. The correct answer is 4. McCarthy posed a greater threat and as a result of his actions, he was formally censured by Congress. The problem with the other three responses is that

they endorse what McCarthy did so they cannot be considered a criticism.

40. The correct answer is 2. The Great Society is best remembered for the creation of the welfare state. Choices 1 and 3 already existed, and 4 is illogical, given the fact that we were engaged in military conflict during this period.

41. The correct answer is 3. The division of the people over Vietnam, as well as the number of casualties, has left America with a fear of committing troops to long engagements. The other three are all clearly false: communist governments still exist in Asia; U.S. policy did not change; and the boycotts have been lifted during recent years.

42. The correct answer is 4. This was a summit in which Carter acted as mediator between President Sadat of Egypt and Prime Minister Begin of Israel. It was hailed as a major advance toward peace in the Middle East.

43. The correct answer is 1. This is most clearly in keeping with Reagan's "trickle-down" theory. Cuts in taxes would spur business productivity and create more prosperity for America.

44. The correct answer is 3. In each of these cases the issue of minorities' rights suffered: slaves labeled as property, separate but equal, and necessity of internment (for Japanese Americans).

45. The correct answer is 4. With educational opportunities, and a diversely stratified society, the opportunities for social and economic mobility are virtually limitless.

46. The correct answer is 1. The progressive income tax is based on how much one makes. The more you make, the more you pay. Although 2 and 4 are desired outcomes, they are not the fundamental purpose of this specific tax plan.

47. The correct answer is 4. Following Washington's policy outlined in his Farewell Address, Americans believed that they should not become entangled in European affairs.

48. The correct answer is 2. As a result of Chamberlain's appeasement at the Munich Conference, Hitler was able to move forward unchallenged in his attempts to conquer Europe.

Essay Questions

(Note: Answers provided are not all inclusive. These are suggested responses and should be used as a guide for the type of answers that would be acceptable.)

Part II

Question 1

Judicial Review—This is the power of the Supreme Court to determine whether or not laws are in harmony with the provisions of the Constitution; and for such laws as are in conflict with the Constitution, to declare them invalid, void, and unconstitutional. This is the method in which the judicial branch of government can "check" the legislative branch. The case of *Marbury v. Madison* (1803) established the precedent of judicial review. An example of how this power was used can be evidenced in the case of *McCulloch v. Maryland* (1819). Maryland's legislators were hostile toward the federally chartered Bank of the United States, so they placed a heavy tax upon the bank's Baltimore branch. James McCulloch, a bank official, refused to pay the tax. In effect, the state of Maryland was attempting to interfere with a branch of the federal government by passing this legislation. The Supreme Court declared the Maryland bank tax unconstitutional. This clearly demonstrated the power of judicial review in determining if a law was constitutional or not.

Impeachment Process—The impeachment process is used to remove unfit persons from the office of the president, or federal judges. This is the method by which the legislative branch can "check" the executive branch. In 1867 the House of Representatives impeached President Andrew Johnson for violating the Tenure of Office Act. With the Chief Justice of the Supreme Court presiding, the Senate heard the evidence. The Radical Republicans failed by one vote to secure the two-thirds majority needed for conviction. The failure to impeach Johnson upheld the American principle of presidential independence of Congress. In 1974, as a result of the Watergate scandal, Congress began impeachment proceedings against President Richard Nixon. When he was informed by Republican leaders that the House of Representatives would overwhelmingly approve the impeachment charges and the Senate would sustain them by far more than the two-thirds majority needed, Nixon chose to resign prior to being impeached. His resignation could be viewed as the power of the impeachment process to control the actions of the executive branch.

Freedom of Expression—Freedom of expression falls under the First Amendment right of freedom of speech, thought, and action. The main purpose of this right is to prevent oppression by the government. In a totalitarian state, expression is monitored, controlled, and suppressed. In a democratic society, it is the right of the people to question the government and to express their views without fear of reprisals. In *Schenck v. United States* (1919), the doctrine of "clear and present danger" was adopted; it put limits on freedom of expression. Charles Schenck published pamphlets urging World War I draftees to resist conscription. He was charged with obstructing the war effort; a violation of the 1917 Federal Espionage Act. The Supreme Court upheld the guilty verdict, arguing that "free speech would not protect a man falsely shouting 'fire' in a theater and causing a panic," and Schenck's writings in wartime created a "clear and present danger" to the American government and people. Clearly this demonstrated that the government could, and would, put limits on those rights granted to us in the Constitution. Another example using this "clear and present danger" doctrine would be the 1951 case *Dennis v. United States*. In this case, Dennis and a group of American Communist party leaders were charged with violating the Smith Act, which prohibited the teaching or advocating "the overthrow or destruction of any government in the United States by force or violence." The Supreme Court upheld the lower court's guilty verdict. However, it could be argued that the Supreme Court was abusing its power and interpretation of the "clear and present danger" doctrine as indicated by Justice William Douglas.

Protection Against Unreasonable Searches—This implies that a person or his property may not be searched without just cause. This was designed to protect Americans from actions such as the Writs of Assistance used by England prior to the American Revolution. In 1961, local police entered the home of Dolly Mapp without a search warrant and arrested her for possessing obscene books. Her conviction initially stood, but the Supreme Court overturned the conviction in *Mapp v. Ohio* (1961). Until this ruling, only the federal government was barred from using illegally obtained evidence. This ruling extended the constitutional rule to apply to the states and their subdivisions.

Equal Protection Under the Law—This implies that all people should be treated equally not only when being protected from criminal elements, but also when being accused of criminal acts. In 1963, Charles Gideon, charged with burglary, was tried in a Florida court. Because he was too poor to afford a lawyer, Gideon requested free legal counsel. The state refused because he was not being tried for a capital offense punishable by death. He was found guilty and imprisoned. Gideon appealed this decision to the Supreme Court on the grounds that he was denied "due process" guaranteed under the Fourteenth Amendment which required the state to fulfill the Sixth Amendment guarantee of "assistance of counsel." The Supreme Court, in *Gideon v. Wainright* (1963), agreed that due process necessitated assistance of counsel be provided even in non-capital cases. Gideon was retried, assisted by a lawyer, and was acquitted. This established the precedent that all people are entitled to legal counsel in criminal proceedings.

Rights of the Accused—These rights protect citizens from incriminating themselves and assures that all people are innocent until proven guilty in a court of law. In 1964, Danny Escobedo was arrested as a murder suspect. The police refused Escobedo's repeated demands to see his lawyer and failed to inform him that he had a right to remain silent. Escobedo eventually made incriminating statements that were used against him to secure a guilty verdict. The Supreme Court, in *Escobedo v. Illinois* (1964), reversed the conviction on the grounds that he had been denied his constitutional rights to speak to his counsel and to be informed of his privilege against self-incrimination. In *Miranda v. Arizona* (1966), the Supreme Court expanded the Escobedo case doctrine to include: before questioning, the police must inform suspects of their rights to remain silent and to legal counsel; must offer to provide counsel if the suspects are indigent, and must warn them that their remarks may be used against them.

Question 2

Representatives of Foreign Nations—One example of this might be the XYZ Affair of 1797. In order to try to resolve American differences with France, President John Adams sent a group of delegates to France. Once there, the delegates were informed by three representatives of Foreign Minister Talleyrand that negotiations could begin only if there were a loan to France of $12 million, a bribe of $250,000 to the five directors then heading the government, and suitable apologies for remarks recently made in Adams's message to Congress. Adams reported the incident to Congress, referring to the three men only as X, Y, and Z. American sentiment was apparent in the popular slogan "Millions for defense, not one cent for tribute." As a result, Congress voted large military funds, especially to build up the navy. In 1798, the United States became involved in an undeclared naval war with France.

Lobbyists—Recently the manufacture, sale, and use of tobacco products have come under a great deal of scrutiny. American tobacco manufacturers have lobbied to gain tobacco subsidies for farmers as well as to prevent legislation interfering with their industry. Their success can be debated either way. It has been successful in maintaining subsidies for farmers, but their products are being more heavily taxed. Another lobby group would be the Common Cause. Their main concern has been corruption in political campaigns. They were successful inasmuch as the Federal Election Campaign Act of 1972, which modified the rules of campaign finance.

Media—Two prime examples of the power of the press in influencing policies and shaping legislation would include "yellow journalism" and the Watergate investigation. The "yellow" press, especially William Randolph Hearst's *New York Journal* and Joseph Pulitzer's *New York World,* sought to increase newspaper circulation by sensational treatment of news from Cuba. Journalists exaggerated stories and falsified news pictures. By its treatment of such news stories, the press enraged the American people against Spain. This, in part, led to the Spanish-American War (1898). In 1972, two newspapers, the *Washington Post* and *The New York Times,* pursued investigations of Watergate. They publicized their findings, voiced their suspicions, and sustained public concern. As a result, the Senate established a bipartisan Committee on Presidential Campaign Activities. The end result was that more than thirty persons were convicted for illegal activities, and the president of the United States was forced to resign.

Political Action Committees—Political action committees, or PACs, work as a unified group to hinder or assist in the passing of legislation. The American Medical Association (AMA) would be an example of a PAC that has worked to attempt to stop legislation from being passed. Being concerned about how Medicare or universal health coverage might affect the quality of caregivers, the AMA has worked successfully to delay legislation involving these issues. The American Farm Bureau Federation would be an example of a PAC that has worked to assist in the passing of legislation. An example would be subsidies for farmers. A prime example of their accomplishments would be the subsidies approved for ethanol.

Political Parties—The main objectives of political parties is to gain control of as many of the three branches of government as possible in order to further their political ideology. An early example of the motives and power of political parties can be seen in the actions of the Federalists. The goal of the Federalists was to strengthen the federal government at the expense of the states. Utilizing the "elastic clause," they were able to accomplish this task. An immediate example would have been the charting of a National Bank. Other examples of political parties shaping the course of government would include: the Radical Republicans in the post–Civil War era; the Democratic-Republicans and Jacksonian Democracy; the Democrats and Great Society Congress under Lyndon B. Johnson.

Unions—The purpose of a union is to provide unified action by labor against management. Samuel Gompers and the American Federation of Labor (AFL) attempted to utilize this unified power, but the government intervened with federal injunctions in labor disputes. Lobbying for a change, the A.F.L. was instrumental in the passage of the Clayton Antitrust Act, which prohibited using federal injunctions in labor disputes "unless necessary to prevent irreparable injury." However, the act did not help unions as much as expected because the courts used the clause provided quite often. The American Federation of Labor–Congress of Industrial Organizations set out to assist their union members by acquiring a federally mandated minimum wage and standardized work week. The A.F.L.–C.I.O. was successful in gaining passage of the Fair Labor Standards Act of 1938, which set the minimum wage at 40 cents per hour and a workweek at 40 hours. Since then the minimum wage has been increased many times in an attempt to keep workers up with the rising cost of living.

Part III

Question 3

George Washington—In his Farewell Address, Washington advised the new nation to develop commercial relations with all nations, but to avoid political entanglements. The United States should avoid permanent alliances, and engage in temporary alliances only under extraordinary circumstances. Some of the reasons for this advice were that the United States lacked military and naval power; might lose its independence if defeated in a war; was internally divided on foreign policy so that any alliance would endanger national unity; and should devote its energies to developing its economy and solving its domestic problems. Although the policy called for was noninvolvement, many interpreted this to mean the United States should follow a policy of isolation. As a result the United States failed to assume the responsibility associated with being a world power until the conclusion of World War II, nearly 150 years later.

James Monroe—During the Napoleonic Wars in Europe, many Latin American colonies asserted their independence from their European masters. At the conclusion of the Napoleonic Wars, Prince Klemens von Metternich organized the Holy Alliance, an ultraconservative organization bent on preserving monarchical forms of government and crushing liberty and equality. Monroe believed the Holy Alliance would attempt to reassert its control over the newly independent colonies of Latin America. Because the United States and Great Britain were developing prosperous trade relations with these newly independent regions, Monroe issued the Monroe Doctrine, which, in effect, banned Europe from interfering in the Western Hemisphere; Great Britain backed up the doctrine militarily with its naval fleet.

Theodore Roosevelt—In 1903 Secretary Hay negotiated a treaty with Colombia to pay that nation $10 million and an annual rental income of $250,000 for the right to build a canal across its northern province of Panama. The treaty was rejected by the Colombian Senate, which hoped for better terms the following year. Rejection of the treaty worried the French canal company (which had agreed to sell its property and franchise rights to the United States for $40 million), inflamed the people of Panama, and enraged Theodore Roosevelt. Roosevelt privately expressed the wish to see Panama independent of Colombia. When a revolt broke out, the United States openly aided the revolt by sending naval vessels to prevent Colombian troops from entering Panama. After the revolution succeeded, the United States was able to negotiate a favorable treaty with Panama. However, the actions of the United States in this incident earned the United States ill will throughout Latin America. In 1921, the United States attempted to placate Colombia with a payment of $25 million.

Franklin D. Roosevelt—On Dec. 7, 1941, Japanese forces launched a surprise attack against U.S. military forces at Pearl Harbor. The next day Roosevelt asked Congress for a declaration of war, which was authorized the same day. Once the United States had declared war on Japan, Italy and Germany declared war on the United States. This officially brought the United States into World War II. After liberating the European Theater of Operations, the United States turned its attention to the Pacific Theater of Operations. In order to bring about a quick conclusion to the war, as well as save American lives, the United States dropped two atomic bombs on Japan in the fall of 1945 (Hiroshima and Nagasaki). This brought about an end to World War II, but at the same time began the start of the cold war, which would last for more than another four decades.

John F. Kennedy—In an effort to achieve some form of foreign policy success Nikita Khrushchev began secretly to bring offensive bombers and missiles into Cuba and to build missile bases. When Kennedy learned of this, he perceived the missiles and bases as a threat to the security of the Western Hemisphere. As a result, Kennedy ordered a blockade by American naval and air forces on shipments of offensive arms bound for Cuba. He further demanded that the Soviets dismantle the Cuban bases and withdraw the bombers and missiles. Kennedy also warned the Soviet Union that if any nuclear missiles were launched from Cuba against the United States, America would reply with a full retaliatory blow against the Soviet Union. The Soviet Union complained, but in the end agreed to dismantle the missile bases and withdraw the offensive weapons. Kennedy agreed to lift the blockade and pledged not to invade Cuba.

Ronald Reagan—In the early years of his presidency, Reagan took a hard line against the Soviet Union, calling it an "evil empire." To ensure that the United States would remain dominant in the cold war between the two superpowers, Reagan began a major military buildup. Reagan sought funds for 100 long-range, multiple-warhead MX missiles; revived the B-1 bomber program canceled by President Carter; expanded the Stealth program; and revived production of chemical weapons, suspended in 1969; and announced his Strategic Defense Initiative (SDI), or "Star Wars." The greatest impact of these events on the American people was that this led to increased expenditures and a rapid rise in the national debt.

Bill Clinton—Bosnia and Herzegovina became an independent republic in March 1992, following a referendum boycotted by Bosnian Serbs, who established their own government. As the violence escalated, the Serbs, with superior firepower, expanded the territory under their control through a program of "ethnic cleansing." Aiming to end the war in Bosnia, the United States sponsored peace talks in Dayton, Ohio, Nov. 1–21, 1995. The agreement reached established a Bosnia and Hercegovina divided into a Muslim-Croat federation (51 percent), and a Serb republic, with Sarajevo as national capital. To enforce the agreement, more than 20,000 American troops were sent to Bosnia as part of a NATO force of 60,000.

Question 4

Boycott—In 1765 the British Parliament passed the Stamp Act, the first internal tax levied on the colonies. At the urging of the Massachusetts assembly, delegates from nine colonies met in New York City to plan united resistance against the Stamp Act. The Stamp Act Congress delegates urged, and many colonial merchants supported non-importation agreements (boycotts). These were pledges not to import British goods until the repeal of the Stamp Act. Parliament finally repealed the Stamp Act in 1766, but reaffirmed its right to tax the colonies by passing the Declaratory Act. When Parliament passed the Townshend taxes in 1767, colonial merchants again resorted to a boycott of British goods. The Sons of Liberty, an organization of colonial patriots, helped enforce the boycott. In 1770 the British Parliament yielded and repealed all the Townshend import duties except the tax on tea.

Civil Disobedience—In 1773 Parliament passed the Tea Act. By this act, Parliament offered colonists the lowest prices ever on tea. However, this would mean that colonial merchants who were smuggling tea from Holland to avoid the import duties would be undersold. It also meant that the colonists would still be paying the hated Townshend import duty on the tea. To protest this action, in Boston, colonists disguised as Indians boarded the British ships and dumped the tea into the harbor. The response from Great Britain was immediate and severe. Boston harbor was closed until all the destroyed tea was paid for, the quartering of troops in any colonial town was authorized, British officials were granted extraterritoriality, and self-government in Massachusetts was drastically curtailed.

Demonstration and Protest March—As a result of the racial discrimination permeating the country, in 1963 some 200,000 blacks and whites demanded further civil rights legislation by participating in an orderly and peaceful "March on Washington." Once

there, they heard the Rev. Dr. Martin Luther King Jr. give his "I have a dream" speech. The intent of the protesters was to demonstrate solidarity and to gain national exposure. This action led indirectly to the passage of the Comprehensive Civil Rights Act of 1964.

Petition—The First Amendment to the Constitution guarantees the people the right to petition the government for a redress of grievances. An example of this occurring would be when Eli Whitney filed a petition to protect him from other manufacturers who were copying his invention, the cotton gin. A disastrous factory fire had prevented Eli Whitney and his partner from making enough gins to meet the demand, and manufacturers throughout the South began to copy the invention. Although Whitney and Miller received a patent on the gin in 1794, not until 1807 was a decision rendered protecting their patent. In 1812 Congress denied Whitney's petition for renewal of this protection. The use of a petition could also be illustrated by any group within a community passing a petition around to achieve some sort of goal, such as modification of a city ordinance. Although not legally binding, it can be quite persuasive to elected officials.

Rebellion—A classic example of this would be the American Revolution. As a result of taxation without representation, oppression, violation of civil liberties, and a myriad of other causes, the colonists decided to rebel against the British Crown. The colonists believed there was no other option available to them after the passing of the "Intolerable Acts" and the response of King George to the Olive Branch Petition. In the ensuing rebellion/revolution, the colonists gained their independence from Great Britain.

Sit-In—In P*lessy v. Ferguson*, the United States Supreme Court adopted the policy of "separate but equal," regarding race-based "Jim Crow" laws. The problem was that whereas facilities were separate, they were far from equal. To protest this decision supporting "white only" and "black only" facilities, civil rights demonstrators in the 1950s and 1960s would go to an area denied to their race and peacefully sit in the area and refuse to leave. Since they were technically in violation of the law they could be, and would be, arrested. The idea was that once they were arrested for violating a law, the law could be challenged in court. Eventually legislation was passed banning segregation.

Strike—In 1894 workers at the Pullman car plant near Chicago went on strike to protest wage cuts of up to 40 percent. To support the strikers, railroad employees refused to handle trains with Pullman cars. Most railroad transportation out of Chicago stopped. Attorney General Richard Olney secured an injunction against the union as a "conspiracy in restraint of trade." President Cleveland also sent federal troops to Chicago allegedly to assure delivery of the U.S. mail. The strike collapsed, but it did show labor leaders that they needed to become more involved in political campaigns and lobbying, which proved to be more successful.

Question 5

Virginia Plan—At the Constitution Convention, Virginia put forth a plan for representation that called for a unicameral (one-house) legislature in which representation would be based on population. Densely populated states liked this plan because it seemed truly democratic, but less densely populated states opposed it on the grounds that it was unequal. In their opposition, New Jersey put forth a plan calling for a unicameral legislature where representation would be based on equality, one state, one vote. In the end, the founding fathers went with the Connecticut Compromise (Great Compromise), which called for a bicameral (two-house) legislature in which representation would be based on population in one house, and equality in the other.

Abraham Lincoln—When Lincoln was elected president, many southerners believed he posed a threat to the southern way of life. Republicans pointed out that Lincoln was more moderate on the issue of slavery than William H. Seaward; the Democrats controlled both the House and the Senate; the Supreme Court was pro-South; and Lincoln had sworn not to interfere with slavery where it already existed. Regardless of these factors, southern states began to secede from the Union, an action that led to the Civil War.

Philippines—As a result of the Spanish-American War the United States annexed the Philippines. The reasons for this were: to gain an entry point into eastern Asia; for trade, raw materials, and investments; to establish a strategic base in the Far East; and, in the words of President McKinley, "to educate the Filipinos, and uplift and civilize and Christianize them." Many Filipinos had expected the United States to withdraw and grant them independence. Emilio Aguinaldo led the embittered islanders in revolt against American rule. After three years of fighting, American forces suppressed the Filipino rebels.

League of Nations—Part of President Wilson's Fourteen Points included the establishment of a League of Nations to promote world peace and security. This was incorporated into the Versailles Peace Treaty, concluding World War I. However, when it came time for the United States to ratify this treaty, Henry Cabot Lodge led an effort to block ratification of the treaty in the United States. Lodge believed that participation in the League of Nations would violate the power of Congress to declare war. As a result of Wilson's declining health and the efforts of Lodge, the United States did not ratify the treaty, nor did the United States join the League of Nations.

Prohibition—In the early twentieth century, proponents of the temperance movement attempted to promote legislation that would prevent the sale, transportation, or consumption of intoxicating beverages. It was their belief that alcohol was at the root of the majority of social problems plaguing the United States. Opponents of this legislation pointed out that the federal government had no right to regulate social norms, and the only result of such a measure would be the advance of the criminal element within society. Regardless, the Eighteenth Amendment was ratified and it made it illegal to sell, transport, or consume alcoholic beverages. As a result, criminal activity increased exponentially, beginning with alcohol bootleggers.

New Deal Legislation—The New Dealers sought to: assist distressed persons through direct money payments, jobs, and mortgage loans; lift the nation out of the depression through aid to farmers, business owners, and workers; and to eliminate abuses in the economy and to prevent future depressions through protection of bank depositors, investors, consumers, the aged, and the unemployed. To accomplish these goals, Roosevelt proposed many new laws during the first three months of his presidency. Using his position as party leader and public orator he was able to secure passage of every major proposal. Some people believed that many of these new laws were unconstitutional, so they challenged them in the courts. In 1935 the Supreme Court declared the National Industrial Recovery Act to be unconstitutional. In 1936 they declared unconstitutional the Agricultural Adjustment Act. In 1937 the Supreme Court adopted a more liberal position and began to rule other New Deal laws as being constitutional, such as the National Labor Relations Act and the Social Security Act.

Roe v. Wade—In 1973 the U.S. Supreme Court passed down its ruling in the *Roe v. Wade* case. This decision stated that the constitutionally implied right to privacy protects a woman's choice in matters of abortion. Many people applauded this decision on the basis that women have the right to make decisions about their own bodies. However, others argued that the unborn child has the right to live. Because of the highly emotional nature of this topic, the results of the decision by the Supreme Court have been quite extreme. Pro-lifers have resorted to everything from picketing abortion clinics to bombing them.

Question 6

Changing Family Patterns—The single greatest change in family patterns in the United States recently has been the rise of single-parent families. This has resulted from two factors: the crumbling of the institution of marriage, leading to ever-increasing divorce rates; and the increasing number of people having children out of wedlock. As a result of these factors, the number of children being left to raise themselves while the parent is out of the house, working, is increasing at an ever-alarming rate. These "latch-key" kids are being provided with little structure or moral guidance. To assist with what is clearly perceived as a problem, legislation has been proposed to make the obtaining of a divorce far more difficult. At the same time, an increased burden has been placed on the school system to provide more support for these children.

Crime—Two interrelated issues that have many Americans concerned in this area today are crimes perpetuated by youths, and drug related crimes. The escalation of gang violence in recent years has caused the death of thousands of gang members, as well as innocent bystanders. At the same time, the potency of drugs has reached a point where addiction is almost instantaneous and quite often the drugs can prove to be fatal. The true victims of this are the children who are never given a chance, such as "crack babies." Beginning with President Reagan and increased under President Bush, the United States has declared a "war on drugs," appropriating billions of dollars for education and prevention.

Health Care Reform—It is hard to believe that in the "most powerful nation in the world," people are being denied basic health care. Because of rising costs in the health-care profession, many people are forced to rely on substandard medical care, or forced to do without medical care. To assist with this problem of affordability, a recent development has been the creation of managed health care, known as Health Maintenance Organizations (HMOs). Although it does not insure coverage for all people, it does attempt to curb the escalating costs of medical care, making it more affordable for many more people. In 1993 President Clinton proposed a universal health plan to Congress in order to assist the estimated 34 million Americans with no health insurance. After a year of national and congressional debate, no plan was passed.

Homelessness—In a nation with one of the highest standards of living in the world, it is hard to understand how some people are denied the basic comfort of a roof over their heads. Many Americans believe this is not only inhumane, but that it goes counter to the American Dream. At the same time, many argue that homelessness leads to potential criminal activity. At the start of the 1990s, estimates of the number of homeless ranged from 600,000 to 3 million. While most Americans agreed with President Bush that this was a "national shame," there was little agreement about how to end it. Some attempts at prevention have been rent-control legislation and construction of low-rent public housing.

Immigration—The United States is a country built by immigrants. Whether one is looking at the original colonists who created the nation, or the Asian workers who physically built the railroads connecting the nation; the country itself is a product of immigration. After the closing of the frontier, and continuing to this day, many Americans have attempted to limit the number of future immigrants coming to this country, both legally and illegally. The main concerns have been that immigrants compete for the scarce number of jobs available, and they are a burden on the welfare system. In 1986 Congress passed the Immigration Reform and Control Act. One of its provisions was that employers would be heavily fined for hiring illegal immigrants, and made it illegal for employers to discriminate against legal immigrants. At the same time, the government tighten controls against further illegal immigration into the United States.

Technological Change—One of the greatest concerns involving technological change is the displacement of workers. The mechanization of tasks has caused many people to lose their livelihoods. At the same time, this technological change has created a demand for more highly skilled employees. Another concern involves global competition. Many Americans believe we are falling behind other nations in this arena. One way the United States has attempted to deal with this issue has been federal spending to increase education in math and science. The hope is that this will prepare the students of today to be better able to compete globally.

Question 7

Excerpt 1—The group described in the song is farmers suffering from declining prices and high loan payments. Basically the song is saying that farmers live on credit. With the interest rates so high, they are unable to keep up the payments, eventually the person holding the mortgage on the farmers' farm forecloses and they lose everything. One way the government has attempted to deal with this problem is the Farm Act of 1973, which guaranteed that farmers would receive a minimal payment on certain crops. If the market price fell below the minimum level, the government would make up the difference in the form of subsidies.

Excerpt 2—The group described in the song is Native Americans. The problem that is being discussed is the confiscation and selling of Native American lands. The author is pointing out that not only has it happened in the past, but it is also happening today. One way the federal government has attempted to deal with this problem is by passing the Wheeler-Howard Indian Reorganization Act (1934). This act ended land allotments, restored unsold "surplus" land to tribal ownership, and began the repurchase of lands for Indian use.

Excerpt 3—The group described in the song is the blue-collar, or immigrant, worker. The problem being discussed is the exploitation and later unemployment of the workers. The author is pointing out that even though they were victimized by management, the union has now made them strong. In looking for legislation that was designed to deal with this problem, one could look at any labor legislation, such as the Fair Labor Standards Act, National Labor Relations Act, or the Social Security Act.

Excerpt 4—The group described in the song are women's suffragettes, or women seeking the right to vote. The problem is that women were being denied the right to vote solely because of their gender. In 1920, the United States passed the Nineteenth Amendment, which gave women the right to vote.

Excerpt 5—The group described in the song are senior citizens, or the elderly. The problem is that they are too old to work, but they are not yet dead. With rising economic prices, many cannot afford the basic necessities of life, such as food and shelter. One attempt to ease this plight has been the passage of the Social Security Act, which ensures all people a moderate income when they reach the age of 65. Unfortunately, Social Security benefits have not kept up with the rising cost of living.

Sample Regents Exam #3

Part I (55 credits)

Answer all 48 questions in this part.

Directions (1–48): For each statement or question, write on the separate answer sheet the *number* of the word or expression that, of those given, best completes the statement or answers the question.

1 The Declaration of Independence states that the fundamental purpose of government is to

1 guarantee the right to vote to all citizens
2 secure for the people their natural rights
3 provide for the common defense
4 assure employment for people who are willing to work

2 Which statement is accurate about governmental power under the Articles of Confederation?

1 State governments had the power to collect taxes, coin money, and control trade.
2 The executive branch of the central government was more powerful than the legislative and judicial branches.
3 The central government was made stronger than state governments.
4 The states with the largest populations had the most votes in Congress.

3 A compromise reached at the Constitutional Convention of 1787 was that

1 states were given the power to make treaties
2 Congress became a two-house legislature
3 slavery was prohibited throughout the United States
4 an individual could serve only two terms as President

4 "To make all laws which shall be necessary and proper for carrying into execution the foregoing powers, . . ."

This clause in the United States Constitution has most often been used to

1 impeach members of the executive branch
2 increase the power of state governments
3 justify the principle of civil disobedience
4 broaden the authority of Congress

5 Before a bill becomes a Federal law, it *must* be

1 reviewed by the Cabinet
2 passed by the Senate and the House of Representatives
3 approved by the Supreme Court
4 signed by the President

6 Which headline refers to a power granted *only* to the Federal Government by the United States Constitution?

1 **"War Declared Against Germany"**
2 **"Reminder: File Income Tax Return Early"**
3 **"New Law Allows Right Turn at Red Light"**
4 **"Law Passed To Raise Drinking Age to 21"**

7 According to the United States Constitution, the reason for conducting a census in the United States is to determine the number of

1 members of each ethnic group
2 people who are eligible to vote
3 people eligible for Social Security benefits
4 representatives to be elected by each state to the House of Representatives

8 The clause of the United States Constitution that provides the legal basis for public regulation of railroads is the

1 equal protection clause
2 commerce clause
3 due process clause
4 supremacy clause

9 "It is the duty of the President to propose and it is the privilege of the Congress to dispose."

This statement refers to the concept of

1 federalism   3 judicial review
2 popular sovereignty 4 checks and balances

10 Presidents can most directly influence the future decisions of the United States Supreme Court by

1 impeaching Justices with whom they disagree
2 encouraging the public to write letters to the Justices
3 vetoing rulings of the Justices
4 appointing new Justices to the Court with Senate approval

11 Political parties and the President's Cabinet are considered to be part of the unwritten constitution because these groups

1 developed through custom and usage
2 represent the people's views more accurately than elected officials do
3 were created by amendments to the original Constitution
4 exist only at the state and local levels of government

12 The decision of President George Washington to use the state militia to put down the Whiskey Rebellion in 1794 demonstrated that the

1 states were still the dominant power in the new nation
2 President was becoming a military dictator
3 Federal Government had no authority to impose an excise tax
4 new National Government intended to enforce Federal laws

13 The most significant effect of minor political parties in the United States is that they have

1 elected many of their party leaders to the Presidency
2 had little impact on the major parties
3 suggested reform ideas that later became laws
4 influenced only local levels of government

14 During the period from 1800 to 1865, the issues of States rights, the tariff, and slavery led most directly to the growth of

1 imperialism   3 national unity
2 sectionalism   4 industrialization

15 After the Civil War, a major goal of the Radical Republicans in Congress was to

1 gain voting rights for the newly freed slaves
2 rebuild the farms and factories of the Northeast
3 restore the white plantation owners to power in the South
4 support the policies of President Andrew Johnson

16 The literacy test and the poll tax were devised mainly to

1 eliminate fraudulent voting practices
2 establish uniform national voting requirements
3 limit the number of African Americans qualified to vote
4 raise money for political campaigns

17 Immigrants to the United States between 1890 and 1930 most frequently experienced discrimination because they

1 spoke different languages and had different customs
2 entered the competition for scarce farmland
3 were better educated than earlier immigrants
4 remained more loyal to their homelands than to the United States

18 During the late 1800's, the theories of Social Darwinism were often used to justify the efforts of

1 Federal officials to control state governments
2 Northern liberals to pass civil rights legislation
3 Southern farmers to increase cotton exports
4 big business to destroy its competitors

19 During the late 1800's, the growing of cash crops by an increasingly large number of farmers resulted in

1 greater isolation of farmers from American economic life
2 a shift from self-sufficiency to commercial farming
3 less food available for export
4 general economic prosperity for all farmers

Base your answer to question 20 on the cartoon below and on your knowledge of social studies.

Boston Globe, May 28, 1898

20 This cartoon deals mainly with the concept of

1 imperialism
2 government overspending
3 isolationism
4 free trade

21 The primary goal of manifest destiny was the

1 abolition of slavery in territories held by the United States
2 removal of European influence from South America
3 expansion of the United States westward to the Pacific Ocean
4 secession of the Southern States from the Union

22 "You furnish the pictures and I'll furnish the war."

In 1898, when newspaper publisher William Randolph Hearst made this statement to artist Frederic Remington, he was suggesting that

1 artists and writers resented being censored by the government
2 artwork made newspapers more interesting to read
3 journalism could be used to shape opinions and policies
4 journalists valued accuracy and objectivity

23 Ida Tarbell, Upton Sinclair, and Frank Norris all shared a belief that

1 monopolies were necessary for businesses to survive
2 reform was needed to control the abuses of business
3 the government should follow a laissez-faire policy
4 the public was unlikely to respond to calls for reform

24 The Granger Laws, the Interstate Commerce Act, and the Agricultural Adjustment Acts are similar in that they all

1 protected the interests of big business
2 turned over significant Federal powers to the state governments
3 forced farmers to join cooperatives
4 attempted to address problems experienced by farmers

25 The main objective of President Woodrow Wilson's Fourteen Points was to

1 establish a military alliance with European nations
2 punish Germany for causing World War I
3 provide for a just and lasting peace
4 encourage open immigration in industrial nations

26 In the 1920's, one reason for placing restrictions on immigration to the United States was that

1 factory owners were hiring only native-born workers
2 Congress was concerned about radical ideas being brought into the United States
3 the United States was overcrowded and could not accept more immigrants
4 many foreign governments demanded the United States close its borders to immigrants

27 Which statement best explains a major cause of the Great Depression in the United States?

1 High income tax rates forced many workers into poverty.
2 Large quantities of foreign imports forced American companies out of business.
3 The government controlled almost every aspect of the American economy.
4 Factories and farms produced more products than Americans could afford to buy.

28 "They used to tell me I was building a dream,
With peace and glory ahead.
Why should I be standing on line just waiting for bread?

Once I built a railroad, made it run,
Made it race against time.
Once I built a railroad. Now it's done.
Brother, can you spare a dime?"

The words of this song suggest that the American dream of economic success

1 can be achieved only through hard work
2 holds its greatest opportunities during periods of war
3 is forfeited by people on welfare
4 can be shattered by forces beyond an individual's control

29 Republican opponents of President Franklin D. Roosevelt criticized the New Deal program on the grounds that it

1 spent more money than was taken in
2 weakened the power of the executive branch
3 failed to include labor legislation
4 promoted the ideas of laissez-faire economics

Base your answer to question 30 on the graph below and on your knowledge of social studies.

Bank Failures in the United States from 1926 to 1937

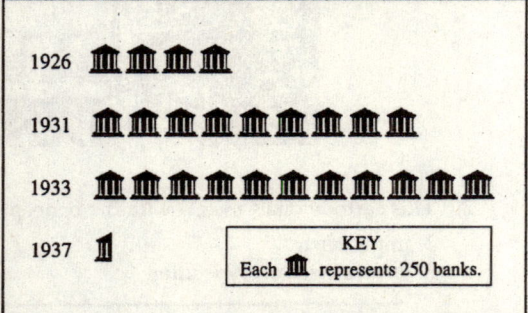

Key
Each 🏛 represents 250 banks.

Visualized American Government, 1957

30 The major reason for the change in the number of bank failures between the early 1930's and 1937 is that by 1937

1 new banking laws had restored public confidence in the nation's banks
2 most people were too poor to have any savings
3 the government had purchased and was now operating the nation's banks
4 most Americans had transferred their savings to European banks

31 President Franklin D. Roosevelt's court-packing proposal was criticized because it

1 attempted to give more power to the judicial branch
2 directly violated the Federal-state relationship
3 threatened the system of checks and balances in the Federal Government
4 violated the constitutional guarantee of the right to legal counsel

32 In the late 1930's and early 1940's, the cash-and-carry policy and the lend-lease policy contributed to

1 ending tensions between the United States and Germany
2 involving the United States in European affairs
3 stabilizing the international money supply
4 expanding North American free-trade zones

33 The main reason for providing aid to Europe under the Marshall Plan was to

1 guarantee American factories a supply of cheap raw materials
2 create disagreements between Western European nations
3 encourage the Soviet Union to withdraw from the United Nations
4 rebuild the economies of devastated European nations

34 Which concept is associated with the formation of the North Atlantic Treaty Organization (NATO)?

1 neutrality
2 isolation
3 collective security
4 appeasement

35 The term "McCarthyism" has come to symbolize

1 unfounded accusations of disloyalty and a climate of fear
2 the protection of the constitutional rights of accused persons
3 integration in public education
4 attempts to encourage totalitarian dictatorships

36 Which trend occurred in United States society in the 1950's?

1 The number of marriages and the birthrate declined.
2 Day-care services for children became widely available.
3 Suburban areas developed rapidly.
4 The automobile became less important in people's lives.

37 During the 1950's, United States foreign policy was characterized by

1 increased trade with Communist China
2 an alliance with the Warsaw Pact nations
3 economic aid to the Soviet Union
4 efforts to block communist expansion

38 In the 1960's, bus boycotts, lunch counter sit-ins, and freedom rides were organized attempts to achieve

1 integration
2 black separatism
3 segregation
4 cultural diffusion

39 Which statement most closely reflects the views of Martin Luther King, Jr.?

1 All Americans have a right to equality. Any means, including violence, can be used to attain it.
2 Unjust laws must be disobeyed and the consequences accepted peacefully.
3 African Americans will never gain equality. We really have no choice but to have the two races separate.
4 African Americans must be patient and aim first for economic advancement. Social and political equality will come later.

40 The Watergate investigation during President Richard Nixon's administration demonstrated that

1 Congress had lost much of its power and influence
2 impeachment is the only way for a President to leave office
3 the military has a great influence on government
4 separation of powers works effectively

41 The Federal Reserve System contributes to economic stability and growth by

1 controlling prices and wages
2 controlling the money supply and the availability of credit
3 regulating the purchase and sale of stocks and bonds
4 regulating the flow of exports and imports

42 Which is a common argument *against* raising tariffs on imported goods?

1 Domestic products are better made than foreign products are.
2 Foreign trading partners may retaliate and reduce their purchases of American-made goods.
3 Foreign products are almost always more expensive than goods made in the United States.
4 Levying taxes on imports may be unconstitutional.

43 The domino theory was used by the United States as a justification for

1 participating in the Vietnam War (1960's–1970's)
2 extending diplomatic recognition to the People's Republic of China (1979)
3 negotiating with Iran to release American hostages (1979–1980)
4 sending armed forces to the Middle East (1990–1991)

44 The reelections of President Abraham Lincoln in 1864 and President Franklin D. Roosevelt in 1944 were similar in that each

1 was later rejected by the electoral college
2 occurred during a major economic depression
3 resulted in a victory for a third-party Presidential candidate
4 showed that the American people were unwilling to change leaders during wartime

45 Sharecropping was a system of farming most common in

1 New England after the Revolutionary War
2 the Middle Atlantic States before the Civil War
3 the Southern States after the Civil War
4 the Pacific Northwest before World War I

46 During the 20th century, economic opportunities for women and minorities in the United States have increased most during periods of

1 war   3 nativist agitation
2 recession   4 overseas expansion

47 In recent years, a trend that many Americans consider a threat to the United States political process is the

1 declining number of minor political parties
2 increasing influence of political action committees and lobbyists
3 rising number of senior citizens who vote
4 decreasing media attention on Presidential election campaigns

48 One similarity between the Open Door Policy of the early 1900's and the North American Free Trade Agreement (NAFTA) of the 1990's is that both were intended to

1 lower tariffs on imports
2 improve relations in East Asia
3 expand economic links between nations
4 relax restrictions on immigration

Answers to the following questions are to be written on paper provided by the school.

Students Please Note:

In developing your answers to Parts II and III, be sure to

(1) include specific factual information and evidence whenever possible
(2) keep to the questions asked; do not go off on tangents
(3) avoid overgeneralizations or sweeping statements without sufficient proof; do not over-state your case
(4) keep these general definitions in mind:

(a) <u>discuss</u> means "to make observations about something using facts, reasoning, and argument; to present in some detail"
(b) <u>describe</u> means "to illustrate something in words or tell about it"
(c) <u>show</u> means "to point out; to set forth clearly a position or idea by stating it and giving data which support it"
(d) <u>explain</u> means "to make plain or understandable; to give reasons for or causes of; to show the logical development or relationships of"

Part II

ANSWER ONE QUESTION FROM THIS PART.   [45]

1 Specific actions taken by United States Presidents on domestic issues have either increased or decreased the role of the Federal Government.

Presidents

Thomas Jefferson	Herbert Hoover
Abraham Lincoln	Lyndon Johnson
Theodore Roosevelt	Ronald Reagan
Woodrow Wilson	

Choose *three* of the Presidents listed and for *each* one chosen:

• Discuss *one* specific domestic action taken by that President that had an impact on the role of the Federal Government in the United States
• Explain how this action has either increased or decreased the role of the Federal Government   [5,5,5]

2 Over the past 200 years, the protections found in the United States Constitution have been both limited and expanded by Supreme Court decisions.

Constitutional Protections

Right to privacy	Right to legal counsel
Freedom of the press	Separation of church and state
Freedom of speech	Freedom of assembly

Choose *three* of the constitutional protections listed and for *each* one chosen:

• Discuss *one* specific United States Supreme Court case that deals with this constitutional protection [The exact name of the case does not have to be given.]
• State the Court's decision in the case
• Explain how the decision either limited or expanded the meaning of the constitutional protection   [5,5,5]

Part III

ANSWER TWO QUESTIONS FROM THIS PART. [30]

3 The United States has followed a variety of policies in its relations with Latin American nations. Some of these policies are listed below.

Policies

Containment
Immigration legislation
Regulation of trade
Territorial expansion
Economic assistance
Intervention

Choose *three* of the policies listed and for *each* one chosen:

* State a major goal of the policy as used toward Latin America
* Discuss *one* specific action taken by the United States to achieve the goal [Use a different action for each policy chosen.]
* Explain how the action affected the relationship between the United States and Latin America [5,5,5]

4 Since 1900, actions taken by the United States Government to solve economic problems have often led to the creation of other problems. Some of these actions are listed below.

Government Actions

Regulating business activity
Setting a minimum wage
Reforming income tax regulations
Setting interest rates
Using farm price supports
Deficit spending
Establishing wage and price controls

Choose *three* of the actions listed and for *each* one chosen:

* Discuss *one* specific economic problem that has occurred since 1900 that the action was designed to solve
* Explain a different economic problem that resulted from that government action [5,5,5]

5 Historians frequently use descriptive titles to characterize various periods in United States history.

Titles

Critical Period (1780's)
Reconstruction Era (1865 to 1877)
Last Frontier (1860 to 1890)
Gilded Age (1870 to 1900)
Roaring Twenties (1920's)
Cold War (1948 to 1990)

Choose *three* of the titles listed and for *each* one chosen:
* Explain why the title is used to describe the time period
* Discuss how *one* specific event or trend during the period illustrates the meaning of the title   [5,5,5]

6 Technological developments often bring about significant changes in American culture. Some technological developments and the aspects of American culture they have changed are listed below.

Technological Developments — Aspects of American Culture

Cotton gin — slavery
Railroad — markets
Elevator — cities
Steel plow — farming on the Great Plains
Automobile — middle-class lifestyle
Television — political campaigns
Computer — education

Choose *three* of the technological developments listed. For *each* one chosen, discuss *two* ways in which the technological development changed the aspect of American culture with which it is paired.   [5,5,5]

7 Reform efforts have played an important role in United States history.

Reform Efforts

Abolition
Labor movement
Temperance
Progressivism
Consumerism
Environmentalism
Women's movement

Choose *three* of the reform efforts listed and for *each* one chosen:
* Identify *one* goal of the reform effort
* Describe *one* action taken to achieve that goal
* Discuss the extent to which the action was successful in achieving that goal   [5,5,5]

Sample Regents Exam #3—Answers

1. The correct answer is 1. Straight from the text itself, the Declaration states, "That to secure these rights, Governments are instituted among Men. . . ."

2. The correct answer is 1. This was one of the fundamental problems with the Articles of Confederation. The states had the bulk of the power, which made the federal government ineffectual. Note that it was possible to have *thirteen* different currencies.

3. The correct answer is 2. This was the Great Compromise, or the Connecticut Compromise. Choice 1 is clearly false; 3 and 4 did not occur until later in history.

4. The correct answer is 4. The "elastic clause" has often been used to extend the powers of the federal government. Examples of this would include chartering a national bank, and the Louisiana Purchase.

5. The correct answer is 2. It is not necessary for the cabinet to review it; the Supreme Court could only declare it unconstitutional after it becomes a law, and state legislatures have nothing to do with a federal law being passed.

6. The correct answer is 1. This is stated in Article 1, Section 7, of the Constitution. Only the federal government, and more specifically Congress, can declare war. Choice 2 is a power shared by both; course 3 and 4 are powers belonging to the states.

7. The correct answer is 4. This is stated in Article 1, Section 2, of the Constitution. The census records population gains and losses among the states. States may gain or lose representatives in the House, depending upon the census totals.

8. The correct answer is 2. Railroads are used for interstate and intrastate commerce. Because they are involved with interstate commerce, they fall under the power of the federal government.

9. The correct answer is 4. This describes the concept of checks and balances. One branch can always check the other to maintain a balance of power. Basically, the quote is referring to presidential appointees. The president proposed his choice, but Congress can refuse the choice, such as the Senate rejecting the president's nominee for ambassadorship or a place in the U.S. Supreme Court.

10. The correct answer is 4. The most direct method to influence future decisions would be to place judges on the court who will vote in line with one's own political ideology. However, judges, once on the court, may deviate from the president's ideological preferences.

11. The correct answer is 1. The statement is true—these items developed through custom and usage; hence the terminology "unwritten constitution." Choice 2 would not be true because elected officials are elected based on their views being representative of those people who elected them. Choice 3 is wrong, because no amendments deal with this. Choice 4 is clearly wrong because we are dealing with the federal level.

12. The correct answer is 4. This was clearly a statement to the people and the world of the resolve of the new government.

13. The correct answer is 3. The best example of this would be the Progressive party. Several of its political platforms, or ideas, later became laws, such as the direct primary election.

14. The correct answer is 2. These were views that were held differently by states in the North and the South. These differences led to sectionalism between the two.

15. The correct answer is 1. The Radical Republicans were primarily concerned with punishing the South. One way to do this was to ensure the voting rights of the newly freed blacks, whom predominantly voted Republican. These radical Republicans were generally opposed to Andrew Jackson's plan of reconciliation with the South.

16. The correct answer is 3. These were tactics designed to prevent the newly freed slaves from participating in the voting procedure. They were part of an overall action referred to as Jim Crow Laws.

17. The correct answer is 1. This is the time period that sees a change in immigration patterns. Old Immigrants, those arriving prior to 1890, came primarily from Western Europe. These New Immigrants, those arriving after 1890, came primarily from Eastern and Southern Europe, as well as Asia.

18. The correct answer is 4. The justification of monopolies was the "survival of the fittest"

aspect of social Darwinism. A business that did not survive competition did not deserve to survive at all.

19. The correct answer is 2. The most logical answer has to be the shift from self-sufficiency to commercial farming, because the question is referencing the increased production of cash crops. Cash crops are used for commercial purposes.

20. The correct answer is 1. Toward the latter part of the nineteenth century, the United States was becoming increasingly involved in the affairs of Cuba, Puerto Rico, the Philippines, etcetera. This involvement took the form of imperialism.

21. The correct answer is 3. The term refers to the ordained mission of Americans to spread from the Atlantic to the Pacific.

22. The correct answer is 3. Hearst was referring to what became known as "yellow journalism." This is the concept that journalism can be used effectively as propaganda, or to "sensationalize" the news. Hearst's yellow journalism probably spurred an American involvement in the 1898 Spanish-American war.

23. The correct answer is 2. These were the muckrakers. Their literary works all attacked the abuses associated with big business, such as the Standard Oil Trust (Tarbell).

24. The correct answer is 4. Each of these items was designed to assist the farmers in one way or another.

25. The correct answer is 3. Wilsonian policy as manifested in the Fourteen Points, was an attempt to achieve a just and lasting global peace. A key example would be the formation of the League of Nations.

26. The correct answer is 2. This is the most logical answer. The main ideas opposed would have been socialism and communism. As for choices 1, 3, and 4, the exact opposite was the case.

27. The correct answer is 4. Surplus products led to a decline in the need for labor. This led to unemployment, further decline in sales, more unemployment, etcetera.

28. The correct answer is 4. This is the most logical answer. Choice 1 proposes the exact opposite effect of hard work; war is not mentioned in passage; and 3 is not true.

29. The correct answer is 1. The expenses associated with the New Deal far outweighed the revenues. Government spending increased substantially. As for the other three alternatives, the exact opposite was the case.

30. The correct answer is 1. Choice 2 would be a result, not a cause; choices 3 and 4 are both false statements.

31. The correct answer is 3. The purpose of this proposal was to increase the influence of the executive branch over the judicial branch. This would have upset the system of checks and balances.

32. The correct answer is 2. These were measures used to assist the Allies, particularly Great Britain, during the war, while the United States remained neutral. Even so, these actions increased the involvement of the United States in European affairs.

33. The correct answer is 4. The Marshall Plan was officially called the European Recovery Program. The idea was to build up the economies of European nations in order to take away the lure of socialism during a depressed economy. About $12 billion in aid was given to Europe.

34. The correct answer is 3. NATO was designed to ensure the collective security of its members. It was in essence a defensive military alliance against a possible Soviet invasion in Western Europe.

35. The correct answer is 1. McCarthyism and the "witch hunt" and the "red scare" were all based on unfound accusations and designed to create an atmosphere of distrust and fear.

36. The correct answer is 3. Suburban areas developed rapidly during the 1950s. As for choices 1 and 4, the exact opposite is true, and day-care services did not become widely available until the 1980s.

37. The correct answer is 4. During the 1950s the United States was following the policy of containment out of fear of the domino theory. If one country fell to communism, then adjoining countries would also topple, like a row of dominoes.

38. The correct answer is 1. Integration is the process of providing someone with civil liberties or membership that was previously denied, based on race. Choices 2 and 3 are the opposite of this, and choice 4 would not be appropriate because the actions described had nothing to do with the sharing of cultural values.

39. The correct answer is 2. King was a strong proponent of nonviolence. This rules out choice 1; his '"I have a dream" rules out 3; and 4 was the view held by Booker T. Washington, not King.

40. The correct answer is 4. This is clearly the best answer because the investigations demonstrated that the executive branch would be held accountable by the other branches.

41. The correct answer is 2. The Federal Reserve system regulates inflation and recession by regulating the money supply and the availability of credit.

42. The correct answer is 2. This is a true statement, whereas the other three are not. One cannot be proven conclusively; choice 3 is false for the majority of products, and the Constitution does allow for taxation of imports.

43. The correct answer is 1. The fear associated with the domino theory was that if one Asian nation fell to communism, then other Asian nations would soon follow. To prevent the first domino from falling, the United States had to stop the communist overthrow in Vietnam.

44. The correct answer is 4. Both of these presidents were reelected during wartime. Choices 1–3 are all false statements.

45. The correct answer is 3. Once liberated, the newly freed slaves had no way of supporting themselves. As a result, sharecropping predominated in the region.

46. The correct answer is 1. During wartime, service people are away fighting the war. At the same time, there is an increased need for war supplies. As a result, economic opportunities greatly increased during these periods.

47. The correct answer is 2. Recently many Americans have become concerned about the power that PACs and lobbyists have on political campaigns, and the influence they exert on politicians and the political process.

48. The correct answer is 3. Both of these items deal with economics, so choice 4 is unacceptable. NAFTA deals with North America (United States, Canada, and Mexico), so choice 2 is unacceptable. The Open Door Policy did not involve tariffs on imports, so choice 1 in unacceptable. Choice 3 is the best possible answer, then, because it deals with economic relations between nations.

Essay Questions

(Note: Answers provided are not all inclusive. These are suggested responses and should be used as a guide for the type of answers that would be acceptable.)

Part II

Question 1

Thomas Jefferson—In 1803 Jefferson was offered the opportunity to purchase the Louisiana territory for $15 million. He was disturbed by this agreement because the Constitution did not specifically give the federal government the power to purchase territory. Because Jefferson believed in a "strict" interpretation of the Constitution, he recommended a constitutional amendment to provide the necessary power. He was warned that such a delay might lead to Napoleon withdrawing his offer. Jefferson consequently agreed to purchase the territory under the presidential power to make treaties. Adopting this "loose" interpretation of the Constitution greatly increased the power of the federal government.

Abraham Lincoln—During the Civil War, Lincoln exercised what many considered to be dictatorial powers. In one instance he substituted martial law for civil law in various states, thereby suspending the writ of habeas corpus and imprisoning southern sympathizers. In another instance he spent federal funds not yet appropriated, explaining that when Congress met, they would approve the expenditures. As often happens, during times of national crisis, the power of the executive branch is often exercised to its fullest capacity, sometimes beyond constitutional limits.

Theodore Roosevelt—Roosevelt, the "trust buster," was instrumental in breaking up several of the larger monopolies and industrial combinations. In order to protect the consumer, Roosevelt urged and secured the passage of the Pure Food and Drug Act (1906) and the Meat Inspection Act (1906). These actions strengthened federal involvement in business and industry.

Woodrow Wilson—In 1913 Wilson called Congress into special session and appeared personally before Congress to request legislations. He used the power of patronage to swing necessary Senate votes, and he appealed directly to the people for their support. During his presidency numerous legislative acts were passed dealing with labor and business: Clayton Act (1914), La Follette Seamen's Act (1915), Adamson Act (1916), and Federal Farm Loan Act (1916). By his actions, Wilson strengthened the federal governments involvement in labor and industry.

Herbert Hoover—In the initial phases of the Great Depression, Hoover rejected measures to combat the depression; direct federal relief for unemployed workers, Bonus Army March, expansion of federal works programs. Hoover believed that government interference in business endangered economic progress and personal liberty. As a result, the government's involvement with labor, industry, and the economy was severely weakened.

Lyndon Johnson—In an effort to create what Johnson referred to as the "Great Society," he pushed for civil rights legislation, conservation legislation, consumer protection legislation, and education legislation. The 89th Congress responded favorably to Johnson's requests for far-reaching legislation. As a result, the federal government became more heavily involved in societal issues.

Ronald Reagan—During Reagan's term as president, he got Congress to make major cuts in social spending; income taxes on individuals and business were lowered, while payroll taxes were increased; stepped up the war on drugs; and continued the process of business deregulation begun during the Carter administration, extending it to airlines and other industries. In August 1981, 11,800 members of the 15,000-member Professional Air Traffic Controllers Organization struck for a shorter work-week, higher pay, and other benefits. The Reagan administration reacted by dismissing all 11,800 strikers and decertifying their union. Reagan's actions increased the government's role in societal issues, business, labor, and the economy.

Question 2

Right to Privacy—In *Griswold v. Connecticut*, the court ruled that the Constitution implies a right to privacy in matters of contraception between married people. In *Roe v. Wade* the court ruled that the constitutionally applied right to privacy protects a woman's choice in matters of abortion. Both of

these cases expanded the meaning of the constitutional protection in question.

Freedom of the Press—In *Schenck v. United States* (1919), the doctrine of "clear and present danger" was adopted which put limits on freedom of expression. Charles Schenck published pamphlets urging World War I draftees to resist conscription. He was charged with obstructing the war effort, a violation of the 1917 Federal Espionage Act. The Supreme Court upheld the guilty verdict arguing that "free speech would not protect a man falsely shouting 'fire' in a theater and causing a panic," and Schenck's writings in wartime created a "clear and present danger" to the American government and people. Clearly this demonstrated that the government could, and would, put limits on those rights granted to us in the Constitution.

Freedom of Speech—In *Dennis v. United States* (1951), Dennis and a group of American Communist party leaders were charged with violating the Smith Act, which prohibited the teaching or advocating "the overthrow or destruction of any government in the United States by force or violence." The Supreme Court upheld the lower court's guilty verdict. This clearly limited freedom of speech. In *Texas v. Johnson* (1989), Johnson burned a flag in front of a Dallas building as a sign of protest. He was convicted of violating a Texas law that made it a crime to desecrate a national flag. The Supreme court overturned this decision when it stated that the Constitution protects desecration of the flag as a form of symbolic speech. This decision expanded the meaning of the protection.

Right to Legal Counsel—In 1963, Charles Gideon, charged with burglary, was tried in a Florida court. Because he was too poor to afford a lawyer, Gideon requested free legal counsel. The state refused because he was not being tried for a capital offense punishable by death. He was found guilty and imprisoned. Gideon appealed this decision to the Supreme Court on the grounds that he was denied "due process," guaranteed under the Fourteenth Amendment which required the state to fulfill the Sixth Amendment guarantee of "assistance of counsel." The Supreme Court, in *Gideon v. Wainright* (1963), agreed that due process necessitated assistance of counsel be provided even in non-capital cases. Gideon was retried, assisted by a lawyer, and was acquitted. This established the precedent that all people are entitled to legal counsel in criminal proceedings. It also expanded the meaning of the protection.

Separation of Church and State—Sarah Prince, a Jehovah's Witness, permitted her nine-year-old legal ward to sell the sect's magazine on the streets. Prince was convicted of violating a Massachusetts law that prohibited a guardian from allowing such child labor. In *Prince v. Massachusetts* (1944), the Supreme Court ruled that religion cannot be used as an excuse for violating child labor laws. This act limited the meaning of the protection. In 1962 Steven Engel and four other parents, representing various religious views, sued to stop the New Hyde Park, New York, school board from requiring their children to recite a short, nondenominational prayer. In *Engel v. Vitale* (1962), the Supreme Court ruled that prayer in school was unconstitutional. This act expanded the meaning of the constitutional protection by further defining the separation of church and state.

Freedom of Assembly—In *Hague v. CIO*, the court ruled that people have the right to use the public streets and parks for the purposes of assembly. This expanded the meaning of the protection to include locations that were authorized. In *Edwards v. South Carolina*, the court ruled that the state has no right to interfere with or make criminal the peaceful expression of unpopular views. This act also expanded the meaning of the protection by removing certain restrictions to what people could do when assembled.

Part III

Question 3

Containment —To prevent European nations from any further colonizing in Latin America or interfering with the independence of the newly liberated regions, in 1823 President Monroe issued the Monroe Doctrine. In effect, this doctrine placed the Western Hemisphere off limits to European colonization and intervention. Now that the newly independent nations were no longer restricted to trade arrangements with their mother countries, the opportunity for trade increased between Latin America and the United States.

Immigration Legislation—The Immigration Reform and Control Act of 1986 was designed to curb the number of illegal immigrants flooding across U.S. borders. Estimates of the number of illegal immigrants entering the country in 1986 ranged upward from the official guess of between 3 million to 5 million. By granting amnesty to many of the illegal immigrants already here and tightening controls against further illegal immigration, officials hoped, in the words of President Reagan, to "regain control of our

borders." For three years after the new law went into effect, illegal immigration declined. However, authorities reported that illegal immigration began to rise again in the 1990s.

Regulation of Trade—In order to increase the ability of Latin American nations to procure American goods, the United States established the Export/Import Bank in 1934. The purpose of this agency was to grant low-cost, long-term loans to Latin American nations for building roads and developing their natural resources. It also provided credit facilities to encourage inter-American trade. While some Latin American nations have greatly benefited from this arrangement, others complain that the United States has forced them to rely to heavily on foreign investments.

Territorial Expansion—Many Americans believed that the nation's "Manifest Destiny" was to spread the continental boundaries from the Atlantic to the Pacific. This meant that the land would have to be acquired from the current owners, Mexico. When the Mexican government decided not to sell the land to the United States, a war ensued. The United States was victorious, but this victory led to distrust of America by Mexico.

Economic Assistance—To prevent future Castro-type revolutions in Latin America and the spread of communism, in 1961 President Kennedy proposed the Alliance for Progress to benefit the Latin American masses. This was to be accomplished via aid, trade, and reform. The Alliance nations agreed to a ten-year, $20 billion aid program for Latin America, with the United States contributing more than half the amount. The Alliance nations agreed to expand trade and to stabilize prices of Latin America's products. Finally, they agreed to improve conditions for the Latin American masses by social and economic reforms. Although the success of the program is debatable, the Alliance received renewed pledges of Latin American support and of United States aid past 1971, the original termination date.

Intervention —In order to save American lives and to protect American economic interests, the United States has felt the need to militarily intervene in Latin America on numerous occasions. A prime example of this would be the sending of military troops into the Dominican Republic in 1965. President Johnson stated this was necessary to prevent the establishment of another communist government in the Western Hemisphere. In response to a United States request, the Organization of American States (OAS) established an Inter-American Peace Force. Combining Latin

American and U.S. troops, the OAS army halted the violence in the Dominican Republic. This has led to strained relations with some Latin American nations that resent the interference by the United States in internal affairs.

Question 4

Regulating Business Activity—Utilizing cutthroat business tactics, entrepreneurs began forming monopolies and trusts. Once these were established, the entrepreneur could control the production and cost of items produced; generally inflating the cost and lowering the quality. Once the "muckrakers" exposed these acts of exploitation and corruption, the government decided it was time to become more involved with what was going on. This involved vigorously enforcing the Sherman Act as well as initiating many new forms of legislation designed to regulate industry and the economy. Industrial leaders responded by promoting business consolidations by forming mergers and holding companies.

Setting a Minimum Wage—In 1938 Congress passed the Fair Labor Standards Act (Wages and Hours Law), establishing a minimum wage for workers at 40 cents per hour. This was designed to prevent employers from slashing workers' wages during slow periods of production and consumption, to levels below the cost of living. The minimum hourly wage has been increased many times in an attempt to keep up with the rising cost of living: $1.00 in 1956, $2.00 in 1974, $4.25 in 1991, $4.65 in 1996. The problem with a minimum wage is that it has forced many small businesses to close down because of the high costs of labor. At the same time, it has led to higher unemployment as management seeks methods to reduce labor costs, whether it be through laying off employees or turning to automation or other labor-saving methods.

Reforming Income Tax Regulations—During the 1980s budget deficits soared to new heights as receipts lagged behind spending. The government had to borrow billions each year to pay for its programs. Under President Reagan, income taxes on individuals and businesses were lowered significantly, while payroll taxes were increased. This increase hit the working-class and middle-class people the hardest. Several families in this category were forced below the poverty level. At the same time, many families found they could no longer survive on a single-parent income, so both parents began working.

Setting Interest Rates—When the country is experiencing inflation, recession, or progress, the Federal Reserve Bank can manipulate the direction of the economy. Established in 1913, the Federal Reserve Bank encourages the healthy growth of the national economy by acting to prevent business extremes: runaway prosperity and inflation, as well as serious recession and deflation. This is accomplished by setting the reserve ratio, discount rate, and margin requirement, as well as engaging in open-market operations. When inflation begins to rise, the Federal Reserve Bank can raise the discount rate, which will slow down business expansion. However, if expansion slows too much, it could lead to recession or depression.

Using Farm Price Supports—With the 1929 Great Depression, farmers were hit especially hard. The average cash income per farmer fell about 70 percent. To assist the farmers, Congress enacted the Agricultural Adjustment Act in 1938. To bring prices up to the 1909–1914 levels, the government gave the farmers direct subsidies, called parity payments. This eased the burden on the farmer, but caused the consumer to have to pay higher prices for agricultural products, as well as placed an ever increasing economic burden on the federal government which was passed on to the taxpayer.

Deficit Spending—During the Great Depression of 1929 and into the 1930s, Franklin D. Roosevelt needed vast sums of money to finance his newly enacted welfare programs. The only way to obtain these funds was through borrowing. This is what causes deficit spending—the government spending money based on borrowing rather than taxation. The problem with deficit spending is that it increases the national debt. During World War II the debt rose to what was then thought to be a staggering amount; in 1945, according to the U.S. Office of Management and Budget, the national debt was $260.12 billion. Between 1981 and 1990 the ceiling on the national debt was raised from about $1.08 trillion to about $4.15 trillion.

Establishing Wage and Price Controls—During the Nixon presidency, inflation was skyrocketing. The Nixon administration attempted to battle the inflation by reducing federal spending, raising interest rates, and establishing temporary wage and price controls. None of the methods worked. The cost of living as measured by the Consumer Price Index rose from 108 in 1969 to 148 in 1973.

Question 5

Critical Period—During this period the founding fathers set out to create a new government for the nation. If they could not resolve the conflicts presented during the Constitutional Convention the recently gained independence would surely be lost.

Reconstruction Era—This was the period following the conclusion of the Civil War. The nation had been torn apart—both literally and figuratively. The Radical Republicans had determined that the Southern states had effectively left the union and were now conquered provinces. If they wished to return to the union, it would only be under their terms. The readmission of the Southern states was paramount to the reconstruction of the union.

Last Frontier—Frederick Jackson Turner, in *The Significance of the Frontier in American History,* argued that the close of the frontier, ending the era of cheap or free land caused many of the problems currently confronting society. Between 1860 and 1890, millions of Americans and immigrants migrated to the American West as settlers. However, once the frontier was closed to further settlement, the "safety valve" for discontented factory workers was gone, as well as land available for new immigrants, were forced to stay in the cities and compete for jobs in the factories.

Gilded Age—In 1873 authors Mark Twain and Charles Dudley published *The Gilded Age* to satirize political corruption, materialism, and the excesses of fabulous wealth. Numerous examples of these can be found during this time period: the Credit Mobilier Scandal, the political corruption under President Grant, the Whiskey Ring, and the Tweed Ring.

Roaring Twenties—The term "Roaring Twenties" has two meanings: first, it refers to the excitement and glamour of the economic prosperity, speakeasies, jazz, flappers, etcetera; it also refers to the speed at which everything was changing. The United States was making the transition from a predominantly rural to a predominantly urban society. Between 1902 and 1929 the production of electricity increased nearly twenty times. By 1929, 70 percent of all American industry was powered by electricity and about 70 percent of all homes had electricity. There were new forms of media, such as radio and motion picture. While many people accepted the social changes of the time, others fought these changes.

Cold War—Following the conclusion of World War II, the world saw the emergence of two superpowers, the United States and the Soviet Union. As the reasons for their being together declined, their ideological differences began to drive the two nations further apart. In the end they would drag the rest of the world into their rivalry. The formation of NATO, CENTO, SEATO, and the Warsaw Pact would in effect cut the world in half between the East and West. The war would continue, but it would be a war without active military engagement. Instead, it would be a war of espionage, clandestine operations, and an escalating arms race.

Question 6

Cotton Gin and Slavery—Slavery was well on its way to becoming a dying institution in the United States. Then in 1793 Eli Whitney introduced the South to the cotton gin. This provided a simple and inexpensive method of separating cotton fiber from the seed. This made the growing of cotton more profitable and increased the demand for slaves, as well as the continuation of slavery.

Railroad and Markets—With the introduction of the railroad, producers and consumers no longer had to be in the same location. Raw materials could easily and cheaply be moved to where they could be utilized, as well as finished goods being sent to markets. As the number of railroads increased, a number of centralized cities emerged, such as Chicago, that would serve as rail stations. One of the greatest impacts of the new railroads was the way they linked the Northeast and the West in a mutually profitable exchange of manufactured goods for foodstuffs.

Elevator and Cities—Prior to the introduction of the safety elevator, the only way for a city to experience growth was horizontally. However, with the elevator buildings could be erected much higher and so there was the beginnings of the skyscrapers. This not only allowed for vertical rather than horizontal growth, but it also led to the creation of large population clusters.

Steel Plow and Farming the Great Plains—With the introduction of the steel plow, the amount of overall arable land available increased tremendously in the Great Plains region. This led to mass migration and settlement of the region. With more people farming, and more land available to be farmed, the overall production of food increased tremendously.

Automobile and Middle-Class Lifestyle—There were two major ways that the automobile affected the middle-class lifestyle. The first way was that it gave the people greater mobility. Using this mobility, many people fled the cities to a new region called the suburbs. They could then live in a more pristine environment and still be able to commute to their place of employment. The second way was the freedom it afforded young people. No longer were young people confined to the parlor or library. They could now take their dates away from the prying eyes of adults.

Television and Political Campaigns—The effects of television on political campaigns has been both positive and negative. Clearly, the use of television increases the visibility of the candidates, but it also increases the use of propaganda as well. Still, many argue that it is a blessing because it does provide for a better-informed populace. Additionally, utilizing television in political campaigns has skyrocketed the costs of campaigns and in many instances it has led to illegal or immoral campaign practices when dealing with obtaining funding.

Computer and Education—The computer is constantly changing the way we view education, as well as how education is being conducted. The computer enables us to provide education at a distance, while escaping the confines of time and space. The computer also allows for increased awareness from a global perspective via the Internet. Many argue that the computer has been the greatest invention to further the education of our children. However, many others argue that using computers in education is creating a group of students incapable of completing basic tasks such as making change or doing simple arithmetic.

Question 7

Abolition—Abolitionists wanted to end the spread of slavery within the United States, as well as put an end to slavery where it already existed. One method used by abolitionists was to violate the Fugitive Slave Law and actively support runaway slaves. One way they did this was by creating the Underground Railroad. The abolitionists were very successful in liberating many slaves, but the end to slavery was something that would take a civil war to accomplish.

Labor Movement—Members of the labor movement worked toward achieving safer working conditions, increased wages, fewer hours at work per week, child-labor legislation, and women-labor legislation. The main tools of the labor movement were unions, strikes, and collective bargaining. Initially, the labor movement was unsuccessful because of government involvement with such items as the injunction. However, once supported by the government, the labor movement gained significant achievements over time.

Temperance—Members of this movement sought to eliminate what they conceived to be the evils associated with alcohol consumption. They attempted to get their message across by using tactics such as demonstrations, marches, lobbying, and violence. In 1920, the Eighteenth Amendment was passed. It prohibited the manufacture, transport, and sale of beverages that had more than 0.5 percent of alcohol. The law was passed, but this action just led to people obtaining alcohol by illegal means, which led to increased criminal activity. In 1933, the Twenty-First Amendment was passed repealing prohibition.

Progressivism—Progressives sought to correct the evils associated with industrialization and urbanization. They wanted to put an end to political corruption, expand government regulation of the economy, and eliminate practices harmful to workers and consumers. Through political lobbying and pressure, progressives were instrumental in achieving numerous legislative acts at both the local and federal levels. Such acts would include: the direct election of senators, fair tax laws, consumer protection laws, child labor laws, etcetera. As to the success of the movement, many historians still debate this. It could be argued that this marked the transition from laissez faire to direct government involvement in the economy. It can also be pointed out that numerous legislative measures were passed that have benefited many members of society. However, the pattern of progress was uneven and varied from state to state. Additionally, the progressives failed to end the power of the political machines.

Consumerism—The main goals of the consumer group have been to protect the consumer in such areas as product safety and truth in advertising. One method used to accomplish this has been the creation of consumer protection agencies such as the Better Business Bureau and Nader's Raiders. These organizations have been extremely successful both in lobbying and providing consumers with information.

Environmentalism—Environmentalists are primarily concerned with protecting the environment in which we live. This would involve fighting against things such as: the use of fluorocarbons, improper disposal of hazardous waste, destroying natural resources, or any form of pollution. The success of environmentalists is debatable. They have been successful in making people more aware of the problems, but not quite as successful in achieving effective legislation to prevent the problems. One area they have been extremely successful in is in the creation of national parks, habitats, and reserves.

Women's Movement—One of the main objectives of the women's movement was to achieve equality between the sexes. An attempt was made to accomplish this through the passage of the Equal Rights Amendment (ERA). The ERA failed to gain the necessary number of states for ratification. However, several steps have been made toward achieving equality by giving the issue national attention.

Sample Regents Exam #4

Part I (55 credits)

Answer all 48 questions in this part.

Directions (1–48): For each statement or question, write on the separate answer sheet the *number* of the word or expression that, of those given, best completes the statement or answers the question.

1 The United States Constitution corrected one of the major weaknesses of the Articles of Confederation by
  1 granting the right of universal suffrage
  2 giving the National Government the power to collect taxes
  3 increasing the powers of state governments
  4 establishing a policy for the admission of new states

2 At the Constitutional Convention of 1787, a major conflict between the delegates centered on the issue of
  1 giving women the right to vote
  2 structuring the Federal court system
  3 setting the length of the President's term of office
  4 determining the basis for representation in Congress

3 Which statement best expresses the meaning of the opening words of the United States Constitution, "We, the people . . ."?
  1 Sovereignty is derived from the consent of the governed.
  2 All citizens are guaranteed freedom of speech.
  3 Federal laws are subject to popular referendum.
  4 Americans favor unrestricted immigration.

4 Federalism is best described as the
  1 authority to make and enforce decisions based on a written constitution
  2 difference in the function of the public and private sectors of the economy
  3 division of powers between a national government and state governments
  4 use of checks and balances between the three branches of government

5 Which institution developed outside the limits of the written constitution of the United States?
  1 executive branch   3 Supreme Court
  2 political parties   4 electoral college

6 **"Senate Fails To Ratify Treaty of Versailles"**
   "President Truman Vetoes Taft-Hartley Act"
   "Senate Rejects Nomination of Robert Bork to Supreme Court"

These headlines illustrate the constitutional principle of
  1 republicanism
  2 executive privilege
  3 due process of law
  4 separation of powers

7 "To the Honorable Senate and House of Representatives in Congress Assembled: We the undersigned, citizens of the United States, but deprived of some of the privileges and immunities of citizens, among which is the right to vote, beg leave to submit the following Resolution: . . ."

— Susan B. Anthony
Elizabeth Cady Stanton (1873)

This statement is an example of a citizen's constitutional right to
  1 petition for a redress of grievances
  2 seek election to public office
  3 receive a speedy, public trial
  4 assemble peacefully

8 The Virginia House of Burgesses, the New York State Assembly, and the United States Senate are all examples of
  1 direct democracies
  2 representative bodies
  3 executive branches
  4 appointed lawmakers

9 Political action committees (PACs) are most closely associated with the

1 spoils system   3 lobbying process
2 Cabinet system   4 appeals process

10 President Abraham Lincoln's post–Civil War plan for reconstruction of the South was based on the theory that the former Confederate States

1 should be treated as conquered territories
2 could be readmitted to the Union only by Congress
3 had never actually left the Union
4 must grant full equality to all people

Base your answers to questions 11 and 12 on the excerpt below and on your knowledge of social studies.

OLD JIM CROW

. . . It's wrong to hold malice, we know,
But there's one thing that's true, from all points
of view,
All Negroes hate old man Jim Crow.

. . . We meet him wherever we go;
In all public places, where live both the races,
You'll always see Mr. Jim Crow.

— *The Nashville Eye* (c. 1900)
(adapted)

11 The author of the poem was describing

1 nativism   3 integration
2 discrimination   4 slavery

12 The presence of Mr. Jim Crow "In all public places" was legally ended by the

1 ratification of the 13th amendment (1865)
2 Supreme Court's ruling in *Plessy* v. *Ferguson* (1896)
3 establishment of the National Association for the Advancement of Colored People (NAACP) (1909)
4 passage of the Civil Rights Act of 1964

13 Which factor was most critical to the building of transcontinental railroads after the Civil War?

1 government ownership of the railroads
2 capital investments by labor unions
3 land and money provided by the Federal Government
4 willingness of Native American Indians to leave tribal lands

14 Which statement best describes a major economic trend in the United States during the period from 1865 to 1900?

1 Many business practices were developed to eliminate competition.
2 Workers determined working conditions and factory output.
3 The gross national product decreased steadily.
4 Basic industries were taken over by the government.

15 During the major industrial strikes of the late 19th century, which action did the Federal Government take?

1 Military troops were sent to substitute for striking workers.
2 Military force and court injunctions were used against the workers to help end the strikes.
3 The Government forced companies to honor their contracts with unions.
4 The Government paid for damage to public and private property.

16 In United States history, a similarity between the "old" and "new" immigrant groups was that both were

1 financially helped by state and Federal Government programs
2 readily assimilated into American society
3 primarily drawn to the United States by economic motives
4 mainly attracted to the Middle West

☞ GO RIGHT ON TO THE NEXT PAGE.

17 Which document is a primary source for information about the Western frontier during the second half of the 1800's?

1 a novel about a farm family in the Dakota Territory
2 a movie presenting a realistic view of cowboys
3 a biography of General George Custer written by one of his descendants
4 a treaty signed by the Sioux Indians and the Federal Government

18 Which headline is the best example of "yellow journalism," as practiced in the late 1890's?

1 **"Maine Sunk in Havana Harbor"**
2 **"Several Sailors Die in Maine Sinking"**
3 **"Maine Split by Enemy's Secret Infernal Machine"**
4 **"Anti-Imperialists Oppose War with Spain"**

19 The Sherman Antitrust Act (1890) and the Clayton Antitrust Act (1914) were similar in that both were designed to

1 regulate child labor
2 limit the power of big business
3 set safety standards in industry
4 restrict the employment of unskilled immigrants

20 ". . . The Pacific is our ocean . . . And the Pacific is the ocean of the commerce of the future . . . The power that rules the Pacific, therefore, is the power that rules the world. And, with the Philippines, that power is and will forever be the American Republic."
— CONGRESSIONAL RECORD, 1900

Which policy is supported by this quotation?

1 imperialism   3 isolationism
2 self-determination   4 humanitarianism

21 The major objective of United States foreign policy toward Latin America during the period from 1900 to 1920 was to

1 improve the standard of living of the people in Latin America
2 support land reform throughout the Western Hemisphere
3 protect the human rights of native peoples in Latin America
4 serve as protector and police officer in the Western Hemisphere

22 The major purpose of the Federal Reserve Act (1913) was to

1 provide a flexible money supply
2 establish government ownership of the banks
3 insure the bank deposits of individuals
4 implement the new amendment for a graduated income tax

Base your answer to question 23 on the map below and on your knowledge of social studies.

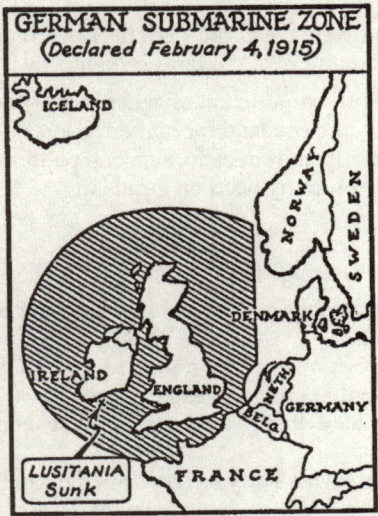

GERMAN SUBMARINE ZONE
(Declared February 4, 1915)

23 The situation shown in the map threatened the United States policy of

1 intervention   3 neutrality
2 containment   4 collective security

24 During the 1920's, the prevailing view of government's role in the United States economy was that the government should

1 control the means of production
2 promote the welfare state
3 play a major role through regulatory action
4 interfere as little as possible

25 The rapid, worldwide spread of the Great Depression of the 1930's was evidence of

1 the failure of government job programs
2 global financial interdependence
3 a shortage of American factories making consumer goods
4 the negative effects of unrestricted immigration

26 During President Franklin D. Roosevelt's first term, what was the greatest obstacle to his New Deal programs?

1 decisions of the United States Supreme Court, declaring some legislation unconstitutional
2 lack of support from the American voters
3 opposition of labor unions
4 refusal of Congress to pass most of the bills favored by the President

27 During the New Deal, the Federal Government attempted to improve the farm economy by

1 reducing the production of agricultural goods
2 opening up more land for homesteaders
3 raising tariffs to reduce foreign competition
4 lowering property taxes on farmland

28 What is one lasting effect of the New Deal?

1 Organized labor continues to grow in size and influence.
2 Many government programs started in the 1930's continue in the 1990's.
3 Women have finally attained equal economic status.
4 The Republican Party has continued to control the National Government since the 1930's.

29 Which action during the 1930's heightened the tensions between Japan and the United States?

1 Japan refused to adopt a democratic form of government.
2 Japan did not allow trade with nations in the Western Hemisphere.
3 The United States placed limits on Japanese immigration.
4 Japan invaded Chinese territory.

30 The Neutrality Acts of the 1930's were primarily designed to

1 avoid the kinds of foreign policy decisions that led to the United States entry into World War I
2 prevent the United States from joining the League of Nations
3 avoid spending money on military development
4 strengthen the economy of the United States

31 Which World War II action was later determined to be a violation of civil liberties?

1 rationing of scarce commodities
2 employment of women in factories
3 internment of Japanese Americans
4 use of a military draft

Base your answers to questions 32 and 33 on the speakers' conversation below and on your knowledge of social studies.

Speaker A: "We must provide arms to the legitimate governments of Greece and Turkey if they are to defeat Soviet-sponsored subversion."

Speaker B: "The first priority is to help rebuild the postwar economies of European countries so that democratic governments can survive."

Speaker C: "Our main goal is to create a system of collective security agreements to deal with any military threats."

Speaker D: "We must continue to build both our nuclear and our conventional arsenals if we are to have any hope of world peace."

32 The central concern of all the speakers is

1 the containment of communism
2 the defeat of the Axis Powers in World War II
3 a ban on the proliferation of nuclear weapons
4 the support of United Nations peacekeeping efforts

33 These speakers' statements would most likely have been made during the Presidential administration of

1 Franklin D. Roosevelt 3 John F. Kennedy
2 Harry S Truman   4 Richard M. Nixon

34 The Red Scare and McCarthyism were similar in that both

1 advocated the development of the arts and sciences
2 supported United States foreign aid programs
3 encouraged nativist ideas
4 promoted economic development

35 In the 1950's and 1960's, the decisions of the United States Supreme Court under Chief Justice Earl Warren tended to

1 expand the rights of individuals
2 reduce government regulation of business
3 deal harshly with persons accused of crimes
4 increase the power of state governments

36 The goal of both Upton Sinclair in the early 1900's and Ralph Nader in the 1960's was to

1 limit immigration to those with skills needed by American industry
2 encourage the growth of American business interests
3 protect the environment
4 expose social and economic problems

37 President Lyndon Johnson's Great Society was an effort to solve the problem of

1 poverty
2 drug trafficking
3 overpopulation
4 illegal immigration

38 During the early 1960's, the United States had to deal with the building of the Berlin Wall, the Bay of Pigs invasion, and the Cuban missile crisis. Each of these events was a direct result of the

1 United States continued support of United Nations decisions
2 continuing tensions between the United States and the Soviet Union
3 United States failure to remain involved in world affairs
4 concern for the safety of Americans living in foreign nations

39 A major achievement of President Jimmy Carter was

1 the worldwide acceptance of his human rights policy
2 the balancing of the Federal budget
3 his handling of international terrorist incidents
4 the signing of the Camp David peace accords

Base your answer to question 40 on the cartoon below and on your knowledge of social studies.

40 Which action was taken in response to the problem identified in the cartoon?

1 The Supreme Court ruled that the Federal Government could not prevent publication of the Pentagon Papers.
2 Term limits were placed on the President by the ratification of the 22nd amendment.
3 Congress passed the War Powers Act.
4 The President was forced to resign as a result of the Vietnam War.

41 Which would be the most appropriate heading for this list?

I. _____
A. Transition from laissez faire to government regulation
B. Democratic reforms of corrupt political practices
C. Concern for the problems of workers and urban dwellers

1 Reconstruction
2 Progressive Era
3 Cold War Era
4 New Frontier

Base your answer to question 42 on the cartoon below and on your knowledge of social studies.

42 The cartoon most clearly implies that since its decision in *Roe* v. *Wade* the Supreme Court has

1 ignored public opinion on the issue
2 experienced serious conflict between female and male Justices over the issue
3 refused to deal with the issue again
4 struggled to accommodate conflicting viewpoints on the issue

43 Which principle is illustrated by the passage of the Sedition Act of 1798, the suspension of habeas corpus in 1861, and the adoption of the Espionage Act in 1917?

1 National interest is sometimes given priority over individual rights.
2 National crises often result in restriction of the powers of the executive branch.
3 The Supreme Court consistently defends the Bill of Rights.
4 Congress expands its other powers when it declares war.

44 One similarity between the League of Nations and the United Nations is that both were created to

1 establish an international armed force to police trouble spots in the world
2 manage the development of industry in economically distressed nations
3 prevent international disputes from escalating into major wars
4 bring democratic government to member nations

Base your answers to questions 45 and 46 on the table below and on your knowledge of social studies.

PRESIDENTIAL ELECTION RESULTS

Year	Party	Candidate	Popular Vote	Electoral Vote
1912	Democrat	Woodrow Wilson	6,286,214	435
	"Bull Moose"	Theodore Roosevelt	4,126,020	88
	Republican	William Taft	3,483,922	8
		Minor Candidates	1,135,697	0
1968	Republican	Richard Nixon	31,785,480	301
	Democrat	Hubert Humphrey	31,275,166	191
	American Independent	George Wallace	9,906,473	46
		Minor Candidates	165,662	0

45 What is the best explanation of the 1912 election results?

1 Americans were unwilling to support third-party candidates.
2 Woodrow Wilson benefited from a split in the Republican Party.
3 Americans did not want to change Presidents while the country was at war.
4 Minor candidates shifted the victory from Theodore Roosevelt to Woodrow Wilson.

46 What is a characteristic of the electoral college system that is reflected in the election results of 1912 and 1968?

1 The two-party system has failed to work in some elections.
2 Electors are not bound to their party's candidate.
3 States with small populations can dominate election results.
4 The "winner-take-all" method can distort the relationship between the popular vote and the electoral vote.

47 "For women working outside the home, it is not new opportunities, but rather new necessities, that have made it happen."

What is the most valid conclusion based on this quotation?

1 The feminist movement of the 1960's gained success in promoting many career choices for women.
2 Because families are smaller, women no longer need to remain at home to care for children.
3 Whether they are married or not, many women must work to provide support for their families.
4 The computer age has actually reduced the number of professional and technical jobs for women.

48 Which statement most accurately describes United States immigration policy since 1920?

1 Any person wishing to immigrate to the United States has been welcomed.
2 Limits have been placed on the numbers of immigrants allowed to enter the United States.
3 Only immigrants with jobs or relatives in the United States have been admitted.
4 Immigrants have been required to speak English before they can be admitted to the United States.

Answers to the following questions are to be written on paper provided by the school.

Students Please Note:

In developing your answers to Parts II and III, be sure to

(1) include specific factual information and evidence whenever possible
(2) keep to the questions asked; do not go off on tangents
(3) avoid overgeneralizations or sweeping statements without sufficient proof; do not overstate your case
(4) keep these general definitions in mind:

    (a) <u>discuss</u> means "to make observations about something using facts, reasoning, and argument; to present in some detail"

    (b) <u>describe</u> means "to illustrate something in words or tell about it"

    (c) <u>show</u> means "to point out; to set forth clearly a position or idea by stating it and giving data which support it"

    (d) <u>explain</u> means "to make plain or understandable; to give reasons for or causes of; to show the logical development or relationships of"

Part II

ANSWER ONE QUESTION FROM THIS PART.   [15]

1 The United States Constitution has remained a living document for more than 200 years. To change with the times, the Constitution has been amended to deal with specific issues.

Issues

Civil rights
Voting rights
Presidential succession
Presidential term limits
Taxation

a Select *two* of the issues listed and for *each* one selected:

- State *one* way a specific amendment dealt with that issue [Use a different amendment for each issue selected. The number of the amendment does not have to be given.]
- Discuss the historical situation that led to the adoption of that amendment
- Discuss a specific impact of that amendment on government in the United States [5,5]

b Some suggested amendments to the United States Constitution are listed below. Select *one* suggested amendment and discuss *one* argument given by its supporters and *one* argument given by its opponents.   [5]

Suggested Amendments

Guarantee equal rights for women
Require a balanced Federal budget
Legalize prayer in public schools

2 In United States history, Presidential elections have been influenced by many factors.

Factors

Political party primaries
Political action committees (PACs)
Voter turnout
Presidential debates
Political party platforms
Campaign advertising

a Select *two* factors from the list. Show how *each* selected factor influenced the 1996 Presidential election.   [5,5]

b Select *one* factor from the list *other than* the factors selected in part *a*. Show how this factor influenced the 1996 Presidential election *or* any other specific Presidential election.   [5]

Part III

ANSWER TWO QUESTIONS FROM THIS PART.   [30]

3 In United States history, foreign policies pursued by various Presidents have resulted in controversy. Some of these controversial policies and the Presidents associated with them are listed below.

Policies—Presidents

Addition of the Corollary to the Monroe Doctrine — Theodore Roosevelt
Support for the Versailles Treaty — Woodrow Wilson
Aid to Great Britain before United States entry into World War II —
    Franklin D. Roosevelt
Use of the atomic bomb — Harry S. Truman
Aid to South Vietnam — Lyndon B. Johnson
Involvement in the Persian Gulf War — George Bush
Aid to Bosnia — Bill Clinton

Select *three* of the foreign policies and the President with which the policy is paired. For *each* pair selected:
• Discuss *one* specific reason the President pursued the policy
• Discuss *one* argument given by opponents of the policy   [5,5,5]

4 Economic and social conditions have prompted the United States Congress to pass various laws to address these conditions.

Laws

Homestead Act (1862)
Interstate Commerce Act (1887)
Pure Food and Drug Act (1906)
Glass-Steagall Banking Act (FDIC) (1933)
National Labor Relations Act (Wagner Act) (1935)
Medicare Act (1965)
Gramm-Rudman Act (Balanced Budget . . . Act) (1985)

Select *three* of the laws listed and for *each* one selected:
* Describe *one* economic or social condition that led to the passage of the law
* Explain *one* way the law dealt with this economic or social condition
* Discuss *one* long-term impact of the law on the United States economy or on American society   [5,5,5]

5 In United States history, controversy has arisen over the reforms proposed by certain individuals.

Individuals

Rachel Carson
Cesar Chavez
Eugene V. Debs
Betty Friedan
Marcus Garvey
Martin Luther King, Jr.
Margaret Sanger

Select *three* of the individuals listed and for *each* one selected:
* State a specific reform proposed by the individual
* Discuss *one* argument given by opponents of this reform
* Discuss the extent to which the individual was successful in bringing about the proposed reform   [5,5,5]

6 Several factors influenced the industrialization of the United States between 1865 and 1920.

Factors

Labor
Transportation
Agriculture
Natural resources
Forms of business organization

Select *three* of the factors listed. For *each* one selected, discuss *two* different ways that factor influenced the industrialization of the United States between 1865 and 1920. [Be sure to include specific historical information in your answer.]   [5,5,5]

7 The cartoons on this page and the next concern current problems in the United States.

   a Select *two* of the cartoons and for *each* one selected:

- Identify the problem dealt with in the cartoon
- Explain the point of view expressed in the cartoon about this problem
- Discuss an action taken either by government *or* by a nongovernmental group to deal with the problem   [5,5]

   b Identify a current national social problem *not* shown in the cartoons. Discuss a major cause of this problem and describe an action taken either by government *or* by a nongovernmental group to deal with that problem.   [5]

Cartoon A

Cartoon B

Cartoon C

Sample Regents Exam #4—Answers

1. The correct answer is 2. Under the Articles of Confederation, the national government could only request funds from the states. Universal suffrage did not occur until much later. Choices 3 and 4 were both components of the Articles of Confederation.

2. The correct answer is 4. Two of the conflicts were over presidential terms and determining the basis of representation. For presidential terms, anywhere from one year to life was suggested. The better of the two answers would be representation.

3. The correct answer is 1. It is stating that the people have determined how they will be ruled. Or, in other words, political power is derived from the people.

4. The correct answer is 3. Federalism is a system by which a dual system of government is created in which powers are divided between the state governments and the central (national or federal) government.

5. The correct answer is 2. Executive branch, Supreme Court, and electoral college are all specifically mentioned in the Constitution.

6. The correct answer is 4. In each instance there is an example in which one branch overrides the decision of another branch of government.

7. The correct answer is 1. In effect, what Ms. Anthony is doing here is submitting a petition for a redress of grievances, those being the denial of a right to vote.

8. The correct answer is 2. Each of these groups represents, or represented, a specific group of people. This would be an example of indirect democracy.

9. The correct answer is 3. The function of PACs is to attempt to influence legislative decisions in much the same way as regular lobbyists do. PCHs usually represent corporations, labor unions, or other special-interest groups..

10. The correct answer is 3. Lincoln believed the nature of the federal union made it impossible for a state to secede from the union. Given this fact, the southern states could not have left the union.

11. The correct answer is 2. "Jim Crow" laws were designed to discriminate against the former slaves by the southern whites.

12. The correct answer is 4. *Plessy v. Ferguson* upheld the "separate but equal" doctrine. The Thirteenth amendment and the formation of the NAACP were steps toward ending discrimination, but it was the Civil Rights Act of 1964 that officially ended segregation.

13. The correct answer is 3. The federal subsidies are what encouraged the construction of the transcontinental railroads. The willingness of the Native Americans to leave tribal lands was never considered a factor; they were simply forced to relocate.

14. The correct answer is 1. This was the major period of the Industrial Revolution in the United States. During this period there was the growth of monopolies, trusts, holding companies, etcetera., which were designed to eliminate competition. Government would not take over businesses in an era of laissez-faire economics. Labor unions were relatively weak. The gross national product (GNP) increased during this era.

15. The correct answer is 2. This is evidenced by the number of times military force was used and the number of times the courts authorized injunctions. The federal government was pro-business during this historical era.

16. The correct answer is 3. America was considered the land of opportunity. With the economic turmoil present in other countries, and the opportunities available in the United States, the numbers of immigrants was always high.

17. The correct answer is 4. A primary source is a factual document written during the period. We do not know when the novel was written or if it is fiction or nonfiction; a movie clearly would not have come from the period in question; the biography might be slanted. The treaty is a factual document written during the period.

18. The correct answer is 3. Yellow journalism involves sensational reporting of the facts to incite an emotional reaction. Choices 1, 2, and 4 are all factual statements. Choice 3 has been sensationalized to create an emotional response.

19. The correct answer is 2. Both of these acts were designed to prevent trusts, monopolies, or other forms of combinations that hindered competition.

20. The correct answer is 1. Imperialism is the policy by which we claim dominance or preference in foreign areas. Here we are talking about the United States's asserting control over the Philippines.

21. The correct answer is 4. A perfect example of this is the Roosevelt Corollary to the Monroe Doctrine in 1904. Theodore Roosevelt asserted that the U.S. had the right both to oppose European intervention in the Western Hemisphere and intervene in the domestic affairs of its Latin American neighbors.

22. The correct answer is 1. The Federal Reserve provides a flexible money supply by setting the reserve ratio and the discount rate. Incidentally, the FDIC insures individual bank deposits.

23. The correct answer is 3. By sinking the *Lusitania* the Germans were threatening our policy of neutrality. The United States either had to accept this violation of freedom of the seas or retaliate.

24. The correct answer is 3. The muckrakers and the progressives believed that the government should become more involved in the regulating of business practices. They attached government's alliance with the corporate community.

25. The correct answer is 2. It was global financial interdependence that allowed for the depression to effect the global economy instead of being confined to one specific region.

26. The correct answer is 1. This is evidenced by the Supreme Court ruling unconstitutional the National Industrial Recovery Act and the Agricultural Adjustment Act.

27. The correct answer is 1. This is evidenced by the Agricultural Adjustment Acts of 1933 and 1938. Reducing production was intended to help farmers receive higher prices for their crops.

28. The correct answer is 2. Prime examples of this would include Social Security, SEC, FDIC, etcetera. The influence of labor has declined in recent years. Women have not attained full economic status; the GOP has not controlled the government.

29. The correct answer is 4. Japan invaded China's northern province of Manchuria in 1931.

30. The correct answer is 1. The neutrality acts were passed by Congress to hopefully prevent the economic and emotional entanglements that, many believed, had involved the United States in World War I.

31. The correct answer is 3. In the 1980s the U.S. Supreme Court overturned its earlier decision and declared the internment of the Japanese Americans as one of the greatest crimes in American history. More than 100,000 Japanese Americans had been placed in these "relocation centers."

32. The correct answer is 1. All of these speakers are referring to the spread of communism or methods to prevent the spread of communism. Containment's arm was to check communist power by both military and economic means.

33. The correct answer is 2. The items the speakers are referring to happened during the presidency of Truman.

34. The correct answer is 3. The "red scare" occurred in the 1920s; McCarthyism occurred in the early 1950s, but both encouraged nativist ideas.

35. The correct answer is 1. The Warren Court served during an era of democratic progress, especially in the area of rights for minority groups and for individuals. The Court's most famous ruling was *Brown v. Board of Education,* which declared segregation unconstitutional.

36. The correct answer is 4. Sinclair's *The Jungle* and Nader's Raders were both concerned with social and economic problems in society.

37. The correct answer is 1. The Great Society involved the creation of the welfare state.

38. The correct answer is 2. Each of these items dealt with U.S.–U.S.S.R. conflict. In the case of the Cuban missile crisis, both superpowers came very close to all-out nuclear war (1962).

39. The correct answer is 4. The signing of the Camp David peace accords was a major advance toward peace in the Middle East, as it involved an agreement between Israel and Egypt.

40. The correct answer is 3. The War Powers Resolution, in theory, places strict limitations on the ability of the president to commit American troops to combat. However, Congress has not forced presidents to abide by those limitations.

41. The correct answer is 2. These were all areas dealt with during the Progressive Era.

42. The correct answer is 4. The cartoon illustrates the precarious position this issue has placed the Court in. As a result, the Court has struggled to accommodate conflicting viewpoints to the best of its ability. The issue of abortion remains one of the most contentious in American society.

43. The correct answer is 1. In each of these instances, individual rights were put aside in order to accommodate the national interest at the time.

44. The correct answer is 3. This is the best choice. Although the other answer choices are possible, the fundamental purpose for creating these organizations was to prevent future aggression. Having been created after global conflicts, the primary emphasis would be on peace, not armed force.

45. The correct answer is 2. The combined totals of the popular vote for republican candidates indicate that the split is what gave Wilson the victory.

46. The correct answer is 4. This is clearly evidenced in both elections where neither winner gained a large gap in popular votes, but they both gained landslide victories in electoral votes.

47. The correct answer is 3. The key here is necessity. More women are working because a single-parent income is no longer enough to support most families.

48. The correct answer is 2. The vast majority of immigration legislation in the last 75 years has dealt with quotas or limitations on how many immigrants can come to this country.

Essay Questions

(Note: Answers provided are not all inclusive. These are suggested responses and should be used as a guide for the type of answers that would be acceptable.)

Part II

Question 1a

Civil Rights—The Thirteenth Amendment abolished slavery. This was an act by the Radical Republicans as a method of punishing the South for having seceded, following the southern defeat in the Civil War. This altered the Three-Fifths Compromise that had been reached at the Constitutional Convention. The Fifteenth Amendment prohibited any state from denying anyone the right to vote based on race. This was passed by the Radical Republicans to counteract the "Jim Crow" laws instituted in the South. The passage of the amendment greatly increased the number of Republican voters and the strength of the Republican party.

Voting Rights—The passage of the Nineteenth Amendment made it illegal to deny anyone the vote based on sex. This was passed following the conclusion of World War I as a way of recognizing the war efforts contributed by women. This more than doubled the number of eligible voters in the United States. The Fifteenth Amendment prohibited any state from denying anyone the right to vote based on race. This was passed by the Radical Republicans to counteract the "Jim Crow" laws instituted in the South. The passage of the amendment greatly increased the number of Republican voters and the strength of the Republican party.

Presidential Succession—The Twenty-Fifth Amendment established guidelines for what would happen if a president or vice-president became disabled or left the office for some other reason. This was enacted as a result of Spiro Agnew's resigning as vice president after pleading "no contest" to income tax invasion. Gerald Ford became vice president, then president after Nixon resigned during the Watergate scandal.

Presidential Term Limits—The Twenty-second Amendment established the two term limit for the office of president. Roosevelt was currently serving his third term, the first president to break the two-term tradition established by George Washington. This limited the number of terms any one person could serve consecutively as president of the United States.

Taxation—The Sixteenth Amendment allowed for a federal income tax. In 1895 the Supreme Court had ruled that the income tax authorized by Congress in 1894 was a direct tax not levied among states in proportion to population and therefore unconstitutional. The new income tax would supplement the federal revenue from tariffs.

Question 1b

Guarantee Equal Rights For Women—Many women argued that they deserved equal protection under the law, equal pay for equal work, and should not be discriminated against because of their sex. Other women argued that the passage of such an amendment would cause women to lose their preferential treatment in child-custody cases, said that labor legislation already ensured equal pay for equal work, and if passed, women would have to fight in combat if the nation went to war.

Require a Balanced Federal Budget—Supporters of this measure point out that this is the responsible thing to do. By not doing so, we are placing an unfair burden on future generations. Opponents point out that it is an unrealistic goal given the global economic situation. Further, it would necessitate increased taxation and extreme budget cuts.

Legalize Prayer in Public Schools—Supporters argue that prayer does not necessarily have to endorse any one religion over another. They further contend that prayer provides a strong moral center for children. Opponents point out that any religion in school violates the "separation of church and state" doctrine. Even if prayer in public schools is allowed, certain religious beliefs would automatically be violated, such as atheism and agnosticism. As for morals, opponents argue that morals are best taught at home by the family, not by the state.

Question 2

(Note: Definitions and examples are given for the terms. These should be used as a guide for answers whether applied to the 1996 election or any other election.)

Political Party Primaries—There are three types of political party primaries: closed primary, open primary, and blanket primary. In the closed primary, only persons registered as members of a particular party may participate. The advantage of this is that it prevents one party from voting for a weak candidate in the other party. In the open primary, voters do not have to declare their party allegiance. This method ensures privacy and allows independents an opportunity to vote in the primary. The blanket primary is used in Alaska and Washington. Voters choose among two or more political parties, crossing back and forth to select nominees for each particular office.

Political Action Committees—Political Action Committees (PACs) provide both legal and illegal campaign contributions to assist in the election of their favorite candidate. At the same time, PACs can introduce new ideas or perspectives to the public that other parties may shy away from.

Voter Turnout—Voter turnout is the percentage of eligible voters that actually vote in a given election. The number of votes cast determines the popular vote. In recent years voter turnout has been on the decline. Many people believe this is because of voter apathy.

Presidential Debates—One of the key arguments involving presidential debates is the question of who will be invited. Clearly, the Democratic and Republican candidates will be invited, but what about third-party candidates? The idea behind the presidential debate is to see where each candidate stands on the issues. Unfortunately, they have been based more on oration ability and personality than anything else.

Political Party Platforms—The party platform is made up of "planks," or the parties' official position on a single issue. A distinction is generally made between wants and needs. Quite often the platform will be designed to meet the wants and needs of specific groups of people. In looking at the various parties one will notice both similarities and differences within each party platform.

Campaign Advertising—Campaign advertising is used both to bolster the image of one's candidate, while discrediting that of the opponent. When the latter is used to excess, it is called a smear campaign. Most presidential elections have centered on campaign slogans such as: "He kept us out of war" or "Fifty-four-forty or Fight." One of the key issues involving campaign advertising in recent years has been the funding for campaign advertising—where it comes from and how it is used.

Part III

Question 3

Addition of the Corollary to the Monroe Doctrine, and Theodore Roosevelt—When the Dominican Republic failed to repay loans to European creditors, Roosevelt opposed European intervention as a violation of the Monroe Doctrine. Instead, he authorized intervention by the United States to protect the European creditors. Opponents of this act argued that no country has the right to use military force to collect debts.

Support for the Versailles Treaty, and Woodrow Wilson—Wilson had helped to draft the Versailles Treaty and was instrumental in assuring the inclusion of his Fourteen Points to ensure future global peace. One of these points involved the creation of a League of Nations and an international peacekeeping force. Henry Cabot Lodge opposed ratification of this treaty on the grounds that placing U.S. troops under the control of the League of Nations would violate the sole power of Congress to declare war. Hence, ratification would be unconstitutional.

Aid to Great Britain before United States Entry into World War II, and Franklin D. Roosevelt—Roosevelt believed this was essential to deter the expansion of dictatorial powers and to assist an ally. If England should fall, there would be nothing to separate the United States from the aggressors except the Atlantic Ocean. Therefore, it was in the nation's best interest to assist England. Others argued that doing so violated the U.S. position of neutrality and could potentially involve it in the war to a greater extent.

Use of the Atomic Bomb and Harry S Truman—Truman justified this action by citing three things: revenge for Pearl Harbor, to save American lives, and to end the war. If the war continued under conventional means, the expected toll of American deaths was predicted to exceed one million from the invasion of the Japanese homeland. Opponents argued that Japan was close to surrendering; it was just a matter of time. Additionally, opponents said there could be no justification for the mass killing of innocent civilians.

Aid to South Vietnam, and Lyndon B. Johnson—When North Vietnam fell to communism, the United States determined that South Vietnam had to be protected at all costs from the spread of communism. The belief was that if South Vietnam fell, then the other Asian nations would fall as well. This was referred to as the "domino theory." Opponents of the United States's involvement in Vietnam argued that there were no clear objectives and so all the United States ended up with was the senseless loss of American lives.

Involvement in the Persian Gulf War and George Bush—When Saddam Hussien's forces invaded oil-rich Kuwait, George Bush equated the act to that of Hitler's use of the blitzkrieg in World War II. He condemned the invasion as "naked aggression." In order to liberate Kuwait and halt the expansion and aggression of Hussien, a multi-national force was authorized by the U.N. Security Council to use force to eject the Iraqis from Kuwait. Some Americans opposed U.S. military involvement because they feared another protracted conflict such as Vietnam. Additionally, the trade embargo, if given time, would weaken Iraq and force its withdrawal from Kuwait.

Aid to Bosnia, and Bill Clinton—Having criticized President Bush for standing by while Serbs, Croats, and Muslims fought a vicious civil war in Bosnia, President Clinton tried to get European nations to openly help Bosnia's government. This eventually involved sending a U.N. peacekeeping force comprised primarily of American soldiers. Some Americans argued that this was an unnecessary risk of American lives.

Question 4

Homestead Act (1862)—This act offered a free 160-acre farm to any settler who would cultivate it for five years. This was deemed necessary in order to meet the increased demand for foodstuffs as a result of the Civil War and urbanization. As a result there was increased westward expansion and agrarian development. The most lasting impact of this act was the further exploitation of the Native Americans.

Interstate Commerce Act (1887)—This act was passed to put an end to the abuses practiced by the railroads. It prohibited railroads from discriminating between persons by special rates or rebates; charging more for a short haul than a long haul; and entering into pooling agreements. Furthermore, it established an enforcement agency, the Interstate Commerce Commission (ICC). Although hindered by weaknesses, the Interstate Commerce Act established the precedent of government regulation of private interstate business and paved the way for subsequent and stronger legislation.

Pure Food and Drug Act (1906)—If one reads Upton Sinclair's *The Jungle*, one is immediately horrified to see what types of things are called food. Industries have been notorious for using sawdust as filler, using chemicals to mask odors of spoiled foods, and other acts harmful to the consumer. The Pure Food and Drug Act forbade the manufacture, transportation, and sale of adulterated and poisonous foods and drugs. Its long-term impact would be that it established the precedent by which the Food and Drug Administration would be established.

Glass-Steagall Banking Act (FDIC) (1933)—During the Great Depression millions of Americans had their savings wiped out when banks failed. The FDIC protects deposits in commercial and savings banks up to $100,000 per account in the event of a bank failure. With this assurance, faith in the banking system had been restored. Unfortunately, the federal government incurred heavy losses when bad investments and fraud caused a rash of savings bank failures in the 1980s.

National Labor Relations Act (Wagner Act) (1935)—During the Great Depression, workers were hurt severely as a result of layoffs and wage cuts. When they attempted to unionize to fight against this exploitation, they found that the unions were not overly effective, and belonging to a union could readily lead to termination of employment. The Wagner Act forbade employers to: interfere with labor's right to organize; interfere in the operation of unions; use "blacklists" to deny active union members jobs; hire labor spies to infiltrate unions; organize company unions; discriminate against union members; or refuse to bargain collectively with employees. By guaranteeing collective bargaining, the Wagner Act was largely responsible for the subsequent growth in legitimate union membership. Between 1935 and 1941 the number of workers in legitimate unions rose from 4 million to more than 10 million.

Medicare Act (1965)—The reason for this act was that persons over the age of 65, as a group, possessed limited finances, suffered disproportionately more from illness, and were therefore most burdened by rising medical costs. This act provided persons over 65 with a basic hospital insurance plan. The only problem is that the costs for Medicare have skyrocketed from $4.7 billion in 1967 to $123 billion in 1991.

Gramm-Rudman Act (Balanced Budget Act) (1985)—Due to deficit spending and soaring interest rates, the national debt has skyrocketed out of control. This act was designed to set a timetable for gradually reducing these deficits. Unfortunately, the money must come from somewhere. This has meant tax increases as well as welfare cuts.

Question 5

Rachel Carson—Carson, in her landmark book, *Silent Spring*, proposed the discontinuation of pesticide use. In examining the issue involving pesticides, proponents argue that this is the most effective method to kill large amounts of insects. However, evidence clearly indicates that the use of certain pesticides definitively harms the environment. When this has happened, the government has banned the use of those pesticides. Three such pesticides that have been banned are: DDT, aldrin, and dieldrin. Additionally, new biocontrol methods are being developed.

Cesar Chavez—Chavez proposed the unionizing of Mexican American migrant workers. The opposition claims that farmers have the right to determine the rate of pay based on supply and demand. By 1970 most of the farmers had signed contracts with his union.

Eugene V. Debs—Debs proposed that employers should not be allowed to lower the wages of rail workers without also lowering rents and other charges. To ensure compliance with this, Debs initiated a strike. Attorney General Olney acted to break the strike by securing an injunction against the union as a "conspiracy in restraint of trade." When Debs violated the injunction, he was jailed for contempt of court. Without effective leadership, the strike collapsed, and with it, the American Railway Union.

Betty Friedan—Friedan, who authored *The Feminie Mystique*, proposed the passage of an Equal Rights Amendment in order to obtain full equality between the sexes. Opponents to the ERA argued that such an amendment would cause women to lose more than they would gain. Labor legislation already assured women equal pay for equal work. However, they stood to lose their preferential treatment in child-custody cases, as well as be required to serve in armed-forces combat. The ERA failed to gain the necessary number of states for ratification. Even so, Friedan was able to increase public awareness about the problem.

Marcus Garvey—Garvey proposed that African Americans return to Africa to create a nation of their own. Many African Americans believed it was unfair that they should have to move to another country to avoid racial violence and discrimination. Garvey's proposal did not encourage many African Americans to return to Africa, but it did increase racial pride among African Americans.

Martin Luther King Jr.—King proposed the end to segregation and full equality for African Americans within the United States. Some Americans believe that blacks and whites should be segregated for a variety of reasons, mainly due to bigotry and intolerance. Even though King was assassinated, great leaps forward were taken to end segregation and toward achieving equality for African Americans.

Margaret Sanger—She proposed that information on contraception should be provided to the general public. Some Americans argued that this involved a moral issue, and as such it should be handled at home by the family. Sanger was instrumental in establishing numerous agencies and organizations to deal with this issue. Planned Parenthood was an outgrowth of her work.

Question 6

Labor—Because of a high birth rate and considerable immigration (1871 to 1880, 2.8 million; 1881 to 1890, 5.2 million; 1901 to 1910, 8.8 million), the American population in the nineteenth century nearly doubled every 25 years. It rose from 5 million in 1800 to 76 million in 1900. This huge increase in population provided industry with a sufficient number of workers and expanding domestic markets.

Transportation—By 1860 the United States had 30,000 miles of railroad track, almost all east of the Mississippi. By 1900 the country had five transcontinental railroads and nearly 200,000 miles of track. This was more than the total trackage in all of Europe. Railroads helped the growth of industry by bringing foodstuffs to city markets, raw materials to factories, and manufactured products to consumers.

Agriculture—Farmers produced both foodstuffs needed for the growing urban centers and the raw materials, such as cotton and wool, needed by the factories. By being able to exploit the farmers by paying low prices for products and exploiting transportation costs, the industrialists were able to realize the profits necessary for continued growth and expansion.

Natural Resources—Nature endowed the United States with an abundance of raw materials: coal, oil, iron, copper, gold, and silver. There are also swift-running streams for water power. Additionally, there is an abundance of fertile soil for raising foodstuffs, lumber, cotton, and tobacco.

Forms of Business Organization—In the early phases of the Industrial Revolution, the key to expansion and growth was profit. To achieve the necessary profit, many industrialists resorted to exploitation of the workers, as well as to cutthroat competition. The competition could take one of two forms: vertical monopolies, or horizontal monopolies. In a vertical monopoly, the industrialist would attempt to take over all aspects of the industry. For example, if you were manufacturing shoes, you would take over the industries associated with producing leather, producing shoes, distributing the items, and selling the items. In a horizontal monopoly, you would take over all industries doing the same thing you were doing. For example, if you were involved with banking, you would take over all banks in the country. Some examples of monopolies would include: Carnegie Steel Company, Standard Oil Trust, United States Steel Corporation, and New York Central and Great Northern Railroads. Other forms of business organizations would include: the pool, the trust, and the holding company.

Question 7

Caption 1—The problem presented is the crumbling of the family structure in America. This is apparent when one reads the caption "Has anybody checked the foundation?" and then sees that the foundation in question is The Family. The point of view being expressed is that the traditional American family that had held the nation together was falling apart. Several efforts have been made to try to deal with this problem: schools providing breakfast for latch-key kids, increases in the number of day care providers, and greater church involvement with families.

Caption 2—The problem presented is the increased number of illegal immigrants coming to America across the California border. This is made apparent by the words "Illegal Immigration" and the guard with "California" written across his chest attempting to hold back the flood that is cracking the foundation of the border. The point of view that is expressed is that trying to stop illegal immigrants from entering California is like trying to hold back a flood. Three recent actions taken by the government have been: passage of the North American Free Trade Agreement (NAFTA) to stimulate the Mexican economy; increased patrols along the border; and instituting heavy fines for people employing illegal immigrants.

Caption 3—The problem being presented is the improper structure, or blatant abuse, of the welfare system. The point of view being presented is that under the current welfare guidelines, one can make more money by staying home and having more children than one can by working. Currently the government is experimenting with a variety of ways to make welfare a form of assistance, not a way of life. One way this is being done is by limiting the time period for which people can receive public-assistance benefits.

**Want more information about our services, products,
or the nearest Kaplan educational center?**

HERE

Call our nationwide toll-free numbers:

1–800–KAP–TEST
(for information on our live courses, private tutoring and
admissions consulting)

1–800–KAP–ITEM
(for information on our products)

1–888–KAP–LOAN*
(for information on student loans)

Connect with us in cyberspace:
On AOL, keyword **"Kaplan"**
On the Internet's World Wide Web, open
"www.kaplan.com" and **"www.score.kaplan.com"**
Via E-mail, **"Info@kaplan.com"**

The Score Edge gives you suggestions for educational activities
and cutting-edge parenting advice each week via e-mail.
For your free subscription to the Score! Edge, visit **"www.score.kaplan.com"**

Write to:
Kaplan Educational Centers
888 Seventh Avenue
New York, NY 10106

Paying for college just got easier...

KapLoan*, the Kaplan Student Loan Information Program, is a free service designed to guide you through the financial aid process.

KapLoan will send you a FREE booklet with valuable financial aid information and connect you with American Express® Educational Loans. With KapLoan and American Express, you'll receive personalized guidance through the financial aid process and access to some of the least expensive educational loans available.

■ **The Federal Stafford Loan**—Eligible students can borrow various amounts depending on their year in college. Loan amounts range from $2,625-$5,500 for dependent students and $6,625-$10,500 for independent students.

■ **The Federal Parent Loan for Undergraduate Students (PLUS)**—Eligible parents may borrow up to the total cost of education, less other financial aid received.

Make the most of your financial aid opportunities.

KapLoan™
The Kaplan Student Loan Information Program

AMERICAN EXPRESS®
Educational Financing